# BLACKNESS IS BURNING

# Contemporary Approaches to Film and Media Series

General Editor
Barry Keith Grant, Brock University

Advisory Editors
Robert J. Burgoyne, University of St. Andrews

Caren J. Deming, University of Arizona

Patricia B. Erens, School of the Art Institute of Chicago

Peter X. Feng, University of Delaware

Lucy Fischer, University of Pittsburgh

Frances Gateward, California State University, Northridge

Tom Gunning, University of Chicago

Thomas Leitch, University of Delaware

Walter Metz, Southern Illinois University

A complete listing of the books in this series
can be found online at wsupress.wayne.edu

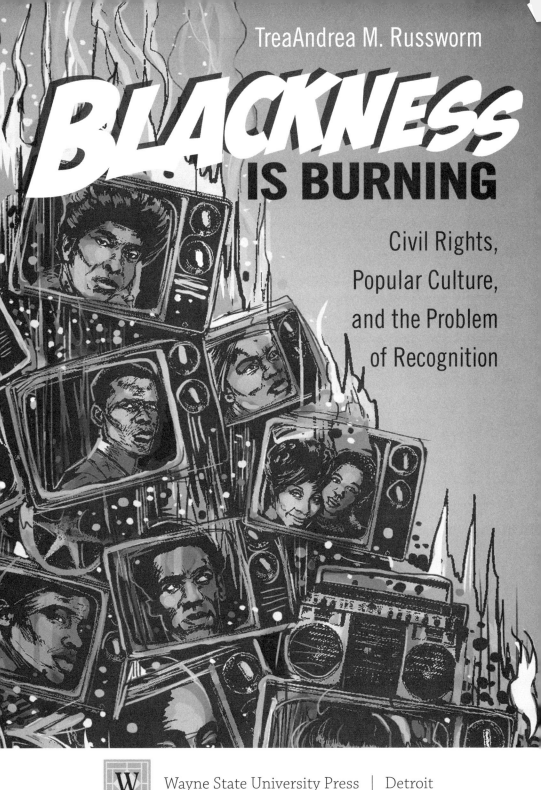

TreaAndrea M. Russworm

# BLACKNESS
## IS BURNING

Civil Rights,
Popular Culture,
and the Problem
of Recognition

Wayne State University Press | Detroit

20 19 18 17 16       5 4 3 2 1

Library of Congress Cataloging Number: 2016940038

ISBN 978-0-8143-4051-6 (paperback)
ISBN 978-0-8143-4052-3 (ebook)

Designed and typeset by Bryce Schimanski
Composed in Chapparal Pro

Wayne State University Press
Leonard N. Simons Building
4809 Woodward Avenue
Detroit, Michigan 48201-1309

Visit us online at wsupress.wayne.edu

# CONTENTS

# ACKNOWLEDGMENTS

*Blackness Is Burning* has been a true labor of love, a testament both to ratchet perseverance and unrelenting faith. Over the long years of writing, editing, and revising the project, I have benefited from an enormous well of support that has helped me brave the book's sobering themes and topics.

I am particularly grateful for the instruction and mentorship I received while at the University of Chicago—when some of the ideas for this project first began to take shape. Jacqueline Stewart, Deborah Nelson, and Lisa Ruddick, as well as members of the greater intellectual community at the U of C, were instrumental in helping me explore some of the original chapter topics and themes. During those years, I also benefited from a predoctoral fellowship from the Consortium for Faculty Diversity and institutional support from DePauw University.

At Wayne State University Press, I have appreciated all of the time and energy the editors and staff have devoted to this project, especially Annie Martin, Bryce K. Schimanski, and Kristin Harpster. As my primary contact, senior acquisitions editor Annie Martin was amazing at every level of development and production, and I am certain this book could not have been in better hands. I also want to thank Barry Keith Grant and the three anonymous readers for their sage and invaluable feedback. Then, too, I am grateful for John Ira Jennings's willingness to design the art for an amazing book cover on short notice. Thank you to everyone who has assisted in the production of this book!

As a teacher and writer, I am ever indebted to the many great teachers who inspired me to pursue a life of learning and writing in the first place:

Marilou Baumgarten, Ameila Barnes, Jeanette Lasley, Sandy Brownell, James Monroe, and Scott Saul. Along these lines, George Monteiro, whose inspiring seminars at Brown University and playful provocation "somebody has to do this, why not you?" will long live in my heart.

At the University of Massachusetts, Amherst, I am thankful for the colleagues who provided me with chapter feedback or engaged with me on the book's central arguments. These colleagues include but are not limited to Jordy Rosenberg, Hoang Phan, Ruth Jennison, Jenny Spencer, Nick Bromell, Jen Adams, Joselyn Almeida-Beveridge, Joseph Bartolomeo, Suzanne Daley, Deborah Carlin, Jane Degenhardt, Randall Knoper, and Donna LeCourt.

I have also been blessed with a circle of family and friends who helped me aspire and persevere. I am especially grateful for the company and encouragement of Karen Bowdre, Laura Furlan, Laura Kalba, Gulru Calmak, Cathy Luna, Gina Valesquez, K. C. Nat Turner, Florence Sullivan, Michael Forbes, Jen Malkowski, Jewel Younge, Fabian Wong, Rebecca Gershenson Smith, and Priscilla Page. This was the Hustle Posse (or legion of superheroes) who helped me discern when to press on and when to Step. Away. From. The. Keyboard. Similarly, the love and prayers of Christ Community Church kept me faithful, especially during the long and dark New England winters. Thank you, friends and faith community!

I would like to extend a special thanks to Tracy Harkless, Armande Millender, and Dr. Gail Thompson. I am proud to consider you kin, and with each of you I know I can always find a home and be myself—with or without books, credentials, or accomplishments. Thank you, family!

To Ron'na Lytle and Mark James, there are, of course, no words to express how much each of you has supported me through this process. Mark, your encouragement and willingness to provide last-minute editing and feedback have endeared me to you even more. I am grateful for having you in my life, and I say this part with utmost sincerity: #thanksChicago! Ron'na, your companionship, care, and pragmatic selflessness throughout these years have been invaluable. It seems only fitting that the next phase of our life together should coincide with the publication of this book and the closing of several necessary chapters on a past well examined.

Finally, none of this would be possible without the spiritual fortitude and daily guidance from my creator, on whom I lean every day. I am humbled to make good on my talents as a testimony of His grace and mercy. Writing this book has been a catalyst for many transformations in my life, and although I am very proud to publish it, I am even more grateful for the powerful lessons learned. Thank you, God!

# INTRODUCTION

This book is about race, civil rights era popular culture, and representations of the theme of recognition—from Sidney Poitier's most famous characters to black mother-and-daughter melodramas to 1960s and 1970s pimp narratives to Bill Cosby's vision of black childhood. Throughout these pages, I demarcate the ways in which the politics of recognition was represented during the era in quasi-psychological terms. That our popular and narrative cultures have a tendency to "psychologize" race and racial identity should come as no surprise, but as I argue here, exposing the psychoanalytic imperatives inherent in stories about recognition proves a useful strategy for both fully engaging and tracing the habit of psychologizing racial identity to a no doubt disappointing end. That end, and this book's central argument, is that humanizing blackness in popular and narrative culture has always been a barely attainable and impossible to coherently sustain cultural agenda.

If psychoanalysis has been a dominant American fascination since Freud's heyday, psychologizing racial identity in popular culture has been common only since the civil rights era, a moment when the demand for the state to fully recognize the rights of African Americans was often communicated as a need to fully recognize the psychological humanity of black people. As the politics of recognition is also a politics of representation, I demonstrate throughout *Blackness Is Burning* that recognition upheld as a social and cultural value encourages a troubling intersubjective view of race. Especially since the basic questions about black humanity and the relational politics of the era have left an uncanny imprint on post–civil rights notions of blackness, I also make frequent comparisons between civil rights and post–civil rights popular representations. As Eve Kosofsky Sedgwick has said of her organizational ambitions, so too does the way I have structured this book represent "a continuing negotiation" between "historicizing and dehistoricizing motives."[1] Fittingly, then, *Blackness Is Burning* began for me during a viewing of a contemporary film that seemed at the time to have nothing at all to do with the civil rights era.

That film was *Antwone Fisher* (2002), a post–civil rights story about how psychotherapy helps a young black man explore and overcome the circumstances of a painful past that includes childhood sexual and emotional abuse. I saw *Antwone Fisher* in the theaters with a group that included my younger brother, who was twelve at the time. As a black film and media scholar in training and with all the hubris of a graduate student, I had made a deal with my brother that I would see almost any film with him as long as we talked about it. My brother quickly caught on that if I seemed particularly eager to see a film, it probably meant that we were in for a long session of "deconstruction" afterward, and this obligatory ritual of "breaking it down" had begun to make him rethink how badly he wanted to see a PG-13 or R-rated film. I do not remember why my brother wanted to go to the movies with my grad friends and me that night to see *Antwone Fisher*, since it was nothing like the other films I took him to see during that school year, films like *8 Mile* (2002), *Bringing Down the House* (2003), and *Bad Boys II* (2003). What I do remember is that we were all crying at the end of the film. Antwone's story was so full of trauma and hardship that there were times when the film's pathos ricocheted heavily somewhere deep inside me; I feared it might all be too much for my little brother. Several times during the screening I wanted to tell him to leave, to go take a break and get some more popcorn, but every time I glanced sideways at him, he was absolutely riveted and more attentive than I think I had ever seen him before. My brother was the only black male among us that night, and when he cried, smiling through his tears as the film's credits ran, I hugged him silently, knowing that there was nothing in my extensive formal education that would give me the language to say anything remotely scholarly or deconstructive about the film as we talked over vanilla shakes and burgers at the ESPN SportsZone in downtown Chicago.

That night our postscreening conversation about *Antwone Fisher* was absent my usual snarkiness. Fresh from an "Advanced Psychoanalytic Interpretation" seminar, I had assumed it was something about how Antwone learns how to apply the lessons of analysis to work through his emotions—specifically his anger—that struck a chord with my brother, who was right at the age when so many black boys become aware that society expects them to be angry and violent. In discovering that I was wrong about what resonated with him, however, I listened to my brother's simple but spot-on analysis of the film. He said, "That movie was about how everybody tried to tear him down. They tried to break his spirit when he was a kid, but he survived. They want us to fail, but we have to show ourselves that we won't." As a young black male watching the film, my brother cried identificatory tears of defiance, then, while I mostly cried hot tears of empathy. Nearly a decade and a half later, this difference as well as what a film like *Antwone Fisher* communicates generally about black hardship and survival, recognition and identification, and our American cultural reliance on psychological knowledge has become essential to how I study and write about race and popular culture.

This film is now referred to fondly in my social circles as "The Black Man's *Color Purple*" because *The Color Purple*'s Celie and Antwone are subjective kinfolk. Both characters have to endure an inordinate amount of hardship en route to proving their humanity.[2] *Antwone Fisher* is a quotidian emotional-uplift narrative and an even more formulaic psychological film drama, but it stands out in a post–civil rights context because there are so few films that are explicitly about psychology, personal and historical trauma, *and* black male subjectivity. The "breaking it down" reflection that I could not have mustered at the time to share with my brother is this: the film is as much about Antwone's discovery that psychotherapy can heal and redeem him as it is about our need for reassurance that the metanarrative of recognition in American culture, which includes some of the most popular stories of black trauma and survival, can heal and inspire others—onlookers and outsiders, friends and therapists, spectators who see themselves in the characterizations as well as audiences who do not. I might have said to my brother that the character Antwone Fisher (to whom I return in the next chapter) needs psychoanalysis, but psychoanalysis also needs him.

*Blackness Is Burning* establishes a cultural context and theoretical trajectory for a film like *Antwone Fisher*. This book is about films and other forms of mass culture that overtly and explicitly connect blackness to the popularly embraced ethos and rhetoric of psychological recognition. Yet, since there are many more stories that establish a much less literal relationship between blackness and the virtues of psychodynamic knowledge, this book is also about the ways in which these things fuse together or—to use a clinical term—"present" themselves in works that are only analogously about the therapeutic potential of intersubjectivity. The way the politics of recognition emerges between civil rights and post–civil rights popular culture is not, importantly, a problem that is unique to visual culture. Although it is tempting to presume that recognizing the racial other as human is a function of the visual, that to recognize means specifically "to see," the attempts to recognize black humanity's psychological distinctiveness have not been bound by a particular form, mode of representation, or intended audience. It is, therefore, an intentional part of my methodology throughout these chapters to place the visual texts (films and television shows) in conversation with other aspects of civil rights era culture, including live performance and black print culture. In forming relationships and connections between the visual and what we have also read and heard, I aim to emphasize the politics of recognition's power and pervasiveness as ideological norm.

## Burning Significations

The title of this book, *Blackness Is Burning*, references and builds on but also ventures beyond the Freudian metaphor of the burning child. Freud begins the concluding chapter of *The Interpretation of Dreams* by recounting a dream that came to him through double hearsay: a patient of his heard about the dream from a person who was lecturing on it and in turn had the same dream herself. Freud knew little about the original context of the dream. He only knew, from his patient's retelling, that the dream was about a father whose son died. As Freud recalls, the father left his son's body under the care of another and, "an old man, who had been installed as a watcher [over the child's dead body], sat beside the body, murmuring prayers. After sleeping for a few hours the father dreamed that the child was standing by his bed, clasping his arms and crying reproachfully: 'Father, don't you see I'm burning?' He woke up, noticed a bright glare of light from the next room, hurried into it and found that . . . the arms of his beloved child's dead body had been burned by a lighted candle that had fallen on them."[3]

About this dream of the child who declares that he is burning, Freud remarks that "the meaning of this affecting dream is simple enough," and he presumes that the father must have fallen asleep feeling anxious about the old caretaker's ability to watch over his child's body.[4] This anxiety filtered through to the father's dream content, making his son appear in the dream as a condemnation of the father's own complicit negligence in what he was simultaneously missing in waking life as the child's actual body burned. Additionally, Freud guessed that the light from the nearby room where the dead corpse was burning, the "bright glare," filtered "into the eyes of the sleeper" and created the father's illusion of wakefulness as he slept, while the ambient light also intensified his perception of the flames and burning visage in the dream. Ultimately, the dream represented an opportunity for wish fulfillment because even though the father went to bed knowing that his son was dead, as he slept, his dead child came alive again. Freud concludes, "The dead child behaves as though alive. . . . It was for the sake of this wish-fulfillment that the father slept a moment longer."[5]

In all, Freud did not spend much time in *The Interpretation of Dreams* analyzing this particular dream; he mostly used it as an opportunity to discuss the existing limited clinical investigations of dreams as psychic processes in general. Perhaps one of the reasons Freud's analysis of this dream seems so incomplete is that Freudian theories, which stress drives and wishes, unconscious behaviors and wish fulfillments, are not at all concerned with the ambition to know the other as real or with the emotional consequences of succeeding or failing at knowing the other as such. What we can take from Freud's cursory treatment of the dream of the burning child, though, is the one thing his analysis makes clear: the child appears to the father as a signifier, as a materialization and embodiment of the

father's guilty feelings and wishful longings. As a signifier, the child represents the father's grasp on reality as well as his fantasies (overt wishes)
and phantasies (less obvious, purely psychic constructions). Freudian
theory cannot account for, however, any of the ways in which the child on
fire might exist in the dream as something other than an expression of the
father's guilt or wish to see his son alive because Freudian interpretation
focuses only on the view and logic of the dreamer, of the dominant subject
or self, and allows for little imagination, agency, or intentionality when it
comes to object, image, or other subjects.

In general, post-Freudian approaches to psychoanalysis, particularly
object relations theory and self-psychology, branches of psychoanalysis
developed by D. W Winnicott, Heinz Kohut, Jessica Benjamin, and Melanie Klein, invite broader possibilities for interpretation that help us at
least consider relationships between subjects and objects, between selves
and others, and, importantly, between equally constituted (or equally
imagined) subjectivities. For instance, how might the child's appearance
function simultaneously as a signification of the father's guilt *and* as a
direct reprimand for the father's failure to see or recognize the child/other
as an autonomous subject in his own right? The child's exact words are
instructive here. Freud did not know what to make of the child's choice of
the word "burning"; he noted only that the child may have used this word
to describe a fever on a prior occasion. Similarly, Freud observed that the
child's comment—"Father, don't you see that I am burning?" was likely
"overdetermined," that the child's words probably "consisted of phrases
that it had uttered while still living" and that this must have referenced
"an emotional occurrence unknown to us." All of this is unremarkable
to Freud. Yet the missing context in this case is everything. If the child's
words referenced conversations between father and son that occurred
prior to the son's death, then the dream and the statement about "seeing"
and "burning" have more to do with the living child and his experiences
with his father than Freud's interpretation of the father's guilt, anxiety,
and longing can account for. Even though Freud suspected that the child's
words were essentially loaded (and therefore not to be taken at face value),
Freud could not imagine a context or history for the dream that could
have reflected more of the child's realities, fantasies, or psychic renderings.

Among the many possible interpretations here, the child's "don't you see" might more accurately have implied or referenced a missed opportunity for recognition, especially if the father had a habit of inattention while his son was living.

If the child appearing on fire could function as an overdetermined invitation for the father to finally learn something about the son's psychological existence and subjectivity, then "burning" carries with it two related potentialities. On the one hand, it signifies a kind of subjective survival that depends on the participation of other subjects—the child rises from the dead to demand recognition from the father. On the other hand, as an agent on fire, the child expresses his own potential to destroy, threaten, or challenge some aspect of the father's identity and consciousness. In this regard, the child might speak as burning with desire and sexual excitement, particularly as a phallic rival.[6] My point here is that these two things are not mutually exclusive: to be a signifier in someone else's imagination does not preclude the simultaneity of "burning" or signifying as something else—as a rival, as independently desirous, or as an entity that simply cannot be "read" or understood at all.

Judith Butler makes a similar assertion about the psychological significance of drag performances. Using a Lacanian framework in her analysis of the film *Paris Is Burning* (1990), Butler emphasizes that the male drag performers in Jennie Livingston's documentary engage gender norms in ways that make clear their investment in dominant cultural ideals. But even as the performers idealize, reproduce, and appropriate normative codes, their drag balls and shows are also "annihilating," "reworking," and "resignifying." The way the performers create meaning with their bodies in their "phantasmatic attempt to approximate realness" is a both/and, not an either/or.[7] That is, Lacan's notion of the symbolic (where the subject comes into contact with language, others, and the law) helps Butler consider the drag performer as a subject who signifies both coherence and incoherence, both iteration and deviation. Butler explains:

> In the drag-ball productions of realness, we witness and produce the phantasmatic constitution of a subject, a subject who repeats and mimes the legitimating norms by which it itself has been

degraded, a subject founded in the project of mastery that compels and disrupts its own repetitions. This is not a subject who stands back from its identifications and decides instrumentally how or whether to work each of them today; on the contrary, the subject is the incoherent and mobilized imbrication of identifications; it is constituted in and through the iterability of its performance, a repetition that works at once to legitimate and delegitimate the realness norms by which it is produced.[8]

As a person who is at a site of multiple, shifting, and competing identifications, the drag performer's complicated and compounding signification is something that we might take for granted in a postmodern and poststructuralist theoretical climate that encourages discourses and interpretations that destabilize bifurcations en route to privileging multiplicity. Yet, in thinking specifically about the psychological contours of a self/subject that might have a both/and relationship to hegemonic systems of meaning, what does it actually look like for a loaded and shifty signifier to engage those systems of meanings in ways that attempt to lock down and stabilize the signifier's signification but ultimately further exacerbate its "incoherence" instead? Plainly, what might it mean for blackness as a trope, like that of the burning child or drag performer, to come up constantly against the force of a system of representation that configures its relationship to psychological knowledge as the real? If another "fact" of blackness is that it functions in the popular imaginary as a similarly "incoherent and mobilized imbrication of identifications," what might this mean for the "coherence" of the representational works that consistently dramatize the proximity of blackness to the metacultural valuation of recognition and intersubjectivity?

## When Blackness Burns: Race and Psychoanalysis

The most compelling part of the Freudian dream and metaphor of "burning" to me, and why I use it as inspiration for thinking about race and popular culture, is the way Freud learned about the dream in the first place. A woman who did not know the child or the father only had to hear about this dream in a lecture to reimagine and redream the entire scenario herself. As Freud noted, his patient "went so far as to imitate it, i.e., to repeat the elements of this dream in a dream of her own in order to express by this transference her agreement with it in a certain point."9 Essentially, as we might put it in a digital cultural vernacular, this random dream "went viral"—with Freud, the lecturer, and the appropriating patient all talking about or dreaming about this one barely intelligible psychic event. Despite the lack of context specificity, despite all of the things no one else could possibly know or understand, this dream traveled and took on a shared, psychically informed and diffuse meaning that depended less and less on the original principal agents and more on how others related to it. The virality of the dream of the burning child, that it could become so captivating and personally meaningful to a random sample of other people, speaks to the high probability of recognition failure and of the attractiveness of that failure. The virality of the dream also conveys the allure and power of transference—the practice of transferring emotions from one person or context to another, of relating to a person or event as if it were something that it is not.

Blackness, as "burning," travels in much the same way, as a mostly shifting and porous, affectively loaded and nonspecific signifier. And so, as this book is about how blackness as a site of meaning depended on the politics of recognition during the dominant relational culture of the civil rights era, when I say that blackness *burns* in popular culture, I am emphasizing all of the things that Freud got right and also missed in the interpretation of this dream. When blackness burns, it *signifies* phantastically because the representations of African American subjectivities are overloaded and *overdetermined* by so many things at once. As significations, the stories and images about black identity are inevitably ripe for cooptation, appropriation, and especially *transference*. If blackness is an open and shifty signifier, psychoanalytic discourse and commonsensical psychological knowledge, on which the intersubjective view of race rests, has worked to try to cohere and make more transferable the incommunicable and noncompliant aspects of the sign. When integrated into public culture, psychoanalytic ideologies, like stories about the success or failure of the recognition of black humanity, aim to secure and fix into place the unfixable. This is not to say, of course, that there is anything wrong or pathological in black culture or with African American subjectivities or experiences—it is that our fallback methods of representing blackness so often return us to the deceptively alluring domain of (lay) analysis. The major consequence of representational modes that return us to the task of seeing blackness survive psychologically or to the metaproject of recognizing black humanity and particularity is that this very process runs always antithetical to the concurrent meanings produced in our other phantastical engagements with blackness as a signifier—the equally compelling and relentless cultural practices of signification, overdetermination, and transference. These cultural practices include, of course, the litany of historical stereotypes of the racial other, like hypersexualizations of black men and women, or the ways in which blackness is often represented as being formed subjectively through trials of sexual violation (as in *Antwone Fisher* and other films that touch on similar issues, like *Precious*) or specifically denied recognition in exploitative sexual economies (as I discuss in chapter 4 with black women in pimp culture).[10]

So too in my theorization of blackness as burning do I intentionally reference that 1960s refrain "burn, baby! burn!" which was popularized by the R&B and soul music radio DJ Magnificent Montague. Montague would famously yell, "burn, baby, burn!" whenever a track had "heat" or would emotionally stir and captivate him. When he shouted "burn!" he was ever confident that his listeners would also experience the song as personally meaningful. The refrain, like the dream of the burning child, traveled transferentially; it was appropriated during the 1965 Watts riots by protestors who chanted, claimed, and recoded it as an idiom of resistance.[11] More than anything, when blackness burns, gesturing meaning multidirectionally, it also always alerts us to black identity's unstable and untenable relationship to the politics of recognition. Blackness burns, then, "freed" by the process of signification and saddled by impending and inevitable transferences, alerting us as it does to the fact that psychological recognition, even if obtained momentarily, can never hold.

I make these arguments about the psychic and cultural value of blackness burning knowing well that writing about psychoanalysis and race is still a vexed and relatively new tradition. Almost without exception, the work done in this vein has centered on black literary traditions. Claudia

Tate, in *Psychoanalysis and Black Novels: Desire and the Protocols of Race* (1998), was among the first to address directly both the long-standing skepticism toward and exclusion of psychoanalytic thought in African American literary criticism. Tate summarized this reluctance in African American scholarship as registering the concern that "the imposition of psychoanalytic theory on African American literature advances Western hegemony over the cultural production of black Americans, indeed over black subjectivity."[12] In acknowledging fully that there have been legitimate biases in the development of many psychoanalytic methods and disciplines, Tate argued that black writers have nonetheless historically engaged and integrated analytic discourses and themes, both into their own lives and as they constructed many of their most canonical characters.

In the past two decades, there has been a modest increase in the production of critical investigations that have sought to go beyond the mere application of psychoanalytic concepts to "the race problem." In this regard, Hortense Spillers in "All You Could Be Now If Sigmund Freud's Wife Was Your Mother: Race and Psychoanalysis" (1996), Anne Cheng in *The Melancholy of Race* (2001), Gwen Bergner in *Taboo Subjects* (2005), and Paul Gilroy in *Postcolonial Melancholia* (2005) have used psychoanalytic principles and ideologies to rethink the phantastical dimensions of slavery and the middle passage, racialized grief and mourning, scenes of racial and sexual awakening, and imperial politics and multiculturalism, respectively.[13] The publication of recent books in this area demonstrates that there continues to be a sustained critical audience within African American studies and cultural studies for projects that centralize the relationship between black culture and psychoanalytic language. For instance, In *Dilution Anxiety and the Black Phallus* (2008), Margo Crawford, in her excavation of American literature and Black Arts poetry, challenges the primacy of castration scenes in the cultural imagination and instead demonstrates psychoanalysis's usefulness for understanding color politics as "dilution anxieties" within black communities.[14] In *Freud Upside Down: African American Literature and Psychoanalytic Culture* (2010), Badia Sahar Ahad persuasively combines literary and biographical analysis in order to make clear the subversive psychological practices and inclinations of some of the most accomplished African American writers, including Richard Wright, Nella Larsen, Jean Toomer, Ralph Ellison, and Adrienne Kennedy.[15]

While these projects have done much to make psychoanalytic inquiry less marginal in discussions about African Americans, *Blackness Is Burning* complements and adds to this discursive history in two important ways. First, as I mentioned, researchers working in this domain have been literary critics and have likewise turned to American and African American poetry and literature to explore race and the predominance of psychoanalytic paradoxes. While the scholarship in this area, from Claudia Tate and Hortense Spillers to Anne Cheng and Margo Crawford, has been so richly productive that we might now willingly concede that the psychoanalytic interpretation of African American literature not only resonates at the level of theory but also makes practical sense, I contend that the way psychological perspectives mesh with and meld into the sometimes insidiously banal mass and popular forms (buddy films, Saturday-morning cartoons, "ghetto" or "street" novels) has made the biggest cultural impact in signifying race as psychological in contemporary American life. And yet, at the time of this writing, there are no book-length studies on blackness, psychoanalysis, and popular culture. We have been slow to investigate the ways in which popular film, television, and fiction have distilled the psychoanalytic into cultural logics about racial difference that are highly reproducible and become only more accessible and consumable as the many established conventions, genres, character types, stereotypes, and common images circulate the psychoanalytic epistemologies. With this project, then, I introduce ways for us to begin attributing the same measure of attentiveness and critical sophistication we have reserved for literature to the popular and mass arts.

Second, this study directly problematizes the way Freudian and Lacanian perspectives have become our go-to models of analysis. An overreliance on Freud and Lacan obscures the fact that sometimes wish fulfillments, unconscious drives, fetishes, phalluses, and symbolic orders simply cannot get to the heart of how we have come to understand our most common conversations about race and identity. In the dense archive of civil rights era popular stories about race, there are repeated themes and concerns—loneliness, the strive for perfection, an alternating sense of depression and exuberance—that take us to affective experiences beyond what either Freud or Lacan cared about principally. Instead of revising significantly Freudian and Lacanian theories to "fit" this examination of race, representation, and recognition, I turn throughout this book to practitioners like Kohut and Winnicott, Benjamin and Klein—thinkers who have remained outside the traditional psychoanalytic study of race. Likewise, if Freud was the theoretical "father figure" of the modernist period and if Lacan has had an equally dominant influence on poststructuralist thought and literary interpretation, the clinical practice of psychoanalysis in contemporary American culture has been composed of many voices, modalities, and influential styles. The mass-cultural appropriation of psychology and psychoanalysis has reflected much more of this complicated (and often contradictory) engagement with contemporary theories that are quite often neither Freudian nor Lacanian in nature or inspiration. This is not to say that Freudian and Lacanian theories do not surface here at all throughout these pages. Aspects of the psychoanalytic canon certainly do get referenced here, but my perhaps idiosyncratic interest in psychoanalysis is most concerned with how it can help us rethink and challenge some of the dominant intersubjective questions that were at the heart of public and popular discourses about race.

Even in the process of engaging these theories, I remain attentive to the fact that there are social and political consequences for the centrality of psychoanalysis in American life. Yet, as I argue, psychological perspective often crops up in texts that are trying to manage the contradictions and consequences inherent in the merging of the politics of recognition with the politics of representation, and this overlap between the psychological and issues of representation becomes clear only after we deliberately make our way through the "hardcore" psychoanalytic tropes. In doing this work, we also expose the ways in which the psychoanalytic models contain and suggest evidence of their own critique; delving further into the theories better enables us to note the times when the ideas also contradict and correlate poorly with black cultural production.

## What This Book Does

Although this study of race and the theme of recognition in popular culture is not comprehensive by any means, I have selected the case studies that appear in this book because each represents a merging of psychology and the politics of recognition that was culturally significant during the civil rights era and has also remained relevant to aspects of black and American popular culture today. In the first chapter, I define and introduce what I mean by the phrase "the intersubjective view of race." In order to establish some of the ways in which such a view is predicated on the assumed relational value of recognizing the other as a psychological subject, I also provide some theoretical and disciplinary context for how social theorists and cultural studies scholars have discussed the related phrases "the politics of recognition" and "the politics of representation." After providing a critical architecture for engaging Hegelian and psychoanalytic notions of recognition, I turn to a brief examination of how the theme of recognition surfaces in a post–civil rights film, *Antwone Fisher*. As I argue, *Antwone Fisher*'s attempt to humanize black masculinity through the lens of analysis, rituals of recognition, and moments of failed recognition has much in common with its narrative predecessors, civil rights era films like *The Defiant Ones* (1958).

In chapter 2, I argue that the mass attraction to Sidney Poitier during the 1950s and 1960s had much to do with the culture of analysis because, as the maid Tilly in *Guess Who's Coming to Dinner?* warns us, "Civil rights is one thing. This here is somethin' else." The limited critical reception of Poitier has focused on his symbolic political significance during the era and much less on what the nonliteral, the therapeutic, and the intersubjective impulse behind that "somethin' else" that appears in the dense archive of his thirty-eight feature films during the era might suggest about his engagement with the politics of recognition. In rethinking the terms of Poitier's celebrity, I argue that Poitier's characters signified or "burned" in these films only sometimes as the racial other fully recognized as human. Mostly, his particular cinema of racial transference, as I call it, displaced conveniently any dedication to representing the racial other's interiority as real. Yet, despite the obvious and assumed feel-good agenda of his films, Poitier's significance as a black film star does not tell the story about

intersubjectivity and recognition that we might expect to see. My examination of three additional Poitier films, *Edge of the City* (1957), *In the Heat
of the Night* (1967), and *Pressure Point* (1962), demonstrates the nuanced
ways in which Poitier's characters were often caught between the competing and contradictory tendencies to idealize, undermine, and recognize
the racial other. As my concluding analysis of *Pressure Point* shows, black
exceptionalism coded as a psychological authority has its limitations, as
quite often Poitier's films communicated a pessimistic assessment of the
country's ability to recognize the other's equal humanity and psychological distinctness precisely because white American men were just as likely
to participate in the intersubjective project as "treatable" and compliant
buddies as they were to appear as untreatable and grossly pathological
subjects who remained antagonistic to any therapeutic mission.

While American film and television history has not exactly produced
a black female film star who has had as much commercial success as Sidney Poitier, the politics of representation and recognition's heavy emphasis on the cultivation of empathy expressed by and directed toward the
racial other has created a succession of black female character types and
stereotypes (i.e., mammies, saints, and martyrs) that have serviced the
American popular imaginary as similar proxies of therapeutic utility—
from Hattie McDaniel's classic performance in *Gone with the Wind* (1939)
to Viola Davis's and Octavia Spencer's more recent performances in *The
Help* (2011). For the most part, however, when it comes to pop-cultural
expressions of the intersubjective view of race, black women have been
much tougher national and analytic subjects. For example, in *Sister Citizen*, Melissa Harris-Perry persuasively describes the unique set of challenges to the politics of recognition in the public sphere that black women
pose, arguing that "African American women lack opportunities for accurate, affirming recognition of the self and yet must contend with hypervis-
ibility imposed by their lower social status. . . . This situation undermines
the intersecting needs for privacy and recognition that underlie the democratic social contract."[16] While Harris-Perry's comments indicate some
of the ways in which dominant perceptions of black women complicate
a cultural investment in the recognition of black humanity, our critical
assessments of the unique challenges facing black women in the United

States tend to colloquialize psychological "harms" and the need for "healing" without accounting for how the psychologization of race in general and appropriation of psychoanalytic themes specifically has compounded black women's fraught engagement with the protocols of recognition.

As psychological subjects, black mothers have appeared in popular culture as the people who are most likely to fail at attempts to establish recognition between equal others. In identifying some of the ways the postwar American appropriation of psychoanalytic theory has informed popular representations of black women, chapters 3 and 4 tell two different stories about "baaaddd black mamas," a trope of all tropes that I use to characterize the representations of black mothers during and since the civil rights era as psychoanalytic in nature. As I read them, baaaddd black mamas have appeared in popular culture as "preoedipal" mothers who are represented consistently as emotionally terrorizing their children. Chapter 3 explores several civil rights era representations of black mother-and-daughter relationships that characterized the mothers as interfering with their daughters' desires for autonomy and pursuit of democratic ideals. I first address the heightened cultural panic around black maternity that pathologized black mothers as unnatural heads of households, a sentiment that was crystallized notoriously in the Moynihan Report but was also more generally expressed by sociologists, psychologists, policy makers, and writers of fiction and autobiography. I argue that family dramas like *Imitation of Life* (1959) and *Black Girl* (1972), novels like Toni Morrison's *Sula* (1973) and Alice Walker's *Meridian* (1976), and autobiographies like Michelle Wallace's *Black Macho and the Myth of the Superwoman* (1978) and Elaine Brown's *A Taste of Power* (1993) represent black mothers as having an innate and assumed inability to recognize others as psychologically distinct. Such works represent black mothers as omnipotently everything and shamefully nothing, while their daughters are equally idealized and repudiated for their attempts to separate from the often-eviscerating repercussions of maternal reach. Reading theories of omnipotence and preoedipality alongside the common narrative representations of black mothers helps us reconsider how some of the most common stereotypes of black mothers, stereotypes like the mammy, matriarch, sapphire, and jezebel have appeared as depressive and destructive figures who make the project of failed, stalled, and aborted recognition captivating, compelling, and compulsively reproducible. As I argue in my concluding analysis of a post–civil rights black family drama, *Precious* (2009), blackness burns around black mothers in popular culture at the site of a double failure of recognition: they are represented consistently as incapable of seeing the humanity of others, and, in turn, they are represented as being unrecognizable as full psychological subjects themselves.

Chapter 4 begins with a brief meditation on the post–civil rights film *Hustle & Flow* (2005). The rest of the chapter situates *Hustle & Flow* in the context of civil rights era pimp culture, an aspect of black popular culture that has remained popular among audiences of both visual and print media. As these comparisons between civil rights and post–civil rights subjectivities suggest, even in works that participate deliberately in realist dialectics of "keepin' it real," the politics of recognition are likely to become even more encumbered by the realm of the unreal or phantasies—needs, wishes, and desires—that stem from interpersonal relationships in the private sphere. While chapter 3 explores mother-daughter relationships, chapter 4 centralizes the relationship between baaaddd black mothers and their sons as I examine the emergence of the pimp as a significant pop-cultural icon that appeared in the 1960s and 1970s black popular fiction by Donald Goines and Robert Beck (Iceberg Slim). In examining closely *Pimp: The Story of My Life* (1967), *The Naked Soul of Iceberg Slim* (1971), and *Whoreson* (1972), I contend that the pimp figure is not just a stable or subversive response to late capitalism, urban plight, and the disenfranchisement of black men as Robin D. G. Kelley and Ronald L. Jackson have conjectured. Instead, I examine the ways in which the foundational pimp narratives from the civil rights era represent the pimp's physical and emotional world, his object world, as evolving from the chronic and catastrophic failure of recognition between black sons and their baaaddd mamas.

In black popular fiction and film (and later in hip hop culture), the successful pimp appears as burning in the popular imagination as an American supercapitalist who, through lawless acts of extreme brutalization and destruction, tries to rationalize and reorder, fantasize and reinvent, the postmodern ghetto around a concerted devaluation of any attempts to recognize the humanity of others. Constructed as a response to recognition failure within the home, the pimp or Mack Daddy who is hailed colloquially as the man with the swift fist and golden tongue—a skilled master of psychological domination—experiences the underworld as littered with a terrifying minefield of people who appear as dehumanized and contaminating objects that he tries constantly, and often unsuccessfully, to ward off. I argue that while it is indeed productive and valuable to destabilize and depart from a cultural investment in the politics of recognition, all too often potentially subversive figures and modes of representation either get caught up in spectacularizing the gloriously brutal ways in which recognition fails or eventually and reluctantly embrace the intersubjective ambition in an attempt to create certainty out of the chaos and nihilism that stems from spectacularizing failure in the first place. Beck's and Goines's canonical pimp narratives do both of these things—the popular fiction documents the pimp's flight from recognition as a set of wacky, unsettling, and patently psychoanalytic triangular desires that pivot around the figure's fantastical relationships with mothers/whores/fags and other underworld men. By the end, chapter 4, like chapter 5, explores some of the ways in which stories about failed recognition, "boundarylessness," or indeterminate postmodern black identities work initially as challenges to the intersubjective view but nevertheless get folded back into it.

In chapter 5, I make clear that Bill Cosby's image was never as unifying as it might have seemed—even prior to the rampant allegations of his sexual misconduct. The chapter explores how Cosby's civil rights era attempts to create humanized blackness in his stand-up comedy routines about black working-class children during the 1960s and 1970s materializes at first as a set of disruptive and competing, contradictory, and productively indeterminate representations of black youthful subjectivities. In critically bypassing this period of Cosby's career, the most influential scholarly considerations of his significant role in American television history (studies written by Sut Jhally, Linda F. Fuller, Janet Staiger, Herman Gray, and Michael Real) have been concerned mostly with analyses of *The Cosby Show*. In part to destabilize the centrality of *The Cosby Show* in written accounts of Cosby's career, my analysis of his earlier career demonstrates that his psychologically significant humor began much earlier than the 1980s. Two decades before *The Cosby Show*, Cosby creatively and repeatedly retold the story of his boyhood using the rich symbolic imagery of psychological possibility and blackness at play. Situating Cosby's early live performances and his first cartoon, *Fat Albert and the Cosby Kids* (1972–85), within the larger public discourses about interiority and childhood, particularly the widespread concerns about the mental well-being of black children, makes clear how Cosby's creation of a black working-class boyhood pastoral was committed to the serious business of refuting popular constructions that imagined the interior life of black children as hollow, psychically unanimated, and damaged by racism and other systemic failures to recognize black humanity.

While Cosby often declined to talk openly about racial politics, he nonetheless spent his entire career integrating commonsense psychological rhetoric into his brand and into his various entertainment properties. As I argue, Cosby's stories, educational programming, and humor depended on central themes of psychoanalysis and especially emphasized the restorative potential of play. Hence, when blackness burns in the typical Cosby production, it is around the conflation of childhood and racial identity as psychological signifiers. In this context, Fat Albert as a proxy for Cosby becomes a grand externalization of a fantastical, "essential," black self that not only can cope with disappointment and setbacks but also can thrive in a space of subjective boundarylessness and indeterminacy. Cosby's intentionally analogous engagement with the politics of recognition produces his version of a type of psychological nationalism that argues for black emotional healing and transformation despite the persistent failure of the state to recognize fully black humanity and dignity. Just as pimp culture dramatized a disavowal of the politics of recognition, Cosby's earlier productions demonstrated what a freedom from the intersubjective wish might look like only to impinge its sign of black children at (free) play with new prohibitory impulses.

In chapter 6, I explore some of the additional ways in which representations of race have continued to merge with psychological epistemologies and psychoanalytic themes in post–civil rights contemporary culture. One reason this tendency to conflate the demand and desire for black equality with personalized accounts of the emotional consequences of failed or successful recognition persists, I suggest, is because retrospective stories about the civil rights era continue to dominate mainstream popular culture. The continued focus on the emotional consequences of successful or failed recognition further predominates in the cultural imaginary in contexts such as the public discourse around Barack Obama's presidency, contemporary films about queer black subjectivity, and popular television shows like *Orange Is the New Black* (2012–present).

I end the book with an open reflection on how the politics of recognition and the intersubjective impulse have continued to inform recent discussions about (and protests of) the racialized conflict and the state-sanctioned violence against black people in Ferguson, Missouri, and in other parts of the country.

1

# RECOGNITION AND THE INTERSUBJECTIVE VIEW OF RACE

In order to explicate what I problematize in this book as the *intersubjective view of race*, it first becomes necessary to trace some of the discursive similarities among notions of recognition, intersubjectivity, and dialogic identity. How is the contemporary black subject formed and understood as a psychological being? What is the relationship between mutual self/other awareness and democratic freedom? Why has this notion of recognizing the other as human, as real and distinct, come to inform so many aspects of our public, popular, and political discourses? The Canadian philosopher Charles Taylor argues in his influential essay "The Politics of Recognition" that the call for recognition is often articulated by marginalized groups as an urgent and fundamental demand because of the largely unchallenged contention that "nonrecognition or misrecognition," be it of a group's or individual's humanity or culture, "can be a form of oppression, imprisoning someone in a false, distorted, and reduced mode of being."[1] Recognition, then, has been discussed as having the potential to impact the very core of human consciousness. Accordingly, there are two arenas in which these demands have played out: in "the intimate level" or private and personal sphere where individuals interact closely with each other and in the "social plane" or public sphere where groups interact with each other and with institutions and representatives of the state. Charting a philosophical history that spans from Jean-Jacques Rousseau and Immanuel Kant to Frantz Fanon, Taylor makes a distinction between "the politics of equal dignity," which is characterized by the demand for recognition of universal human dignity, and "the politics of difference," which demands the recognition of individual and group particularity. Taylor explains that, "with the politics of equal dignity, what is established is meant to be universally the same, an identical basket of rights and immunities; with the politics of difference, what we are asked to recognize is the unique identity of this individual or group, their distinctness from everyone else."[2] So, although the universalist emphasis on human equality often contradicts with the demand for individual and collective distinctiveness, both have come to inform ideals governing liberal democracy. Perhaps because it is so easy to marry appeals for the recognition of human dignity to claims about cultural distinctiveness and the demand for equal rights on a collective scale, there remains, as the social and political theorist Nancy Fraser argues, a pressing need for rethinking how recognition works both in theory and in practice. Fraser specifically notes that this need has only intensified as the desire for recognition continues to "drive many of the world's social conflicts, from campaigns for national sovereignty and subnational autonomy, to battles around multiculturalism, to the newly energized movements for international human rights."[3]

As Taylor's and Fraser's remarks about the scope, stakes, and various implications of a politics of recognition indicate, there are varied theoretical and disciplinary approaches to the topic of recognition that span from legal studies and social theory to philosophy and psychology, from African American studies and cultural theory to studies of media and representation.[4] Given the multiplicity of perspectives on this topic, it is necessary to be as clear as possible about to *which* politics of recognition we are referring at any given moment. In this regard, Fraser's discursive interventions are particularly useful for the ways in which she highlights some of the common interests evident in how social scientists, cultural theorists, and media scholars have approached the topic. While Fraser is ultimately critical of any politics of recognition that displaces "the politics of redistribution," she rightly centralizes G. W. F. Hegel's notion of the desire for a mutual or reciprocal recognition of conscious beings as a paradigm around which many of the various conversations about recognition intersect. The Hegelian view of recognition, explains Fraser, "designates an ideal recip- rocal relation between subjects, in which each sees the other both as its equal and also as separate from it. This relation is constitutive for subjec- tivity: one becomes an individual subject only by virtue of recognizing, and being recognized by, another subject. Recognition from others is thus essential to the development of a sense of self. To be denied recognition— or to be 'misrecognized'—is to suffer both a distortion of one's relation to one's self and an injury to one's identity."[5]

I discuss the psychoanalytic evolution of Hegel's notion of mutual recognition more extensively in chapter 2, where I reposition Sidney Poitier's career in relation to rituals of recognition and analysis. For now, evident in Fraser's concise summary of Hegelian recognition is the pro- cess's inherently dialogic design. Both self and other, dominant group and marginalized group, come to know their importance, cultural distinctive- ness, and very psychological existence by participating in a dialectic that is supposed to reciprocally emphasize difference and sameness. When the reciprocity of that dialectic is broken, however, misrecognition (failed or false recognition) dominates the exchange and tragically compromises the participants' abilities to see accurately or relate equitably.

In fact, as Fanon reminds us in *Black Skin, White Masks*, intentional and strategic misrecognition is a defining feature of colonialism. What Fanon calls the "fact of blackness"—the interpretation of the racial other's out- ward appearance as a pejorative prism of difference—has historically been used as the very catalyst for precluding recognition even though, under the Hegelian model, the psychological consciousness of the other is sup- posed to signal some measure of ontological sameness, thus creating that delicate balance of difference and sameness on which the potential for rec- ognition rests. Fanon rightly interprets the way others hail him as a "dirty nigger" and as a "Negro" as the confirmation of a failed recognition—one that reverberates psychologically by creating in him an internalized sense of a "crushing objecthood."[6] The failed recognitions and misrecognitions of blackness are confirmed continually by the dominant group's illusions or phantastical projections (as in "the Negro is ugly; look, a nigger, it's cold, the nigger is shivering, the nigger is shivering because he is cold").[7]

As a psychoanalyst, Fanon invariably stresses the dialogic or intersubjective nature of recognition between the races, and in the *point culminant* of his analysis, he deploys a Hegelian logic to argue that unless successful mutual recognition is achieved, a compulsive obsessiveness with the self/other and the quest for recognition will persist.[8] Importantly for Fanon, "a world of reciprocal recognitions" will be formed neither passively nor necessarily nonviolently. The struggle for, and belief in, this kind of dialogic and intersubjective recognition requires, as Fanon concludes, a willingness to "accept conclusions of death, invincible dissolution, but also the possibility of the impossible."[9] Although there have been some insightful reinterpretations of Fanon, from Kara Keeling's compelling notion of a "cinematic Fanon" to Glen Sean Coulthard's understanding of Fanon's "self-affirmative challenges to colonial humanism," here I stress what Fanon nonetheless envisioned as a humanist ideal.[10] Even in the face of all that can and is likely to go wrong in an intersubjective or dialogic process of recognition, despite the highly consequential outcomes of "death," "dissolution," and "impossibility," Fanon eloquently echoes here the persistent hope that the struggle toward true human interconnectedness can make the impossible (reciprocal recognition) possible.

Along these lines, if recognition failure has the potential to create "crushing objecthood(s)", popular culture has been discussed as a site on which battles for recognition are ardently fought. As Fraser puts it, in the cultural and political terrain, "the politics of recognition aims to repair internal self-dislocation by contesting the dominant culture's demeaning picture of the group."[11] It is in the cultural domain "that members of misrecognized groups" have sieged opportunities to challenge and reject "distorted, dominant imagery" by creating "new self-representations of their own making," representations that aim to correct and replace the "internalized, negative identities."[12] It is perhaps for these reasons that cultural studies theorists have typically distilled the politics of recognition into the phrases "the politics of representation" or "the cultural politics of representation."[13] Stuart Hall, for instance, who famously theorized popular culture as a "theater of popular desires" and "popular fantasies," also seemed to take for granted that motifs of recognition are an inevitable part of a culture born of a marginalized group's response to dominant cultural distortions.[14] Hall stresses that "the ways we have been positioned and subjected in the dominant regimes of representation were a critical exercise of cultural power and normalization, precisely because they were not superficial. They had the power to make us see and experience ourselves as 'Other.' Every regime of representation is a regime of power formed, as Foucault reminds us, by the fatal couplet, 'power/knowledge.'"[15]

In calling misrecognition a "truly traumatic character of 'the colonial experience,'" Hall's assessment of a politics of representation frames it as dialogic, much like the politics of recognition. If cultural identity is, as Hall understands it, a function of "being" and "becoming," or a process that is both inwardly and outwardly defined, then popular culture like film, television, music, and pulp fiction matters in this context because it is the arena in which cultural identity is both formed and expressed. Similarly, though less interested in the dialogic or intersubjective imperative of recognition, television and media studies scholar Herman Gray persuasively argues in "Subject(ed) to Recognition" that while the state was "was once the primary *site* of struggles for civil recognition and social equality, the media remain the crucial site where different sectors of disenfranchised populations and communities continue" to pursue "greater visibility as a measure of cultural justice and social equality."[16]

Popular culture, like the basic tenets of liberal democracy, can also easily conflate claims related to the recognition of dignity with a superficial valuation of difference. While the African American demand for recognition and representation, "black freedom struggles," as Gray summarizes succinctly, "have always included the demand for representation and recognition as human beings by slaveholders, the state, and public institutions within civil society, law, and culture," what I critique in this book as the intersubjective view of race overemphasizes and often sensationalizes the role that individuals and interrelatedness can play in these processes.[17] As more comprehensive than the intersubjective emphasis on recognition, the long history of the African American struggle for recognition has been defined by the "access to and affirmation of black humanity" (as evident in the autobiographical writings of Frederick Douglass) and the "assertion of interiority . . . that expressed a yearning for freedom" (most famously argued by W. E. B. Du Bois).[18] The civil rights era marked a point of particularly high concentration and visibility for arguments in this regard, and the struggle for recognition was expressed, challenged, and affirmed in landmark legal cases like *Brown v. Board of Education of Topeka*, in Malcolm X's call for "black recognition on a global scale," in the speeches and activism of Martin Luther King Jr., and in the efforts of "countless ordinary men, women, and children" who protested oppression and inequality throughout the era.[19] While the civil rights era without question marked an equally significant moment when the politics of recognition and the politics of representation intertwined, Gray remains critical of how popular culture has remained a site where "representations of the modern civil rights subject and the discourse of racial justice as multicultural and color-blind" proliferate.[20] As he further explains in critiquing this politics of representation,

> Indeed, the liberal subject of the modern civil rights movement is not the same as the neoliberal subject of the post–civil rights, postnetwork era. . . . I want to suggest that in the post–civil rights, postnetwork television period, the press for more visibility and authentic representation is concerning. I suggest this because the alliance of difference and power instigates a yearning for *representation as an end in itself* that perfectly expresses the logic of market choice, consumer sovereignty, self-reliance, and cultural diversity. In short, the *incitement* to media visibility and the *proliferation* of media images that it generates is a technique of power. Notwithstanding the collective achievements of the modern civil rights movement, this modern form of power now operates in a conjuncture where the cultural politics of representation articulated by the American civil rights movement four decades ago is no longer productive in the same way.[21]

Gray is correct, I believe, in arguing cogently that "we are experiencing a 'waning' in what a cultural politics of representation can yield."[22] Like Gray, I am critical of the politics of recognition, especially as it appears in representational culture. Yet it is not only the neoliberal black subject who has been affected by the "conditions of impossibility" that characterize the politics of representation's thematization of recognition. Rather, the politics of recognition and representation have always functioned as "a modern form of power," as a "regime of power formed." More specifically, the theme of recognition, to draw from Saidiya V. Hartman, as Gray does, produces many protracted "scenes" of subjection that in the end only reinforce dominance, depressiveness, and a futile migration toward unattainability.[23] What does it mean to see and read again and again accounts of the impossible—true intersubjective recognition—framed as either barely and ephemerally achieved or as horribly and tragically dissolved? What cause for celebration of the intersubjective view is there in the tiny measure of hope and possibility that exists between tenuous achievement and colossal failure?

As I argue throughout *Blackness Is Burning*, even though the actual subjects of a civil rights and post–civil rights social order are not the same legal and social subjects, just as the call for increased representational visibility across popular cultural forms in either of the two historical periods remains similar, so too is there much continuity between the *representations* of civil rights era black subjectivities and popular *representations* of post–civil rights black subjectivities. Simply acknowledging that the civil rights era was a key moment when the fight for recognition heavily influenced the cultural domain tells us little about how those works imagined and dramatized the theme of recognition in the first place. At this point, it may be helpful to work our way backward, historically speaking, and look more closely at how a post–civil rights text, *Antwone Fisher*, dramatizes recognition (and failed recognition) between black characters, before then considering how a classic civil rights era text, *The Defiant Ones* (1958), casts a similar intersubjective logic around an interracial dyad.

## Blackness and the Therapeutic Struggle for Recognition

Within the first five minutes of *Antwone Fisher*, after the title character, Petty Officer Antwone Fisher (played by Derek Luke), is unable to control his violent temper and punches one of his white commanding officers in the face, he is instructed by his superiors to undergo psychiatric evaluation and treatment with one of the navy's psychiatrists, Dr. Jerome Davenport (Denzel Washington). Although the entire story revolves around the rare dramatization of two black men in analysis, one as analysand, the other as analyst, right from the start, the story acknowledges that black people might have good reason to run kicking and screaming from any attempts at "psychiatric" intervention. Perhaps justifiably so, Antwone's black male friends lambast him for having to go to the "nut house" and "shrink clinic," and Antwone initially lies to his love interest about his whereabouts during his weekly hour-long appointments with Davenport. Antwone's opening comments to his psychiatrist are incendiary. When asked what brought him to analysis, Antwone retorts, "Why something gotta be bothering me? Cuz I jumped on a white boy? Something must be wrong with me? Send him to the psychiatrist. Nigger tried to kill his master. He must be crazy!" The dialogue consolidates and succinctly references a deep black cultural mistrust of clinical psychology and articulates the suspicion that psychoanalysis not only has the potential to function as a disciplinary mechanism designed to undermine the mental and emotional competence of people of color but also might serve as a more general tool of indoctrination and oppression.

Despite Antwone's skepticism toward psychotherapy, analysis works for the character just as we might expect it would. Psychiatric treatment, therapeutic consultation with another black male, changes Antwone Fisher. It softens him. It helps him better understand and rechannel his chronic feelings of rage, or as his analyst says, "You have to use that energy [anger that stems from trauma] to better yourself." And so after Antwone learns to talk about the painful details of sexual abuse and dehumanization that were a part of his childhood in the foster-care system, he falls in love and becomes more adept at controlling his emotions. He travels from the safety of his naval base in San Diego to Cleveland to confront his abusive foster mothers, track down his biological mother, and connect with an enormous, welcoming extended family he never knew he had. At the film's end, Antwone becomes friends with his therapist, and by the time he yells the film's signature line, a battle cry—"I'm still standing, I'm still strong!"—we are convinced that he is now better poised to lead a happy and productive life.

My quick summary of the film's plot does not fully capture the emotional and cultural impact the film made during the time of its release.

Denzel Washington, who made his directorial debut with the film, and the real Antwone Quenton Fisher, who wrote the screenplay based on his life and best-selling memoir, *Finding Fish*, were praised for bringing a story about the physical, sexual, and emotional abuse of black boys to public view. Upon its release, the film's star, Derek Luke, admitted that he too was a survivor of childhood sexual abuse, saying, "I was molested, and I have my own personal fight. That was a challenge for me, even now talking about it. But my whole thing was to bring justice to the Antwones of the world."[24] Different from the 1990s films like *Boyz n the Hood* (1991) and *Menace to Society* (1993) that emphasized the effects of gang violence, racism, and the biases of an American criminal justice system, this film tried explicitly to tell a story about black male interiority that could be made more intelligible by our shared—if reluctant—belief in the useful potential of talking therapy.

In trying to make black interiority communicable, *Antwone Fisher* dramatizes a set of rituals that invite an *identificatory* spectatorship from some of its viewers and an *empathizing* spectatorship from others. As two of the film's most affecting scenes suggest, both of these responses are ultimately about the emotional upside and benefits of recognition. The first of these scenes appears as Antwone's most significant analytic revelation. The actions take place immediately after he has been thrown in jail for fighting again: this time he erupts because his shipmates goaded him for being a virgin. Davenport visits him behind bars, and when he probes Antwone about his explosive and regressive behavior, asking whether he is in fact a virgin, Antwone, overcome with emotion, begins to recount the most traumatic moments of abuse from his childhood. After a close-up of Antwone's anguished expression, the events on-screen flash back to when he was a child of six or seven years old. In the flashback, Antwone's physically and verbally abusive foster mother, Mrs. Tate, has left him alone with Nadine, another adult black woman. With the two alone in the house, Nadine approaches young Antwone, slaps him, and pushes him against the wall. She orders him to kiss her and then tells him to "get on downstairs and drop 'em." The camera, which shifts between stationary and tracking positions, does not visualize fully the reenactment of childhood sexual abuse; it zooms in tightly on the basement window once Nadine and Antwone have gone down below. Perhaps because this violation of Antwone's humanity cannot be represented on-screen due to the age of the child actor, the dialogue and other diegetic sounds we hear confirm that a gross violation of the character's subjective will and consciousness is occurring. There are sounds of Nadine slapping him and impatiently instructing, "Come on, pull them down. Pull them right over my feet." She says, "Get close. You don't have to be afraid. Now touch me." And then, after some time has transpired, with a wide tracking shot, the camera follows young Antwone running frantically from the house, shirtless, belt unbuckled, shaking. At the end of the flashback, as the action shifts back to the present, the adult Antwone interjects, "She made me. She made me do those things. I was only a little boy. If there was something I wouldn't do, she would beat me." As the adult speaks for the child in the present, the camera focuses unwaveringly on Antwone's face. His lips are ashen, his face tightly grimaced.

Both parts of this scene, the shots of Antwone's visceral pain in the present day as well as the flashback to him as a vulnerable boy, are important to the film's emotional and intersubjective logic. As Davenport's initial interrogation of Antwone at the start of the scene suggests, the volatile young black man behind bars was motivationally inaccessible and unintelligible without the disclosure of these traumatic details of his past.[25] That is, in order to either identify with or have empathy for what might otherwise appear as a stereotypical representation of black masculinity, Davenport needed to finally learn of Antwone's survival of chronic attempts to destroy his humanity and will. If Antwone's foster mothers play an important role in repeatedly failing to recognize his subjective distinctness, Davenport is poised in this analytic breakthrough as a more suitable subjective partner who can fulfill that dialogic imperative. While the Hegelian model normatively pits the two relational subjects in direct conflict with each other so that it is the "violence" of their coming together that each must survive in order to establish a partial or mutual recognition, in this case, Davenport's position as a witness serves a similar purpose: he models the task of recognizing the other as real that the black women in Antwone's past are vilified for spectacularly failing to do. Irrespective of whether we identify with or empathize with Antwone, watching (and hearing) him survive destruction in his most vulnerable state creates a spectatorial pleasure and investment in wanting to see him survive in the present and future.

The way the scene is edited further stresses Davenport's participation in the dialectic. Before and immediately after the flashback, all of the tight close-ups of Antwone's face visually unify the child's trauma with the man's interior logic, his rage and his pain. Only a few carefully edited shot-reverse-shots of Davenport's shock, concern, and compassion create breaks in the camera's concentration on Antwone's facial expressions. These brief visual interruptions create a small distance, a mediation, between Antwone's consuming pain and Davenport's performance of empathetic listening. The final shot of this therapeutic exchange is a compelling wide shot of both black men still behind bars. After Antwone has confessed the details of his painful past, he hunches over in exhaustion, disheveled and dressed as a civilian, while his therapist, dressed neatly in the navy's service uniform, sits upright across from him, patiently waiting in their collective silence. The image captures Davenport's willingness to go behind bars—into another man's emotional prison—so that he might do the difficult but rewarding relational work of humanizing the otherwise stock personification of black masculine rage. The two men framed together also create a visualization of black pain and hardship's purported proximity to success and survival, as Antwone's brutal experiences have brought him into contact with another black male who has achieved the professional and emotional competence that he seeks. The image holds. Davenport's complete attention is held captive by Antwone's recitation of adversity; Antwone, emptied at last of explosive affect, is "held" by Davenport's compassionate silence.

This breakthrough in analysis paves the way for Antwone to travel to Cleveland to confront other aspects of his past. Yet the film does not end during this visit, after Antwone has confronted his abusers, located his biological mother, and connected with an affirming assortment of extended family members—as we might expect it would. The film ends not at its highest melodramatic point of cathartic release when the long-lost family welcomes Antwone to dine with them in a celebratory feast (as he has dreamed they would). Instead, the story ends with Antwone and

Black masculinity and talking therapy, *Antwone Fisher*

his therapist speaking to each other on the naval base as friends. Echoing a discourse of reciprocity that informs psychoanalytic theories of transference, the final exchange between analysand and analyst stresses what the patient, by being a compliant and treatable subject, has taught the doctor. In this reunion between patient and doctor, after Antwone provides a synopsis of his latest demonstration of survival and resiliency, Davenport, beaming proudly, confesses that analysis with Antwone has touched him "to the core" and helped him address his own personal secrets, including issues that have been affecting his marriage. He says, "One day a young man came into my office and into my life, and he blew up that little secret, and he put me to shame in a way I never thought possible. Because of you, Antwone, I'm a better doctor. And I'm learning to be a better husband. You don't owe me anything. I owe you. You're the champ, son. You've beaten everybody who has beaten you. I salute you." The film ends with both men marching off together.

These final scenes of action encourage the two modes of spectatorship that are an inherent part of psychologizing of race, one mode based on identification and sameness, the other derived from an acknowledgment of difference and the cultivation of empathy. For those who will identify with Antwone either because the specific experience of overcoming childhood abuse resonates with their own experiences or because they identify with what the film more generally references as the plight of being African American in the United States, the process of recognizing Antwone's humanity helps affirm their own similar personal narrative of resiliency, or as Antwone says triumphantly to his foster mother, "I'm still standing, I'm still strong! And I always will be." In this case, the exercise of recognizing Antwone's humanity and dogged ability for surviving perpetual attempts at destruction motivationally reminds and assures these viewers of their own ability to survive real and symbolic destruction.

Comparatively, for spectators who do not see themselves as what Luke called "the Antwones of the world," recognizing Antwone's humanity in his distinct and unique history of surviving destruction paves the way for the kind of recognition that produces empathy. Davenport's final conversation with Antwone stresses the added benefits that stem from this actual or simulated engagement with a "surviving" other. As Davenport makes clear in his concluding words of praise, Antwone's story of hardship is so extreme that it puts him "to shame" by comparison, and the shameful examination of his life beside Antwone's inspires him to want to be "a better doctor" and a "better husband." The doctor's empathetic response that is fundamentally self-bolstering and self-serving indicates how tenuously achieved the recognition of a distinct other will be. That is, in the process of relating to and using Antwone's experiences as motivation to improve his own life, the doctor is already, just as recognition is achieved, casting the other into a different, fantastical position of subject/object status that begins to serve other emotional aims. As twin responses to the dramatization of black hardship, both identification and empathy only maintain a momentary engagement with a real and truly autonomous subject since the benefit of either outcome of recognition is that the process always teaches us more about ourselves than it teaches us about others. Further, in this post–civil rights context, the intersubjective value of recognition is predicated on a three-part cycle of first seeing black subjectivities fail (and fail spectacularly) to be recognized by others, be those others "baaaddd" black foster mothers, the state, or other antagonists. In the second part of the process, recognition is thankfully, joyfully, attained only to give way to new and competing fantasies of self and other by the third phase, as indicated in this example by Davenport's final idealization of Antwone.

## "Get Back on the Train!": Civil Rights and the Promise of Recognition

*Antwone Fisher*'s on-screen story takes place in the year it debuted, 2002, but the filmmakers intentionally brought civil rights era themes and references and the metadiscourse of analysis to its contemporary audiences. Fisher, who was born in Cleveland, Ohio, in 1959, experienced the events that are portrayed in the film when he was a child during the 1960s and 1970s; his experiences in the navy as a young man happened during the early 1980s. As such, the film's dramatization of Antwone's psychoanalytic discoveries was based on events that took place during the most formative moment in the American cultural history of bringing analytic themes to bear on "the race problem." The real Antwone Fisher came of age during a time when the stated democratic mission of inclusion was being constantly exposed as duplicitous, as extending unevenly across racial lines. This postsegregationist judicial climate was marked by the many well-documented and televised outbreaks of civil disobedience, including when the 1965 march from Selma to Montgomery, Alabama, became "Bloody Sunday" as news crews captured the violent and excessive use of force on peaceful protesters. Although this history is not referenced directly in the film version of Antwone Fisher's story, his early childhood experiences were a part of the social and political milieu that also witnessed the nonpeaceful protests of the Watts rebellion of 1965, the Detroit riot in 1967, and Cleveland's Hough Riots in 1966 and "Glenville Shootout" in 1968. Throughout this period of national transition and civic unrest, the call for more realistic, dynamic, and diverse representations of blacks in mass culture had never been louder. A dynamic range of mass-cultural representations of blackness formed alongside the various cultural renaissances of the era, including the Black Arts movement and the cadre of filmmakers known as the L.A. School of Rebellion. For example, there were novels and films that emphasized militancy and resistance, as seen in *The Spook Who Sat by the Door* (1969 novel; 1973 film) and *Sweet Sweetback's Baadasssss Song* (1971) as well as the more complicated representational ambitions of black independent filmmakers appearing in the late 1970s, like Halie Gerima's *Bush Mama* (1979) and Charles Burnett's *Killer of Sheep* (1979).

Rather than engage the artistic and political tradition of a 1960s and 1970s black counterculture or an overtly resistant representational culture to tell Antwone's story, however, both the screenwriter and the director (Fisher and Washington) decided that the film should be stripped of its specific temporal markers in order to market it as a socially relevant contemporary tale that was, decidedly, *not* about the civil rights era.[26] As Fisher explains, "I was born in 1959 but for the movie's sake, we decided [to change it] so that children—kids—would find it contemporary. If we did it like I grew up in the '60s and '70s, then some kids might say, 'Well, that's an old story.' And people might say that a long time has passed since then. But we wanted it to be current so that people would identify with it more."[27] Fisher and Washington believed ardently that something about this story would be communicable and valuable to contemporary audiences as a current-day tale. Yet *Antwone Fisher*'s relational politics is very much "an old story" that has much in common with mainstream productions from the civil rights era—films and television shows that emphasized black humanity, universalism, and the value of interpersonal relationships, such as *Nothing but a Man* (1964), *Julia* (1968–71), and *Roots* (1977). Part of what made Antwone's civil rights era experiences transplantable and relatable to later audiences is the fact that although much had changed in American cultural and political life between the era and 2002, the simple and captivating habit of relating to blackness through the humanizing language of analysis had not.

Although *Antwone Fisher* represents black humanity as formed through a brutal cycle of destruction and survival in an intraracial context, the film's general theme of the intersubjective utility of blackness connects it to civil rights era popular narratives and discourses about race. Take Sidney Poitier's career, for instance, and his performance in the now-classic interracial buddy film *The Defiant Ones*. By way of plot summary, Poitier plays Noah Cullen, an escaped convict who is chained to fellow escapee Johnny (played by Tony Curtis), a white man. Although the men are initially hostile toward each other, their extended run toward freedom and mutual survival of a lynch mob and a manhunt draws them closer together emotionally. The film's plot actions are fairly simplistic: the men fight, they talk, and they run in a repetitious cycle until at the end of the film, their newly formed homosocial bond is put to the ultimate test: is each man willing to sacrifice his own claim to freedom for the other? In the first part of this test, Johnny discovers that his new mistress has sent Cullen in the wrong direction through a marshy swamp instead of toward his desired location. Johnny, in rejecting a future with a white woman who clearly has no regard for his black friend's humanity, opts to sacrifice himself; he plunges headlong into the swamp to rescue Cullen. This part of the plot is particularly implausible, however, given Poitier's cinematic penchant for playing exceptional black men. That is, we are never fully convinced that Cullen is in any real danger since throughout the story, he has appeared superiorly competent, physically skilled, and generally more adept at surviving obstacles than any of the story's white characters. As James Baldwin complained in his critique of the film, "It is this which black audiences resented about *The Defiant Ones*: that Sidney was in company far beneath him, and that the unmistakable truth of his performance was being placed at the mercy of a lie."[28] For Baldwin, that "lie" is that Poitier's Cullen needs Johnny as much as Johnny needs him.

Narrative deceptions and implausibilities notwithstanding, the second part of the film's test of the characters' mutual empathy presents Cullen with a chance to save Johnny. Only, of course, "save" is not exactly the right word to describe what happens at the end of the film. After Johnny finds Cullen in the swamp, the two men, with a group of law officials and tracking dogs closing in on their location, finally make it to a departing freight train. Famously, and perhaps predictably, Poitier's Cullen makes a safe leap onto the platform of the moving train; Johnny, who is wounded, does not. Instead of riding the train to freedom, Cullen jumps off, and since Johnny can no longer run, the two men await recaptivity together. Notable in the scene's upbeat tone and mise-en-scène are the characters' mutual expressions of contentment and joy. They embrace. Cullen sings. Johnny smiles. They share a cigarette. Evident in this moment, as Baldwin also observes, is the homoerotic consequence and charge of male homosocial bonding and union. So too might we take note of how historical tropes of black masculinity, like the "noble savage," further overdetermine the pair's physical and emotional configuration in the film's final frames. While these readings are certainly warranted, the more overt point the film aims to make is that the promise of recognition that their interracial union introduced in the first place seems finally realized: both men, in choosing the other, acknowledge and affirm their mutual humanity as something valuable and more appealing than their individual freedom. We might even see in the film's final depiction of interracial union a snapshot of what Fanon described when he envisioned "a world of reciprocal recognitions" that can only form after the bouts of life-threatening conflict on which "the monument" of recognition is built. Specifically, perhaps wistfully and even a little sardonically, Fanon wrote that he could "already see a white man and a black man *hand in hand*."[29]

*The Defiant Ones* (like several of Poitier's films) is particularly good at representing some version of the emotional payout of two characters approaching recognition. If *Antwone Fisher* uses the tools of formal analysis to create the conditions for recognizing black humanity, this civil rights era film uses the interracial dyad to perform a similar analytic task. Only, just as the revelatory joy expressed at the end of *Antwone Fisher* was inseparable from what Davenport stood to gain from coming into contact with a surviving black other, the ending of *The Defiant Ones* seems to unintentionally capture an imbalance of gains and losses inherent in the buddied dialectic. Does the film's representation of the characters' joyous union represent subjective recognition finally achieved? Is *this* even what recognition between two equal subjects looks like? While I more thoroughly address the film's representation of recognition and analytic expertise in

Joyous recognitions, *The Defiant Ones*

chapter 2, for now, even if we might assume that interracial intersubjectivity has been achieved by *The Defiant Ones'* ending, the unequal costs of recognition for each character is woefully downplayed.

That both men should seem so unconcerned about their impending recapture was both unconvincing and profoundly disappointing to Baldwin, who writes at length about the film in *The Devil Finds Work*. Baldwin's thoughts are particularly helpful for delineating the difference between how empathizing and identifying spectators might differently perceive the film's celebration of mutuality, or as he frankly comments, "Liberal white audiences applauded when Sidney, at the end of the film, jumped off the train in order not to abandon the white buddy. The Harlem audience was outraged, and yelled back *Get back on the train, you fool!*"[30] Since the two men were not the same social and legal subjects in 1958, their mutual disavowal of corporeal freedom rang hollow for a potentially identifying audience. Yet the theme of recognition, and its accompanying intersubjective view of race, seemed plaintively clear to Baldwin as he further considered the significance of the emotional work the characters were created to perform. He explains: "Of course, what the film is now attempting to say—consciously—is that the ordeal of the black man and the white man has brought them closer together than they ever imagined they could be. The fact, and the effect, of this particular ordeal is being offered as a metaphor for the ordeal of black-white relations in America, an ordeal, the film is saying, which has brought us closer than we know. But the only level on which this can be said to be true is that level of human experience—that depth—of which Americans are most terrified."[31] Baldwin well summarizes here that the psychological work of recognizing mutual humanity serves as a metaphor for the era's "black-white relations." He also importantly expresses grave skepticism about whether such a project is achievable, given what he identifies as mutual recognition's creation of a terrifying depth of human experience.

In addition to creating an emotional state that is potentially both terrifying and joyful, the other thing that mutual recognition seems to cultivate here is the very type of regulation and subjection that Herman Gray assigns to representations of recognition in the post–civil rights era. If the pursuit of recognition might bring with it a further policing of the neoliberal black subject, we can see with this civil rights era text that the promise of recognition and the certainty of subjection were closely aligned during the era as well. In fact, the most obvious consequence of recognition in *The Defiant Ones* is disciplinary regulation. If both buddies consciously free themselves using a Hegelian dialectic, they do so only to be subjected to the state's disciplinary actions—as they are indeed recaptured by law enforcement in the final seconds. To return for a moment to the homo-erotic charge around the buddied pair, to the way they cradle and comfort each other in the final shots, and especially to the ways in which black masculinity is so often discussed as "feminized" in these types of inter-racial bonding stories, capturing and framing racial identity as such has the potential to only further exacerbate racial subordination—not free-dom—as Roderick Ferguson has theorized about the intersections among race, sexuality, and the denial of state privileges in "The Nightmares of the Heteronormative."[32] This is all to say that a "recognized" black subjectivity is also a more concretized, more easily normalized and contained subjec-tivity, a social and psychological being that may in fact have less access to other, nonpsychological freedoms. That blackness should end up in "pro-tective custody" as a function of the "cinematic terms of Black subordina-tion" in the interracial buddy film is something that the film scholar Ed Guerrero differently critiques in his reading of 1980s buddy films.[33] In the case of *The Defiant Ones*, it is the intersubjective imperative and promise of recognition, of finally knowing the other as real, that proves to be the red herring for the newly formed black subject. Suffice to say, post–civil rights buddy films have only continued to frame and reframe versions of this psychological dialectic, from *Beverly Hill Cop* (1984) and *Rocky II* and *III* (1979, 1982) to the more recent cycle of Kevin Hart films, such as *The Wedding Ringer* (2015) and *Get Hard* (2015).

As *Antwone Fisher* and *The Defiant Ones* indicate, both civil rights and post–civil rights narratives thematize recognition in ways that suggest how psychological transformation will serve the interpersonal domain and the public sphere because these works offer some vision of how these new subjects will function at home and in society at large as empathetic, enlightened, subjugated friends/lovers/citizens. Yet the civil rights era remains the most ideal place to trace some of the additional and less

obvious ways in which blackness and the inherently psychological implications of recognition correlate precisely because intersubjectivity, as a chief
rallying cry, democratic ideal, and organizational tactic, was such a central
theme of the civil rights movement. Accordingly, Benjamin DeMott, in
writing about one of the major derivatives of civil rights public discourses
on race, argues that while the era ostensibly exploded "the myth that some
humans are more human than others, whites more human than blacks,"
Americans have since come to value "the friendship orthodoxy" in which
whites and blacks are encouraged to "work toward recognition of their
fundamental commonality" in order to "see through superficial differences to the needs and longings that all share."[34] DeMott suggests that the
politics of recognition have been more or less reduced to frequent public
calls for teaching "ourselves how to get along together and how to become
friends."[35]

This belief in the transformative potential of the politics of recognition was conveyed during the civil rights era in increasingly intensified
emotional terms. Even though Baldwin was critical of how representational culture promoted the theme of recognition in films like *The Defiant
Ones*, this did not stop him from being optimistic that political progress
and mutual psychological transformation would coincide in the public
sphere. Writing in 1955 in *Notes of a Native Son*, Baldwin argued ardently,
"The time has come to realize that the interracial drama acted out on the
American continent has not only created a new black man, it has created
a new white man, too. No road whatever will lead Americans back to the
simplicity of this European village where white men still have the luxury
of looking on me as a stranger. I am not, really, a stranger any longer for
any American alive. . . . It is precisely this black-white experience which
may prove of indispensable value to us in the world we face today. This
world is white no longer, and it will never be white again."[36] Baldwin is
hopeful here that the social and political progress of the civil rights movement would lead to the creation of new American psychological subjectivities. When Baldwin claims, for instance, that white people no longer
have the "luxury" of seeing him as "a stranger," he is not just talking about
general political progress and activism; he is conveying the understanding that the "drama" of interracial conflict is also a movement toward a

form of recognition that can at last free him from Fanon's fact of blackness (chronically un/misrecognized objecthood). Baldwin does not simply
stress his equal right to full democratic participation in this reflection;
rather, he instead emphasizes a "black-white" intersubjective experience
that eradicates the existence of subjective strangers. Yet, if we read these
comments against what Baldwin said about *The Defiant Ones*, especially
since he wanted Poitier's character to get back on the train, Baldwin's view
of black subjective agency is one that takes recognition and separates it
from the repetitious cycle of continual discovery and rediscovery. We can
note here too the nuance in Baldwin's vision of civil rights era psychological transformation. His is decidedly *not* one of an equal, mutual recognition that stems from the Hegelian model. In the context of the civil rights
social and political order, what Baldwin seems to call for here is a more
one-sided recognition. That is, he is much less focused on knowing white
subjectivity's nonstrangerness and is instead more concerned with whiteness's ability to finally recognize him. From this perspective, the "failure"
of mutual recognition could serve as a more satisfying correction of a
long-standing historical imbalance of failed recognitions. Baldwin's hope
for white subjectivities to change psychologically, essentially the wish for
transformation that deemphasizes mutuality, is another example of how
intersubjectivity functioned as a more complicated and contradictory
theme during the era.

Throughout *Blackness Is Burning*, I take an extended look at the disparate and competing ways in which representing recognition and recognition failure appeared in civil rights era popular culture while also
attending to, as Richard Iton has discussed, the unique ways in which
popular works can generate "attention around a specific issue" and at
the same time mobilize "broader and less coherent sentiments."[37] When
it comes to the civil rights era's cultural engagement with the politics of
recognition, the popular works' broad and incoherent sentiments contain
as much doubt and anxiety around humanizing and recognizing blackness as they contain hope and possibility. What the repeated circulation
of narratives about black recognition (either as "failed" or as "realized")
did do, however, was further cement and popularize Hegelian dialogic
interrelatedness, from which the associated psychoanalytic discourses of

intersubjectivity stem, as a vaunted cultural ideal. Mutual recognition as ideology forms the foundation of what I critique in this book as the inter-subjective view of race—the melding of the politics of representation and recognition around a set of psychologically significant rituals, symbols, and cultural practices. This intersubjective view of race (which includes but is not limited to the "interracial dramas" of the civil rights era) is a way of thinking about racial difference that emphasizes private and social engagement, the exploration of interiority and affect. It centralizes inter-personal relationships and personal transformations as the basis for the recognition of black humanity. The way these notions of citizenship and humanism converge around the psychological makes the related represen-tational culture that has been dedicated to the realist expression of this process every bit as fantastical and nonsensical as it is personally inspiring and democratically reflexive.

If the intersubjective or dialogic understanding of recognition takes for granted that there are multiple subjects who desire some form of recip-rocal interrelatedness, and if part of what popular culture does—even when it is overtly political—is tell stories about individuals instead of sys-tems, then we can also say that the theme of recognition's place in popu-lar culture is as psychologically discursive and referential as it is anything else. The transitional nature of American public and private life from the late 1940s through the 1970s, during what Jacquelyn Dowd Hall has iden-tified as the "long civil rights movement" and the years I refer to in this book as "the civil rights era,"[38] was also the moment in American social history that witnessed the unprecedented increase in the public aware-ness of psychoanalysis, particularly non-Freudian theories like object rela-tions theory and self-psychology. Even though historians have written colloquially about "mourning" and "healing" when talking about national identity and racial conflict during these years, our most respected written accounts of the civil rights era have shied away from engaging psycho-analysis's concomitant history and influence on the times.

Yet the fight for freedom and black recognition during the civil rights era was inseparable from a pervasive American cultural engagement with, and development of, psychological perspectives. As concepts like self-help, repressed trauma, father figures, and guilt complexes were becoming a part of everyday vocabulary from the 1940s onward, mainstream films like *Home of the Brave* (1949), *Intruder in the Dust* (1949), and *Pinky* (1949) were representing black identity as a psychological drama that was rife with inner turmoil and conflicts about a sense of belonging. During the 1950s and 1960s, Sidney Poitier, as the country's biggest black film star, was discovering that he was "hooked on psychoanalysis" in part because something in the language and practice of psychotherapy gave him a way to grapple with the era's unique "anxieties and tensions" and his personal "ghosts of times past."[39] Meanwhile, other civil rights era African American iconic figures like Eldridge Cleaver, Amiri Baraka, and George Jackson were creating terms like "white omnipotent administrator" and appropriating concepts like ego satisfaction and wish fulfillment to describe their engagement with capitalism, racism, and legal bias. With these references and cultural histories in mind, any critical effort that seeks to truly understand how recognition resonates as an important cultural theme in popular culture cannot overlook the rise in visibility of the psychological expert in the postwar years or the ways in which civil rights discourses about race overlapped with a cultural boom in analysis.

If we are tempted to identify the way race so often gets discussed in psychological terms as a particularly insidious cultural habit, what happens when we actually apply psychoanalysis to the cultural obsession with knowing, wanting to know, or not being able to know the racial other as human? As I develop in chapter 2, Poitier's career is instructive for the ways in which it both utilized the discourse of analysis and dramatized some of its gross limitations.

# 2

# SIDNEY POITIER AND THE CONTRADICTIONS OF BLACK PSYCHOLOGICAL EXPERTISE

As the most visible black Hollywood star during the long years of the civil rights campaign, Sidney Poitier appeared in thirty-eight films—from his first film, *No Way Out* (1950), to his last film of the era, *A Piece of the Action* (1977). Poitier was, by all accounts, charismatic and consistent in modeling a newly humanized image of black masculinity. His performances have received the highest of accolades possible for any actor, including an Academy Award for *Lilies of the Field* (1963), an honorary Oscar for a lifetime of "representing the industry with dignity, style and intelligence" in 2002, and more recently, a Presidential Medal of Freedom conferred in a historic ceremony by Barack Obama in 2009. Many critical accounts of Poitier's career have situated these achievements in the context of Hollywood's long-held and persistent commitment to stories that project a sanitized version of liberal humanism's engagement with racial difference.

When read in relation to the political movements of the era, Poitier's films have been lauded for disrupting old celluloid stereotypes of African Americans and also dismissed as being anachronistic by the late 1960s. In this regard, Thomas Cripps has thought of him as "a bland antidote to racial tension," a genre onto himself who represented "waxy-smooth liberal politics."[1] Other film historians like Aram Goudsouzian, Donald

Bogle, and Ed Guerrero have stressed that by the late 1960s, despite Poitier's meteoric commercial success, the actor profited from films that were simply out of touch with the social agendas of resistance and protest, of dissension and critique, that were a part of the urban racial conflicts that led to the 1965 Watts riots and the widespread urban rebellions of 1967 and 1968.[2] This critical frame for viewing Poitier treats him as something of a civil rights era mirage, as Hollywood stars are wont to be.

Despite the perceived political innocuousness of Poitier's most popular films, however, his characters were often signifying and representing a much more complex stream of meanings than the few analyses of his career have considered. This chapter examines the interracial buddy film's penchant for psychological drama. The kinds of scripts Poitier received, his training as a method actor, and Hollywood's direct and analogous relationship with psychoanalytic discourse are all factors that contributed to the kind of star he became. As I argue through an analysis of four civil rights era buddy films, Poitier's image was caught between the therapeutic ambition of the "idealizing transference" (where real subjects never exist) and the magical lesson of black survival (where real subjects are momentarily found).

## Genre, Introspection, and "Problem" Films

While there are many different kinds of performances and projects that make up the totality of Sidney Poitier's dynamic career, his social problem and buddy films easily constitute his biggest contribution to cinematic history. Poitier's filmic habit of playing the "buddy" to white men (and women) is the reason he has become so definitively associated with a kind of integrationist humanism that implicitly defines black humanity's value in terms of how beneficial it is to others. If there is a critical consensus about Poitier's career, it is, as Peter Roffman and Jim Purdy describe in their history of the social problem film, that Poitier's characters were both unduly giving *and* unrealistically accomplished. His character type "either nobly sacrificed himself for whites" or "over proved himself in order to be accepted in white society."[3] It is evident at the surface of some of the more common critiques of Poitier's career that his popular image of black masculinity is a patently intersubjective one simply because his

characters (whether sacrificial or exceptional) affirmed that there was tremendous value in the personal interactions between the dominant self
and racial others or between whites and blacks. Roffman and Purdy, in
their brief discussion of Poitier's role in the history of American social
problem films, especially note that since Poitier's image was so static for
so long, his image carried "late forties conventions through to the sixties
and seventies."[4] While I argue that we might consider the dramatization
of the intersubjective view of race as the most important ideology that
Poitier's image "carried" from the 1940s through the 1960s, what are the
other, more formal conventions and aspects of film history that enabled
his image to implicitly psychologize race and frame race relations in terms
of interpersonal experiences? What specifically about film culture and the
history of the social problem film made it not only possible but even obligatory to link blackness with psychological epistemologies?

The thematic features and general tone of social problem films or
"message movies" emerged as a part of a production trend in the decades
before Sidney Poitier became a box-office star. Starting in the 1930s as an
attempt to cut studio costs by streamlining production budgets, Warner
Bros. Pictures became the first major studio to experiment with producing
a new dramatic form: cheap, gritty dramas that often took plot inspiration directly from sensational newspaper headlines as a way to dramatize
the trials of everyday American life. Since the thematic focus of problem
films varied so greatly, we can think of the early run of films as spanning
any number of different genres, from crime and gangster films to family
melodramas. Topically, these films, including acclaimed productions like
Warner Bros.'s *I Am a Fugitive from a Chain Gang* (1932), *They Won't Forget*
(1937), and *Angels with Dirty Faces* (1938), as well as MGM's *Fury* (1936),
explored social issues ranging from racketeering and chronic unemploy-
ment to mental illness and alcoholism.[5] Although these downbeat films
were taken seriously for the ways in which they indicated the need for
social reform, social problem films have also been critiqued for largely
"burbanking" those issues, or using current events to draw an audience
and then ultimately sidestepping the systemic roots of those problems.[6]
As message movies were replete with quasi-moralistic critiques, there was
also often a subtle or explicit indication that the underlying cause of the

"problem" under review could be attributed to an individual psychic insta-bility that usually stemmed from the character's troubled personal history or familial relationships.

While the social problem film as a production trend showed signs of fading at the end of the Great Depression, there was a resurgence of the type during the 1940s with films like *The Grapes of Wrath* (1940), *The Best Years of Our Lives* (1946), and *Salt of the Earth* (1954). Increas-ingly, films that were fashioned as social critiques became even more directly and analogously imbricated in psychological discourse. This shift toward couching social critique in psychological terms was espe-cially evident during the height of McCarthyism and Cold War hysteria when the House Un-American Activities Committee and its blacklisting practices contrived to stifle some of Hollywood's most critical voices. In a political context when critiques of America could be construed as dis-loyal, the problem film "had to speak with discretion."[7] Brian Neve has observed that by the mid-1950s, message movies in general were "more often psychological than social," particularly those films that could also appeal to a younger audience.[8] In this regard, films that showcased mar-ketable youth talent—like *On the Waterfront* (1954), *East of Eden* (1954), and *Rebel without a Cause* (1955)—could attract younger audiences by making implicit psychosocial critiques of a societal lack of awareness of the interior depth and emotional complexity of America's youth. In con-trast to a prevailing vision of an older generation of American men, the younger American male was represented in these works as highly intro-spective and intersubjective: he valued self-awareness and interconnect-edness with like-minded individuals. We might also situate the influx of American "art or mood films" of the 1950s, films such as *A Streetcar Named Desire* (1951) and *Sunset Boulevard* (1951), and the male melo-drama or "male weepie," like Vincent Minnelli's *The Cobweb* (1955), as having some proximity to the problem film's tradition of drawing heavily on psychological models. Each of these genres and subgenres, as the film historian Thomas Schatz reminds us, shared a thematic proximity with "Freudian psychology and existential philosophy," as "each stressed the alienation of the individual due to the inability of familial and societal institutions to fulfill his or her particular needs."[9]

Another reason Hollywood film came to play such a central role in the popularization of psychological discourse is the fact that many writers, directors, and actors were personally and professionally invested in analysis. As Stephen Farber and Mac Green explore in their research on the film industry and psychological discourse, from the 1930s through the 1960s and the golden age of the studio system, there was general infatuation "with the Freudian cure" among Hollywood creative talent.[10] During the studio system's heyday it was common for directors and actors to include psychoanalysts and psychiatrists within their intimate social circles and also, famously, on production lots during the shooting of major films in order to help pacify notoriously volatile stars.[11] As a result, many Hollywood films across genres and subgenres—including screwball comedy, romance, westerns, noir films, and of course, social problem dramas— would integrate some version of a "pop" or lay psychoanalytic logic to further explain character motivation and conflict. This conscious integration of psychology and cinema remained popular even during the years of the early parts of the civil rights era, and some era directors, like Hitchcock, stayed personally and professionally intrigued by the world of analysis for an entire career.

Representations of blackness appeared on-screen in the social, cultural, and political context of the social problem film's psychoanalytic history in two competing ways: either as wounded black humanity, which was consistent with the white emotional fragility emphasized in male weepies and psychological thrillers, or as emotionally solvent— as therapeutic experts in an otherwise emotionally (and morally) bankrupt society. Most notably, 1949 was the year of the black-themed psychosocial problem film—with the debut of *four* such films, *Pinky*, *Home of the Brave*, *Intruder in the Dust*, and *Lost Boundaries*. As Michelle Wallace notes in her brief review of these films, "the institutionalization in the forties of a psychoanalytic/psychiatric discourse in the US was central to the formation of conventional notions of masculinity, sexual difference, family, and personality in dominant film practice."[12] Each of these films approached the familiar generic framing of societal problems (race in this case) by asking and trying to answer a series of psychologically informed questions about the mind of the racialized other. Were black people suffering from any additional psychological burdens? Did they secretly wish to be white? Were inferiority complexes holding them back from reaching their true economic potential? Or was the "black psyche" a bedrock of emotional stability from which nonblacks could learn important lessons about life, liberty, and the pursuit of happiness? As an extension of these prevalent assumptions about black interiority, the central narrative "diagnosis" in *Pinky* is that the main character, who passes because she feels both socially and emotionally encumbered by racial hierarchies, is too concerned with what others think about the incongruities between her skin tone and her race. The film concludes that Pinky's interior logic is too outwardly defined; her inability to lead a content and productive life amid what is portrayed as the emotional and economic prosperity of the postwar years is attributed to her gross oversensitivity.

Similarly, in *Home of the Brave*, a military Freudian psychoanalyst tells a tragically paralyzed black war veteran, Peter Moss, that it is his conscious and unconscious hypersensitivity to American racism and bigotry that has caused his physical and emotional symptoms. A round of aggressive psychotherapy and a resulting "thicker" psychological armor, his analyst concludes, will prepare him for the inevitable slights of a slow-to-change racial social order. Both *Pinky* and *Home of the Brave* use psychological rhetoric to pathologize black interiority and also to set up a causal relationship between society's influence and individual resiliency. Black emotional health represented in this way appears as precondition to recognition, or since the black characters are portrayed as needing internal transformation, any recognition of their humanity on an external scale is treated as either secondary or unnecessary. In this way, both films use the rhetoric of analysis to ultimately reinforce and maintain racial and class hierarchies.

Both *Intruder in the Dust* and *Lost Boundaries* feature the inverse of this psychological logic: whites, not blacks, are saddled by emotional issues that impede progress toward recognition. Based on Faulkner's novel, *Intruder in the Dust* features Lucas Beauchamp, a black landowner who is prejudicially accused and tried for murder. Once a lynch mob of white southerners forms to protect their rights and privileges relative to Beauchamp's, the film quickly becomes a moralistic parable about white destructiveness and internalized toxicity. Beauchamp's comparative decency labors to signify a greater need to reform the emotional location from which white racism stems. In using the racial other as a benchmark for proper civic and interpersonal behavior, the film represents white emotional retardation as the impediment to other forms of recognition. Thus, the white characters in *Intruder* quickly realize, "He [Beauchamp] wasn't in trouble, *we* were in trouble." Such narratives present the need for collective moral conversions as indistinguishable from the need for personal psychological transformations. Likewise, *Lost Boundaries* presents a fair-skinned black couple who find the black community to be painfully ostracizing because of their skin tone. Black communal rejection forces the couple to migrate and pass as a white couple in a small New England town. The average white American, who is represented as racist but also as valuing intersubjective exchange (unlike the black community), becomes the therapeutic subject of interest that the couple's presence promises to change before any measure of recognition can be initiated.

As a cinematic production trend, introspective films like the four 1949 psychological race dramas helped establish the cultural climate and set of narrative conventions against which Sidney Poitier's performances could be affirmatively measured. While W. E. B. Du Bois, Paul Robeson, Canada Lee, Ruby Dee, Ossie Davis, and other African American activists and entertainers were antagonized, undermined, and blacklisted during the 1950s because of their vocal critiques of American racism and McCarthyism or because of their political affiliations, Sidney Poitier found work in the types of films that continued the project of psychologizing the race problem. While he was not targeted directly by HUAC or blacklisted like the Hollywood Ten during the government's notorious regulation of the film industry, Poitier insists that his refusal to sign a loyalty oath during the filming of *Blackboard Jungle* (1955) made him an FBI target throughout "the fear and panic of those terrible cold war days of madness."[13] Part of Poitier's strategy for dodging the Red Scare's assault on the film industry involved aligning himself with influential Hollywood personalities like Richard Brooks, David Susskind, John Cassavetes, and Stanley Kramer—men who were "left of center" and who could also provide him with roles that were subtler and analogous in their themes, style, and modes of social critique.

## A Cinema of Racial Transference

As a part of the what Poitier called the "dream fabric" of the 1950s, he starred in five buddy films in just one year, between 1957 and 1958: *Edge of the City*, *Something of Value*, *Band of Angels*, *The Mark of the Hawk*, and *The Defiant Ones*. As psychological dramas, each narrative suggested that racism was not about race and had little to do with an actual racial other. Instead, Poitier's buddy films from the 1950s emphasized that a host of frustrations and personal failures contributed to racial bias, bigotry, and poor black-white relations. The civil rights era interracial buddy film used the popular discourse of psychology and the metaphor of analytic treatment to address the fate of struggling American prodigal sons, men who were failing to rise to the demands of the state because of their basic inabilities to cope with their personal histories. The central quasi-psychological lesson that these buddy films promoted is that the racial other, by representing superior competence and expertise, could personally teach his wounded, misguided, and emotionally insolvent buddies how to match his emotional competence.

MGM's 1957 *Edge of the City*, which David Shipman has called the "first American film mainly concerned with an inter-racial friendship," centralizes heavily the most common type of relational arrangement that appears in nearly all Poitier films: interracial friendship masked as an idealizing transference.[14] In *Edge of the City*, Poitier plays dock worker Tommy Tyler, who befriends Axel, a transient white army defector with a haunting emotional past. As the men work together on the docks in New York, Axel first reluctantly but then almost compulsively confides in Tommy about his troubled childhood and aversive relationships with male authority figures. Tommy, for his part, teaches his white buddy how to integrate into the upbeat, racially mixed community and helps him discover simultaneously the desire to let go of past fears. The film demonstrates that there are usually three types of characters who propel the drama of a Poitier buddy problem film: untreatable recalcitrant racists (in this case Charlie, a violent supervisor), treatable but scarred buddies (Axel), and Poitier's men of expertise (the racial other). The actions of Poitier's characters are always singularly directed toward the reform of their buddies while comparatively critiquing the antipsychological nature of the untreatable racists who often try to interfere with the process of therapeutic friendship. At the film's conclusion, when Poitier's Tommy is murdered on the docks by the antipsychological nemesis, Axel has grown enough under Tommy's tutelage to overcome his fear of confronting authority figures so that he can stand on the right side of justice in his friend's memory and honor.

Although Aram Goudsouzian has noted that the silent phone calls that Axel makes to his mother "increased his psychological peculiarity," none of the brief written summaries of the film have explored its psychological messages and themes.[15] Yet *Edge of the City* makes plain its investment in psychotherapy, as characters use popular terms like "guilt complexes" and Axel becomes preoccupied with learning how to express his discontent with his chronic depressive emotional state. Additionally, extensive dialogue between the two characters provides ample opportunity for talking therapy, as the film is organized around five scenes of lengthy, quasi-analytical conversations that focus exclusively on Axel's emotional pain. Over the course of several other deeply reflective but also one-sided exchanges, Axel reveals that the only way he knows how to feel "ten feet tall" is to prove himself through achievement by trying to please a host of authoritarian figures—his father, his former military sergeant, bosses, the "Charlies" of the world. Axel speaks at length about his emotional vulnerabilities and confides in his analytic friend, as if embarrassed: "The thing is, T, a guy has to do something before somebody can love him. A guy has got to prove himself first. Why else would I be this way? Why else would I be chasing around like this, looking for something?"

During these conversations, Poitier uses method acting to exhibit calmness and deadened affect.[16] With the method, Poitier sought to represent a measure of himself in his performances by trying to create a cinematic experience "where real life and fine art mimic each other."[17] The method, both by its nature and in the way Poitier interpreted it, emphasized an immersive style of acting that intentionally blurred the boundaries between actor and character so that emotional reactions on-screen were tied to an actor's personal experiences, feelings, or aspirations. Christine Gledhill argues that method acting helped create recognizable stars, particularly during the 1950s, precisely because the style of acting seemed to humanize both the actor and the character at the same time. As Gledhill notes, "in this respect, the Method is the contemporary performance mode most able to deliver 'presence,' the goal at the heart of both melodrama and stardom."[18] Similarly, Linda Williams describes the 1950s as the

> moment in American moving pictures when popular psychology and the "method" became the reigning form of the assertion of personality, when morality itself became explainable by Oedipus. At this point the eruption of symptoms and unconscious gestures began to substitute for the more straightforward bodily expression of good and evil and everyone became a victim of unconscious desires. Thus Robert Stack's famously swallowed voice, squeezed frame, and hunched way of holding a martini in *Written on the Wind*, so much commented upon by critics, was typical of a whole generation of Oedipally beset protagonists whose virtue was now revealed in somatic symptoms.[19]

As both Williams and Gledhill indicate, method acting in the 1950s was often highly demonstrative, since like melodrama, it functioned as a mode of excess. It emphasized actions and character demeanors that could be perceived as inseparable from the star's persona. The on-screen behaviors were also intended to be heavily symbolic so that they could work to clearly delineate a character's motives and "raw" personality.

For Poitier, who firmly believed that the method helped him "become part of the collective unconscious, part of the dream fabric of the culture," the method could allow some of the "coolness" of his personality and budding star persona to show up in the character on-screen.[20] Ironically, though, the way Poitier established his "presence" as a star in scenes of talking therapy was to demonstrably perform detachment and neutrality. Rather than emote purposefully or profusely in scenes devoted to excavating the white buddy's emotions, in playing the on-screen character who was *not* the primary focus of attention or "treatment," Poitier characteristically performed an exaggerated reticence and blandness. Throughout all of the confessional moments in *Edge of the City*, Poitier's Tommy listens to Axel patiently. He procedurally projects cool neutrality. Like a classical analyst, Tommy listens silently and only occasionally makes a quiet, pointed comment that assures his buddy of his expertise and full attention. The blank, cool-mode stares make his character look bored, further accentuating the one-sidedness of these interactions, as these moments have little to do with creating the conditions for mutual recognition. Instead of signaling anything about the racial other's interiority, humanity, or distinctiveness, Poitier's performance of cool-mode listening works antithetically to how other method actors would have used the technique, since the deadened affect is used solely to draw out the white buddy's humanizing self-discoveries, not his character's.

As the therapeutic partner, Tommy establishes his clinical expertise in his limited but enlightened dialogue. His words convey a wisdom and emotional maturity that his white buddy especially needs to hear. For example, throughout these moments of talking therapy, Axel reveals that he is constantly searching for valuation outside himself and also that he holds Tommy's feedback in high esteem. In one conversation, after listening blankly to Axel's recitation of his issues, Tommy musters a little animation, clinching his facial muscles slightly, and challenges Axel's penchant for externalizing his ambition with a simple, leading question: "Now, *why* are you?" Bewildered but contemplating the seemingly provocative question, Axel cannot answer, so the question triggers a transitional crossfade to the next scene and to yet another exploratory bit of dialogue that concludes with Tommy's most significant spoken intervention. In a diagnostic, matter-of-fact tone, Tommy says to Axel, "You are worthy of being loved. You don't have to do things to be loved." Tommy's comparative emotional proficiency permits him to colloquially counsel Axel that anything that can be measured externally, in the social or relational domain, is secondary to the ability to internalize the feeling of greatness and grandiosity on the private, self-conscious level. Again, though, Tommy shares these insights as if reciting basic principles of social-psychological discourse.

If method acting is one way in which a process of transference, or psychic redirection of one memory, action, or intention from one context to another, informs the performance mode of the Poitier buddy film,

Blank affect, *Edge of the City*

Cool-mode listening, *Edge of the City*

transferential behaviors also inform how the characters act on-screen. In interpersonal transference, prior experiences and old feelings are "transferred" from their original relational context to a new person who serves as a substitute for the original relationship or context. Transference by its nature always brings past experiences and issues to the present. Heinz Kohut's notion of an idealizing transference is particularly useful for thinking through what has been popularized in these dramas as a friendship with a helpful, exceptional racial other. Kohut founded self-psychology (a branch of psychoanalysis that focuses on the self's relationship to others) while writing case histories about Americans who failed to experience postwar life as joyful and meaningful. As the branch of psychoanalysis that has become the most influential in American clinical practice since Freud's writings, Kohut's theory is distinct from the Freudian tradition of repression and drives in the way that it emphasizes the role that idealization and empathy play in the construction of the self and in relationship dynamics. Self-psychological theories offer an interpretive rubric for better understanding the compulsion to idealize others. In this relational schema, the most central mechanisms of the self rely on the internalization of other people, mostly of what is perceived as the best in others—whether those "others" are people, ideals, or institutions. Although misrecognizing other beings as perfect is an important part of psychic constitution, some people, Kohut argued, struggle with bringing the self's own abilities into a realistic harmony with how others are perceived. Held in the highest of esteem, these "idealizable figures" appear to represent everything the self lacks but yearns to have. As Kohut put it, "a person who suffers a lack in the area of internalized ideals continuously attaches himself to others."[21] These idealized figures ("self-objects" or "imagoes") are treated as absolute in their goodness and flawlessness; there is never any ambiguity allowed when it comes to their status as essential and good. Under ideal circumstances, the fantasy of the other as a perfect object eventually helps the self construct its own more balanced sense of grandiosity, ability, and esteem. The individual comes to reason, "'I am perfect.' 'You are perfect, but I am part of you.'"[22] This association with the other's perfection begins the cycle of letting go of that connection in order to locate esteem and ability within the self's ontological domain.

Yet, as in nearly all psychological processes, the self has to struggle mightily to give up that idealizing transference because externalized grandiose objects play a tremendously satisfying role in the self's fantasy life. In this regard, reviewers and critics have long commented on the fantastical, unrealistically superior attributes of Poitier's characters. As many have pointed out, Poitier's characters are never even minimally bad. When *Edge of the City* debuted, reviewers identified Poitier's embodiment of black exceptionalism and expertise as a new character type. A *Time* magazine reviewer remarked, "Surprisingly enough in a Hollywood movie, the Negro is not only the white man's boss, but becomes his friend, and is at all times his superior, possessing greater intelligence, courage, understanding, warmth, and general adaptability."[23] The idealizing transference that the reviewers seem to describe here works in other ways throughout the film. For example, a crucial aspect of Axel's perpetual search for validation is that he feels responsible for his brother's accidental death. Coincidentally, there is much symmetry between his lost brother and his newfound black friend, or so he supposes in forming the friendship with Tommy. In another scene of masculine introspection, Axel describes his younger brother as someone who "everybody loved." Axel says, "He made me feel special. . . . He was everything I wasn't. He had this great sense of humor. . . . He laughed all the time. Whenever my old man would come at me, Andy would come in joking all the time." As a convenient and receptive replacement for Axel's brother, Tommy also has a great sense of humor, he is always available for lengthy conversations, and on several occasions he proves willing to defend Axel before imposing authority figures. Axel transfers the emotion, trust, connection, and admiration he has only felt for Andy to Poitier's Tommy by the midpoint of the film. Once the shift in Axel's idealizing transference from his dead brother to Tommy is complete, Axel begins to truly benefit from the relationship. That is, Axel begins to succeed in both love and work, he reconciles with his estranged parents, and he comes to realize that both his guilt over killing his brother in a car accident and his resentment toward his father are impediments to the personal and professional life he wants to have.

What Linda Williams has theorized as an American need for blackness to provide a "melodramatic racial fix" is evident in the way the idealizing transference casts the racial other into the role of the analytic expert who provides insight, skillfully listens, and rarely interrupts. In a similar vein, E. Ann Kaplan reads cinematic transference as a normalizing process in her review of psychoanalytic Hollywood films. Kaplan explains that "Hollywood's turn to psychoanalysis may be seen as a specific kind of transference phenomenon that unconsciously served some of its own needs—especially those of normalizing race and gender so as to reduce

unconscious threat, unconscious conflicts about race and gender for dominant (white, male) culture."[24] Although Kaplan is writing about films that
literally dramatize the relationship between psychotherapist and patient,
we can also see how a normalizing agenda surfaces in even an analogously
therapeutic relationship. The cool black expert certainly does help Axel
improve his lot in life, and at the same time, any threat that the black
analytic expert might pose because of his superior skill set is fully sub-
sumed when he dies in order to teach his patient/buddy the final lesson
of self-sufficiency.

## From Destruction to Recognition: *The Defiant Ones* Reconsidered

Narratives of racial transference necessarily create idealized figures that
are known and valued primarily for what they represent to the people
around them. The cinema of transference's tradition of producing narratives with a penchant for idealizing but not "seeing" the racial other is
precisely where we should situate the complaints that charge that Sidney Poitier portrayed neither ordinary nor "real" black men. That Poitier
should be received as exceptional and decidedly not real is not surprising,
though, as I have argued, in light of the psychic role that idealized figures
typically play. If Freud, Kohut, and other post-Freudian analysts described
transference as an inevitable component of human relationships, popular
modes of storytelling codified this type of responsiveness around blackness at a moment when mass-culture industries like film were responding
to calls to produce realistic, relatable, and recognizably human black characters. Yet, while psychoanalytic notions of transference and idealization
help explain the representational appeal of elevating blackness during the
1950s and 1960s, particularly as a response to historical stereotypes and
"negative" imagery, transference and idealization are not the only psychoanalytic concepts that made Poitier characters so uniquely and powerfully
therapeutic. The trope of the perfect black companion who encourages
his buddy to become a better, more emotionally attuned, person so that
the white patriarchal subject can in turn function as a better American is
complicated elsewhere in Poitier's oeuvre by the transparent and competing wish to see the racial other as "real" and autonomous, even if only
for a moment. As films like *In the Heat of the Night* and *The Defiant Ones*

demonstrate, the desire to see the other as real gets communicated in the buddy narrative as a cinematic spectacle of destruction and survival.

As I argued in chapter 1, a film like *The Defiant Ones* stands out in Poitier's career because of the way it romanticizes and generally valorizes interracial friendship as a metaphor for American social progress, interracial tolerance, and racial equality. If we pay closer attention to the film, however, we see that its representation of intersubjectivity is formed around scenes of physical contest and violence. Fisticuffs battles are a central feature of the film's action and literalization of racial tension. The fact that Poitier's character, Noah Cullen, and Tony Curtis's Johnny are two convicts who are chained together for most of the film gives them ample opportunity to experience the sweaty and celebratory, heated and cherished, work of intersubjective engagement. The brief bouts of physical contest between the two characters occur often, particularly following a moment that showcases masculine vulnerability achieved through talking therapy or empathetic bonding. Hence, immediately following a scene in which Johnny and Cullen talk about their innermost fears and desires, the two men face the direct violence of a lynch mob. When the mob rounds up the interracial buddies and vows to exact the "old-fashioned prayer meeting" form of lynching justice because the convicts have inadvertently injured one of the townsfolk, Johnny—symbiotically in blackface—tries to distinguish his subjectivity and social privilege from the "buddy" to whom he is chained. To save himself, Johnny says, "Don't you understand? You can't go lynching me. I'm a white man." The sideways look that Poitier's Cullen gives Johnny is brilliantly achieved. The look, far from the blank or calmly empathetic stares of the transferential black object, is a layered mixture of shock, disappointment, and even mockery. In absence of dialogue, his look says, "Are you crazy? Everyone can see that you are not recognizably a white man standing here next to me—in blackface, no less."[25] Verbalizing some of what Cullen's look implies, the mob leader says to Johnny, "I'll tell you what kind of white man you are," and then he instructs Cullen to spit on Johnny. When Cullen silently refuses, the ringleader slaps him; Cullen defiantly spits in his face. Eventually the interracial buddies escape from the mob and run off, still chained together. Johnny's articulation of how his subject position differs from Cullen's

("Why, you can't lynch *me*") not only is an overt attempt to separate him-self from the intersubjective ritual of bonding with the racial other but also offers up Cullen as a to-be-destroyed object. It is immaterial that the mob lynches neither man in this scene. What the characters' survival of the mob's violence most exhibits is an added dimension of contradictory nuance in their relationship. Whereas in other scenes between the two men, empathy and idealization are the norm, here Johnny is willing to be complicit in his friend's murder, and Cullen's affect and visceral reactions conversely communicate his own motivations, feelings, and agency.

In other scenes, the film showcases the aggression and violence of the buddy dyad through the more literal dramatization of fisticuffs battles. For instance, in the exchange immediately following the buddies' near lynching and escape, Johnny rightly detects that Cullen is angry about Johnny's attempts to sacrifice him. Poitier again departs from the char-acteristic cool mode of performance that characterizes his exceptional therapeutic men when they are being idealized, with Cullen unleashing a fiery verbal diatribe, at the height of which he spews at Johnny, "You are nothing!" Cullen does not give voice to a culturally assumed and feared black male rage that confesses to always hating white men. Instead, Cul-len's comment to Johnny, who has already confessed to fearing that "everybody is alone," is apparently more frightening than black male rage. "You are nothing" is really the self's most debilitating fear, and here Cullen enlivens that accusation by confirming the *white* self's nonexistence. To deny this accusation of nothingness, to defend his self-existence through bodily insistence, Johnny responds with his body, tense and lunging for-ward. Cullen, eager for the physical contest that can back up his words and already in a fighting stance, issues a battle cry: "You said we were going to tangle together, and that time is now!" What ensues is a lengthy rumble in which the two men take turns pummeling and choking each other.

Eroticism, feminizations, and romantic allusions are par for the course in masculine bonding scenarios, and as the buddies struggle and tumble down a muddy embankment, still chained together, still fight-ing, their sweaty contest no doubt evokes an elemental erotic charge that would be consistent with what Eve Kosofsky Sedgwick has argued about homosociality as well as what Kaplan has noted about the erotic contours

Visualizing destruction, *The Defiant Ones*

Visualizing survival, *The Defiant Ones*

of transferential experiences.[26] Additionally, both the lynch mob and the fisticuffs battle recall what Robyn Wiegman has called "the lynch motif and the interracial male adventure," or plot conventions that represent the masculine "bond's defiance of the history of enslavement, lynching, and segregation."[27] These same conventions help create a "mapping of the feminine in relation to the masculine" as a way of "instantiating or alleviating racial hierarchies among men."[28] There is indeed a charge to these moments, erotic or otherwise, and the pair's actions are further complicated by how evocations of historical tropes of black masculinity, such as the feminized genteel nobleman or the primitive sexualized black buck, also inform the performance of black masculinity on-screen.

The racial body, analytic expert or otherwise, cannot escape these gender inscriptions, erotic associations, and historical tropes, particularly as visual technologies work uniquely to anchor them.[29] As I discuss in chapters 3 and 4, psychoanalytic or therapeutic codes compound rather than limit readings that are attentive to how stereotypes of race, gender, and sexuality work together to instantiate or deny black humanity. The less-often-examined "formations of power" evident in this aspect of Poitier's performance of analytic expertise, however, have to do with the way the violence and fisticuffs battles in a film like *The Defiant Ones* visualize aggression and attempted annihilation only to alleviate those tensions with displays of mutual triumph and survival. The physical battles assist rather than detract from the intersubjective mission, and Cullen's word-for-word, punch-for-punch, participation in these contests demonstrates to Johnny that blackness will not be easily dismissed. These are pedagogical lessons intended to teach Johnny something about Cullen's equal durability and self-constancy relative to him, or as Cullen charges in the middle of their fight, "That's right, white man. Kill me! Only it ain't so easy to kill me! Is it?" This assertion voices the hopeful social fantasy that 1957 is a time when white men cannot kill black men with impunity. The comment and Poitier's heated affect and reciprocal aggression are also loaded analytically to express something particular about the buddies' mutual subjective existence. If these moments of contest and triumph are notably different from *Edge of the City*, in which Poitier's idealized analytic expert dies in order to teach Axel one final lesson about white masculine psychic grandiosity, how are more durable and surviving others formed and insisted in intersubjective interactions that are also implicitly about the politics of recognition?

## Three Variations: Recognition, Intersubjectivity, and Mutuality

There are three different modalities of recognition that correlate with this aspect of destruction and survival in Poitier's popular dramas. The first of these models is Hegel's master/slave (or lordship and bondage) dialectic—to which I referred briefly in chapter 1 as simply dialogic recognition. Rethinking the Hegelian model here in terms that emphasize the process of two *unequal* social subjects coming together provides an additional way to think about the relationship of Poitier's characters to the politics of recognition. A more complete Hegelian reading of Johnny and Cullen's relationship than I provided in my introduction to these concepts in chapter 1 properly historicizes the interracial dyad as a reconfiguration of master-slave power relations. This version of the Hegelian model makes clearer some of the ways in which the white "master" in the buddied pair needs the black "slave," both materially and ontologically, as it is the slave's labor (in this case, Cullen is always far more resourceful on the lam than is Johnny), coupled with his subordinated social and economic position, that teaches the master mostly about himself. Writing in *The Phenomenology of Mind*, Hegel explains that "self-consciousness is faced by another self-consciousness, it has come *out of itself*. This has a twofold significance: first it has lost itself, for it finds itself as an *other being*; second, in doing so it has suspended the other, for it does not see the other as an essential being, but in the other sees its own self."[30]

   In other words, the master recognizes himself in the slave, losing himself, at first, in the process. This "loss" of the self is necessary for him to become a truer and more enlightened version of himself. This transformation is formed only with the participation of the other. Eventually, in order for the dyad to assure certainty of their existence, they prove "themselves and each other through a life-and-death struggle"; it is only in "staking one's life" that the "freedom" of recognition is won.[31] In Hegel's ideal of mutual recognition, both participants in this process would acknowledge the freedom and rationality, dependence and independence, of the other. However, because of the many opportunities for objectification, particularly of the slave, and the continued power imbalances inherent in the dyad, either or both can fail to make it to the double, sovereign, form of mutual recognition.[32]

Hegel is especially useful for thinking about visions of interactivity and intersubjectivity that bond men together across social hierarchies. For instance, it will not do for "masters" to garner this process of recognition from "others" of the same class and position of power, for those types of interactions would not be with a distinct enough other to induce that first level of (one-sided) recognition. The inherent one-sidedness of master-slave interrelatedness has been discussed in African American criticism in similar terms. For example, Toni Morrison and the literary critic Kenneth Warren have argued that the trope of darkness and the construct of an Africanist presence occupy a defining position in American literature, where the historically oppressed character provides an important countersubjectivity against which the master/subject measures himself.[33] This variant of recognition is formed through violence and aggression but also through what we might think of as "counteridentifications" since, as Morrison stresses, Mark Twain's Huck comes to know who he is because of Huck's counteridentification with Jim—through the general "parasitical nature of white freedom."[34] But for Hegel's more complete process of recognition, it is not just that the self learns about itself through counteridentifications; the self actually sees itself in the similarities and differences of the other. Even though achieving this level of recognition is arduous, Victoria Burke stresses that Hegel's more complete process of recognition is one of profound personal awareness, consciousness, enlightenment. As Burke argues, "It [the master] thus becomes aware of its own consciousness as a consciousness, and is thereby self-conscious rather than merely conscious."[35] Both master and slave also, in coming more fully into contact with their mutual dependence, experience what Hegel calls a "dialectical reversal," in which the psychological power imbalance between the two is amended by the realization that the master has been less capable and less significant than the slave all along.[36]

There are several aspects of Hegel's notion of recognition that are dramatized in Poitier's therapeutic performances as the buddy and analytic expert to white men. Most immediately, when we think of how his characters were framed through the lens of perfection (black exceptionalism and psychological expertise), we note the fluidity among the "magical Negro" stereotype, the psychoanalytic concept of the idealizing transference, and

Hegel's dialectical reversal.[37] Each of these notions accounts for why the "slave" or black character might appear as so comparatively more confident and competent than the "master" or white male counterpart. Yet the magical Negro, idealizing transference, and dialectical reversal also serve the ideological purpose of creating empathy for the disheveled white male's consciousness, which is framed as experiencing such tremendous, if agonizing, growth. Further, since the buddies survive a series of literal life-and-death struggles together, we can also see how the buddy dyad in *The Defiant Ones* only grows stronger in their connection as a direct result of tumbling through the muddy banks of conflict and aggression. Relatedly, as the story progresses, Johnny, who began the film as laconic and barely intelligible, also becomes more proficient at expressing his interiority, motivations, and consciousness. Even though we can see that there are actually several layers or levels of recognition that make up the master/slave dialectic, what stands out in Hegel's formulation is just how difficult it is to complete the full cycle and arrive at a mutual recognition.

A second, psychoanalytically constructed, understanding of how recognition works comes from D. W. Winnicott's notion of destruction/survival. This is a process of discovery that again stresses the perspective and consciousness of the subject or dominant self. As Winnicott notes, "The subject says to the object: 'I destroyed you,' and the object is there to receive the communication. From now on the subject says: 'Hullo object!' 'I destroyed you.' 'I love you.' 'You have value for me because of your survival of my destruction of you.'"[38] The Winnicottian process can be summarized this way: the self tries to attack, limit, or even control the other, while the other proves to be outside the self's psychic domain by successfully surviving the enacted aggressions. For Winnicott, both "destruction" and "survival" in this context are largely metaphorical, where the amount of destruction (a form of the self's boundary testing) cannot be unreasonably excessive because that would fatally exclude the other from the process. As a psychoanalyst, Winnicott, certainly much more so than Hegel, emphasizes the feelings and emotions that ensue from either the success or failure of the destruction/survival trial. Winnicott discovered that a social world where positive (idealizations) or negative projections (abjections) of other people replace the process of knowing and experiencing other people as psychologically distinctive ultimately creates a terrifying emotional world for whoever is doing the fantasizing.

Since fantasies of annihilation reinforce intense feelings of self-abjection, despair, and loneliness, the other's survival of destruction assures the self that the self is not alone, thus adding to the subjective quality of life. If this cinematic tradition of interracial storytelling frames the idealizing transference as a part of a hopeful project of national repair (in analogously suggesting that the emotional skill set that the process creates can be beneficial to other citizens), these same works emphasize that there is simply joy for the individuals involved in the practice of establishing cold, liberating contact with others. As such, films like *The Defiant Ones* use aggression not so much as a tool to evoke suffering; rather, aggression and violence surface as pedagogical opportunities for the racial other to model intrapsychic durability. The Winnicottian model of recognition that produces a "surviving" other is inherently cyclical—both members of the dyad would inevitably want to maintain the tension of constantly having to learn the other's distinctiveness. Hence, at the end of *The Defiant Ones*, the buddied pair happily forsakes their freedom in order to continue to experience the cycle of destruction/survival. Similarly, other Hollywood films, especially civil rights era retrospectives, imagine the intersubjective bond as something that at least one of the participants (usually "the master") wants to prolong and maintain.[39]

The feminist psychoanalyst Jessica Benjamin's conception of mutuality, the third variant of recognition, both includes and deviates from the Hegelian and Winnicottian models. Physical and metaphorical violence in this vein serves as a similar test of discovery and as a test of self-distinctiveness, but the confirmation of a distinct and separate interior life of the other person takes on added importance here. In this process of recognition, both self and other *must* recognize the autonomous desires of each other, and the lopsided potential of a one-sided recognition is critiqued for its role in creating psychologies and epistemologies of domination. Benjamin argues that mutuality indeed requires moments of contest, boundary testing, and "violence." It is a process that requires, "finally, contact with the other," a process in which both subjects can "engage in an all-out collision" with each other en route to discovering "the shock of the fresh, cold outside."[40] For Benjamin, this is a "collision" with another's agency and autonomy that distinguishes "two subjects recognizing each other from one subject regulating another."[41] If two distinct selves can indeed use destruction/survival rituals to learn of the self and other's complementary codependence and independence, the nature of the relationship will inevitably change. Thus, even if we can see the "parasitic" nature inherent in these models of recognition, mutuality proposes that it should not be exhaustively so and that the relay between self and other is to be mutually satisfying and beneficial. Although we may not be convinced that at the end of *The Defiant Ones*, when Cullen jumps off the train to be with Johnny, there is no longer an idealizing transference (which decidedly interferes with recognition), at least the circumstances (the fact that they stay together) seem ideal for paving the way for this process of mutuality to unfold. Yet, as we may recall from my reading of the film in chapter 1, this outcome carries with it additional consequences for the racial other's subjection to the authority of the state. In the end, regardless of whether the characters succeed at the master/slave dialectic or the Winnicottian model or even the gold standard of recognition—mutuality—they end up as more easily tracked, disciplined, and "known" by the state. Despite the allure of recognition, then, it is not a subversive social status.

## *In the Heat of the Night* and the Magic of Black Object Survival

While Poitier's performance in *The Defiant Ones* contains inflections of all three types of recognition, his performance in *In the Heat of the Night* is a good example of how the politics of recognition produces therapeutic lessons about what I call Poitier's knack for signaling *black object survival*. Despite playing initially with limited release in the South, *In the Heat of the Night*, Poitier's most acclaimed film of the era, won five Academy Awards in 1967, including Best Actor for Rod Steiger and Best Picture, and excelled over the other top films of the year: *Guess Who's Coming to Dinner* (another Poitier film), *Bonnie and Clyde*, and *The Graduate*. The imminent threat of racialized violence influenced both the film's plot and production. For example, the main reason *Heat* was shot on location in 1966 in southern Illinois instead of Mississippi, where the narrative events take place, is because Poitier refused to film in the Deep South. As he told the director,

Norman Jewison, "I am not going to work in a city where I can't move about, where I can't eat if I want to."[42] Even in Sparta, Illinois, and Dyersburg, Tennessee (where they traveled to shoot the plantation scene), the cast and crew received mixed and hostile reception because of *Heat*'s overt dramatization of southern bigotry and racism during an already intense period of social unrest. Consistent with other Poitier buddy dramas, the plot of *In the Heat of the Night* brings a black man, Poitier's Virgil Tibbs, into close relational contact with a white man, Rod Steiger's Chief Gillespie. Much to their mutual chagrin, the men are forced to work together to solve a murder case. The story positions the men as diametric character opposites: Tibbs, a northerner, is refined and fastidious; the Chief, like *The Defiant Ones*' Johnny, is gruff and antagonistic. Initially within this narrative frame, the Chief is represented as a reluctant companion: he does not want Tibbs around, but he realizes he needs him—evoking a bit of Hegel's dialectical reversal. Though the characters seem as if they could not be further apart at the start of the film, the plot moves them closer together with scenes of mutual combat, talking therapy, and the constant threat of violent southern racism that marks Tibbs's interactions with all other townsfolk.

As is typical of the Poitier vehicle, Tibbs, dressed in a stylish suit, appears as a cut above, in terms of acumen, class, and professionalism, than anyone else in Sparta. This aspect of the film's mise-en-scène and character presentation sets up the expectation that there will be a familiar idealizing transference of his blackness. What we see instead are metaphorical dramatizations of his character's object survival and other complementary gradations of recognition. The most obvious instance of initiating recognition takes place in the film's most famous scene. This is, of course, the moment when Tibbs slaps a white man. This "slap heard around the world"[43] has been seared into popular memory through a repetitive and compulsive recasting of those few seconds in contemporary film award shows, like when Poitier received his lifetime award, during yearly Oscar montages, and in various other film-tribute reels that commemorate Hollywood's history. The scene's actions are simple: Poitier's Tibbs accuses Endicott, a wealthy white southerner, of committing murder (it turns out later that Endicott is innocent). Appalled, Endicott slaps him. Without hesitating, Tibbs backhand slaps Endicott across the face. That there is no pause in Tibbs's reaction slap further emphasizes his will, agency, and right to hit back. Endicott's open-palmed slap is slow and indignant; his hand connects with an unflinching and almost expectant Tibbs. Comparatively, Tibbs's instinctual backhand slap is swift but protracted, graceful and stylized. The blow nearly topples its unsuspecting target, as upon contact, Endicott careens off to the side. Both slaps are a part of the same continuous medium shot, providing a clear, unobstructed view of the slap's significance. When, in reaction to being slapped by Tibbs, Endicott says, "There was a time when I could have had you shot," his words acknowledge his recognition of a change in their power (master/slave) relations. Tibbs "survives" in this moment because he does not fold to either Endicott's aggression or the probable state-sanctioned violence that might (and eventually does) ensue. Instead, his participation in this version of an analytically loaded fisticuffs contest makes a powerful statement that times have changed; his humanity now belongs to a protected realm of the social order that has been previously inhabited only by whites. The slap threatens to *force* a one-sided recognition in favor of the racial other.

Yet Endicott, like most racist antagonists in Poitier's films, is portrayed here as having limited intersubjective ability—he neither invites nor copes well with these psychosocial trials. Clearly this now-classic moment of cinematic black object survival was never intended to advance the racist's (or identifying spectators') consciousness beyond any archaic form of recognition. If the moment communicates a demand and a desire to be seen, then the way the slaps and facial reactions are edited together stresses for whom this particular psychological lesson is most important. As Tibbs slaps back, two witnesses are prominently included in the deep focus of the same frame: Chief Gillespie and Endicott's black butler. The butler, who has just arrived with a tray of lemonade, reacts symbiotically, as if he is viscerally connected to *his* master. As Tibbs's hand makes fresh, hot contact, the butler jumps in horror, winces in agony, and almost falls sideways, as does Endicott. The butler exists not only to give the other master a slave but also to quell any deep anxieties that what is happening with black subjectivities and recognition extends to all blacks regardless of

Signaling survival, *In the Heat of the Night*

Witnessing survival, *In the Heat of the Night*

class or occupation. Clearly the "old" social order still has its participants, subjects and objects alike. While the butler and Endicott are implicated in the film's tepid critique of racial hierarchies, the Chief, as the more important master present in this double master/slave dialectic, watches the contest with an expression that wavers between shock and stoicism, wonder and bewilderment. Despite the Chief's exterior performance of reluctance and petulance, his consciousness, more consistent with Hegel's vision of the mind, is a more malleable subjectivity that can grasp some of the beneficial potential inherent in the demonstrative ritual being worked out before him. The very next shot after the slaps, practically a jump cut to the Chief's face, emphasizes as much. The cutaway to the Chief's mixed but receptive expression accompanies his transformative inaction: he is utterly immobilized and resists retaliation on Endicott's behalf—even though Endicott asks him to interfere.

The complicated political, social, and psychological significance of the "slap heard around the world" is only further compounded by Poitier's transferential behind-the-scenes actions and motivations. For example, originally *In the Heat of the Night*'s script did not call for Tibbs to strike back; Poitier insists that he demanded that his character respond with matching violence. He also drew on personal experience to express part of himself in the symbolic dialectical exchange. In order to play Tibbs's reaction to Endicott's other-limiting aggression in just the right way, he reminded himself of a time when as a teenager in Miami in the 1940s he was harassed and humiliated by two white police offers. As Poitier explains, "I could too easily remember that Miami night with the gun pointed at my forehead, that fifty-block march with those guffawing cops in the patrol car behind me. I told the director that the script needed to be changed."[44] Calling forth memories of his own experiences with state-sanctioned dehumanization and instances of failed recognition gave Poitier the "pure, raw experience" he needed to play the scene, or, as he put it, "I had to find a way to get me to raw organic experience emotionally."[45] These extradiegetic motivations for playing the scene in the way that he does indicates why this moment in *In the Heat of the Night* has such rich potential to resonate in complex and overdetermined ways. That is, Poitier's use of personal memory suggests some of the ways in which fictionalized dramatizations of black recognition have a highly compoundable and referential physic life of their own. Even though the slap might play out as tiny act of survival in the film, since it is linked so securely to the politics of recognition outside the diegesis of the film, it also burns and encodes other reverberations of personal and collective histories of, and suppressed desires for, black retaliation and retribution. In evoking a measure of transference to play the scene, then, Poitier the man was able to perform and display a corrective sense of empowerment and autonomy that he did not feel as a teenager being intimidated by the police.

The way Poitier performs his characters in moments like these has garnered some notable critical attention. In describing Poitier's relationship to violence and aggression in civil rights era films, some scholars have minimized the subtext of "indignant" survival in these eruptive, demonstrative scenes. For instance, Aram Goudsouzian notes that Poitier displays a muted "cool boil" whenever he is angry, and Thomas Cripps has argued that these liberal integrationist films only permitted Poitier to "play to the edge of his control, as though simmering beneath a surface of repressed stammers and catches in the throat that functioned like volcanic fissures through which hidden powers seeped."[46] While this style of performance might not signify the strongest form of resistance in a political vein, Poitier's "heated" but controlled affect is nonetheless appropriately measured in the context of recognition battles. In recalling Winnicott's emphasis on the emotionality of destruction/survival scenes, we can note that performing just to a certain edge of controllability is important since extreme reactions in either direction threaten to undermine the process altogether. A heated affect that communicates resistance, agency, and subjective survival is more in line with how a parent might firmly discourage and withstand the tantrums of a child. Notably, this register of expressibility strategically differs from the even-more-heightened affective response that would be appropriate in a literal battle to death. Poitier's method of communicating "hot," instead of "cool," therapeutic responsiveness in this regard is not far from Martin Luther King Jr.'s notion of "sweltering with the heat of injustice."[47] Although the performance method may be rightly criticized for being politically benign, as far as political actions are concerned, the degree of outrage of Poitier's characters makes perfect sense in the context of communicating and displaying a more human black subjectivity.

As both racial transference and object survival are features of the intersubjective view of race, the difference between recognizing and idealizing is a fundamental tension in *In the Heat of the Night*. Lest the performative moments of black object survival be idealized for the ways in which they ultimately benefit the Chief, the film also dramatizes the Chief's anxious desire to deflate Tibbs's relative superiority and seeming perfection. As both failed mutuality and failed master/slave paradigms indicate, if unimpeded objectification or perfection persists, recognition cannot succeed. Recognition requires balancing the knowledge of the other's independent consciousness against the impulse to idealize and fantasize, and we see some of this struggle in the Chief's orientation to Tibbs. Fittingly, in the scene immediately following the slap, as the two characters verbally spar about Tibbs's actions, Tibbs grips the hood of a car and yells, "I can pull that fat cat down! I can bring him right off this hill!" The Chief squints at Tibbs as if seeing something new and exclaims, "Oh, boy . . . man, you're just like the rest of us. Ain't ya?" The subsequent cut to a medium close-up of Tibbs's face reveals something like disgust or embarrassment at having his desire for revenge plainly exposed. While Tibbs clearly finds it intolerable (and no doubt a different kind of misrecognition) to be identified as "just like" southern racists, the desire for personal retaliation is coded here as unprofessional, as a now-glaring imperfection in Tibbs's character. This discovery is delightfully satisfying to the Chief, who only reluctantly accepted Tibbs's professional assistance and expertise in the first place.

Narratives that accentuate both a dependence on and a denial of the relative perfection of the magical Negro function consistently with how Benjamin describes some of the challenges inherent in the struggle for mutuality. As she writes, "This insight [of intersubjective theory] allows us to counter the argument that human beings fundamentally desire the impossible absolutes of 'oneness' and perfection with the more moderate view that things don't have to be perfect, that in fact it is *better* if they are not. It reminds us that in every experience of similarity and subjective sharing, there must be enough difference to create the feeling of reality, that a degree of imperfection 'ratifies' the existence of the world."[48] Similarly, the Chief certainly feels better discovering the black surviving object's degree of imperfections. Knocking the exceptional other down to the level of "just like us" reflects an underlying anxiety that seeks to reassuringly limit the scope of black achievement and grandiosity. Yet the Chief's discovery of Tibbs's ratifying imperfections also seems to allow the character a break from the taxing emotional work of maintaining the racial idealizations in the first place.

Perhaps one of the more frustrating facts of Poitier's career is that those persistent idealizing transferences are never kept neatly at the margins of works that also visualize and confirm recognition. In this regard, although Poitier's Tibbs is only analogously therapeutic in *In the Heat of the Night*, the film does include its share of strong allusions to a specifically analytic transference. For instance, weary after the heated scenes of contest and survival, the buddied pair retreats to the Chief's house, where he lounges on his couch and Tibbs sits across from him in an armchair—a spatial configuration that unmistakably maps the master/slave paradigm onto an analyst/analysand dyad. The scene opens with the Chief stretched out across the couch, lost in a moment of rare, deep reflection. To loosen some of his inhibitions and gruff reluctance to talking about his feelings, the Chief takes quick sips from a tumbler of bourbon. He admits that Tibbs is "the first human being" who has ever been in his house; then he proceeds to ask Tibbs questions about psychological well-being. The Chief says, "You know a lot of things, don't you? Just what do you know about insomnia?" He recites a litany of his personal problems, most of them about his chronic state of loneliness, or as he says, "I got no wife, got no kids. I got a town that don't want me." The Chief appears in this scene slightly drunken, visibly forlorn. Tibbs sits perched on the edge of his armchair, listening silently and hardly emoting. After the Chief's sad succession of confessions about the barren nature of his relational life, he, increasingly despondent and staring off into the distance, begins to ask Tibbs questions about *his* personal life, like "You married?" Tibbs sighs in response, reclines his chair, and gives the question some silent consideration before admitting that he was almost married once.

At this point in the conversation, after first relating to the racial other as a psychological expert by assuming that he knows "a lot of things," including about insomnia and loneliness, the Chief attempts to fold this encounter with talking therapy and psychological expertise into an even stronger idealization by assuming that they are emotionally alike. That is, the Chief assumes that surely Tibbs's interior and emotional life resembles his. As such, after learning that Tibbs never married, just as he has not, the Chief presumes, "But don't you get just . . . a little lonely?" When Tibbs responds with sarcasm, "No lonelier than you, man," Tibbs decisively disrupts the Chief's use the racial other/analyst/buddy in a transferential way. In coming into painful contact with that abrupt image dissolution, the Chief responds in kind by trying to find some comfort in a more stable master/slave relation. Specifically, he says, "Well don't get smart, black boy. I don't need it. No pity!" Their analytic session concludes with Tibbs running off to finish solving the murder on his own, or as he says to the dejected Chief as he departs, he is going off "where whitey ain't allowed." Tibbs's words establish his physical and emotional need to remain separate from the Chief's projections and fantasies.

*In the Heat of the Night*'s couch analysis scene provides the emotional catalyst for the narrative's movement into resolution. The entirety of the analytical exchange dramatizes how even the most compelling transferences might be offset by a successful modeling of the other's boundary setting, agency, and competing motivations. Unlike the end of *The Defiant Ones*, where the promise of mutuality can only be realized in the perpetuity of the destruction/survival cycle, *In the Heat of the Night*'s story ends with a mutual relinquishing of the parasitic demand for continued discovery. Like *The Defiant Ones*, this film also ends with a train departure. This time Poitier's character happily and proudly boards—and does not disembark—the train. In fact, even though there are lingering close-ups of both men's faces as they say good-bye, both facial expressions reflect a bit of that Winnicottian joy in "seeing" the other go away. As it is the Chief who calls out to the departing black surviving object first, Tibbs takes his time responding with a slowly emerging grin that the Chief quickly returns with a sanguine smile of his own. While it is certainly much less disruptive to the social order of the town for Tibbs to leave than it is for him to stay and try to force cyclical one-sided recognitions of his humanity with the Endicotts of the area, the fact that Tibbs does leave is much more consistent with how we can imagine the ideal of mutuality would play out in narrative form. In this case, if mutuality does succeed, that process also links the buddies to the state's disciplinary agenda since both are, conveniently, police officers and will live to patrol their respective communities with a newly cemented appreciation for the personalized and contained upswing of the intersubjective view of race.

## Conclusion: When Analysis Fails

As therapeutic figures, Poitier's characters modeled a set of behavioral protocols that kept blackness vacillating between transference and recognition, depending on which lesson his buddy most needed to learn in a given moment. Part of what Poitier's films did, then, with the consistent modeling of the contradictory processes of racial transference and object survival or recognition as treatments is insist that to be an American during the civil rights era meant to be a treatable subject. If the ideology of American exceptionalism calls for an insistence on national supremacy that is realized domestically as individual achievement, emotional stability, familial harmony, moral superiority, and democratic idealism as aspirational benchmarks, Poitier's extensive filmography of other social problem films from the era indicated that there were still, nevertheless, a host of untreatable subjects who would undermine any intersubjective vision.

For example, in *No Way Out* (1950), Poitier plays a doctor whose impeccable bedside manner and soft-talk model of racial transference fail to placate or transform his patient's supremacist retaliations. Both *Band of Angels* and *Something of Value*, buddy films released in 1957, the same year as *Edge of the City*, also cast real doubt on the white buddies' ability to internalize the messages that would ease their personal or existential traumas and grievances so that they could work toward any greater cause. In *Band of Angels*, Poitier's Rau-Ru, a slave who wears tailored suits and who is ridiculed for talking "fancy," criticizes his white master/buddy for extending "cruel" kindness and companionship that does nothing to eradicate colonial rule. In *Something of Value*, Poitier's Kimani dies accusing his buddy of betrayal and incompetence, and as he dies, he begs his "buddy" not to raise his African child as his own. The cautionary Cold War drama *The Bedford Incident* (1965) further dramatizes the consequences of white people failing to heed the advice of black analytic authority. The film ends with everyone dying in nuclear annihilation because an antipsychological naval captain has not valued the advice of Poitier's character to pay attention to the emotional welfare of his crew. In *Brother John* (1971), rather

Departing black object survival, *In the Heat of the Night*

Departing mutuality as relief, *In the Heat of the Night*

than befriend a hostile southern cop as Tibbs does in *Heat*, Poitier's John abandons all opportunities to discover and discuss his potential buddy's personal disappointments and past traumas. Instead, Brother John forcibly beats the white cop into submission and compliance rather than participate in the kind of ritualistic and stylized fisticuffs battles that aim to produce recognition and mutuality in his other films.

To take a closer look at how some of the goals of the psychological dramas that frame blackness as an analytic authority ultimately falter, I turn here to *Pressure Point* (1962), a film in which Poitier actually plays a psychoanalyst. This film best demonstrates some of the ways in which films can both rely on and undermine the rhetoric of racial integration as a model for transformative psychology. While Poitier's characters are suggestively and analogously therapeutic in other films, here he is cast as making deliberate use of psychoanalysis as a liberatory personal and civic practice. Like many Poitier films, *Pressure Point* advertises a telling climactic clash between black and white men, or as the film's theatrical trailer promises, "Sometimes white-hot rage and black fury can reach the pressure point." The unchecked "white-hot rage" in this case, played by Bobby Darin, is an unnamed prisoner in a psychiatric hospital who hates blacks and Jews. As the film's personification of "black fury," Poitier plays Darin's unnamed and reluctant psychoanalyst. With a narrative frame that dramatizes a comparison between the social and emotional climate of the 1940s and the 1960s, only the beginning and end of the film are set in 1962; most of the action of the story is told through flashbacks from 1942, when Poitier's character, exceptional within his profession, served as the only black doctor working in the psychiatric ward of the prison. In 1962, the older Poitier character, who has excelled over the years enough to become the prison's "Chief Psychiatrist," retells the story of his most difficult and notorious patient as a way of providing an instructive lesson for a younger white analyst who has been assigned to treat a black man who hates white people.

In this way, not only does the film establish a connection between the therapeutic culture of the 1940s and race relations in the 1960s, but the peculiar temporal and narrative frame is also notable for how it decontextualizes and conflates anti-Semitism and black rage.[49] Andrea Slane well summarizes the social context that shapes *Pressure Point*'s particular mix of political psychology as it relates to the era's race relations, arguing that, "at the end of the war, when the massive magnitude of Nazi atrocities became widely known, the notion that anti-Semitism is incompatible with democratic society did gain a greater foothold, as did liberal humanist antiprejudice rhetoric in general. Indeed, the movement for the greater civil rights of African Americans also benefited from the mainstreaming of liberal antiprejudice rhetoric wrought in the opposition of fascism and democracy."[50] In infusing "antiprejudice rhetoric" with psychological discourse, *Pressure Point* endorses the popular 1950s view that racism was a psychological pathology.

Within this narrative and ideological frame, prototypical Poitier soft talk and talking therapy—the familiar moments when his characters encourage nonreciprocal free association as a way to facilitate the excavation of deeper needs and hurts—are presented in this film as a tedious but necessary process that once again has the potential to spur individual change. In trying to effect this change, the doctor finds psychoanalysis directly helpful, and he notes that "after several extremely difficult and slow months of analysis," he reaches "a knowledge, a beginning" that helps him understand his white patient's hostility toward Jews and blacks. Using a clinical style of analysis that is a convoluted amalgamation of popular psychologies, the doctor eventually deduces that the patient's anger and intolerance has been created by a sadistic "alcoholic father," a frail and "clingy" mother, general "sociopathic tendencies," the death of an imaginary childhood friend, and the patient's longing for an appropriate authoritative figure to idealize and emulate—some of the same kinds of emotional problems and traumas that other Poitier buddies faced during the era. In this case, the would-be buddy, desperate for male guidance, joins a supremacist group that worships and idealizes Hitler. This idealizing transference with Hitler's image is misplaced, reasons the doctor, and in order for him to recommend the patient's reintegration into society, for the doctor to be convinced that the patient can be a productive American citizen, the patient has to redirect his idealizations and use "healthier" transferential objects to initiate a complete personality change. As the doctor informs him, "All I can do is help you to remake yourself." The doctor's prescription for treatment proposes that anti-intersubjective worldviews must be transformed one noxious, "rotten" personality at a time.

In the early part of the analysis, the formal psychoanalytic setting creates a hopeful synergy between trauma resolution, personal morality, and national loyalty. As the story progresses, however, and the analyst learns more about the patient's crimes and intended crimes against blacks and Jews, the doctor's internal dialogue reveals a grave skepticism about whether this presentation of whiteness as a pathological emotional condition is in fact curable. Further, as Kaplan notes in her brief reading of the film, the doctor's own countertransference, his personal reactions and associations to the patient, break his veil of psychoanalytic neutrality and threaten to compromise his willingness to become the central figure of the patient's transference.[51] That is, the type of racial transference that is actively encouraged in other Poitier films falters here, in part because the racist patient resists transference but also because of the black psychological expert's disgust with pathological whiteness. As the doctor reflects, "Everything about the man, everything he believed and stood for, alienated me, repelled me." Despite this repulsion, the doctor remains professionally committed to the case and does his best to limit the countertransference by masking his internal frustrations with an outward projection of nonjudgment.

Poitier's training as a method actor works well in this context to portray a doctor who needs to ultimately mask the countertransference of his personal thoughts and beliefs. As an actor, Poitier conveys this struggle in his long, contemplative silences and blank stares. When the patient makes inflammatory remarks, the doctor stares on with a labored, almost caricatured, visceral blankness, as he fixates unemotively on his pair of round glasses and preoccupies himself with adjusting or cleaning them. The performance of emotional detachment in these moments serves to create the doctor's intellectual maturity and distance relative to white psychosis. Typically, in other Poitier films, the psychotherapeutic cool-mode moments of deadened affective listening serve as the prelude to an inevitable, emotional fisticuffs battle or as a buildup to a heated verbal tirade, both of which produce a momentary engagement with black humanity and recognition, as in *The Defiant Ones* and *In the Heat of the Night*. While in other films Poitier's method of performing cool-mode affect gives way to a measured performance of dignified outrage, this combination of hot and cool method acting works here to passively encourage transference with the cooler affect or to communicate his bristling struggle with countertransference in the more heated moments of exchange.

And yet, in a climactic scene that evinces the black psychological expert's inherent difficulty in succeeding as either an idealizing transference or an object of recognition, the doctor does strategically boil and contrast deadened affect with eruptive response. A familiar confrontational pedagogical moment does indeed happen in *Pressure Point*, but the way the action of the scene unfolds makes the film more like *No Way Out*, *The Bedford Incident*, *Brother John*, and the other Poitier films that raise psychiatric concerns about the nation and its citizens but ultimately express an ambivalence about psychology's practical utility. As these films indicate that the black exceptional other's psychological authority will be thoroughly undermined by systemic bias, ironically, in one of the few films in which Poitier's role as a therapeutic expert is literally construed, his character is portrayed as needing to abandon analytical tools altogether. Toward the end of *Pressure Point*, the doctor makes the painful discovery that not only has the analysis and treatment of racism failed to remedy individual trauma, but the very system in which he has invested his hope has betrayed him. In the final scenes of the film, a psychiatric review board composed of his white and Jewish colleagues surreptitiously holds a meeting with the doctor's patient without the doctor's knowledge. Just as the board is on the verge of unanimously agreeing that the patient has been reformed and no longer poses a threat to society, Poitier's character interrupts the proceedings and delivers a measured speech about his colleagues' inappropriate usurping of his power. He further argues that his patient is only manipulating the system, only mimicking what he knows the board wants to hear. The patient dismisses his analyst's claims, telling the board that it is the doctor who is racially biased, "sensitive," and revenge prone.

The scene turns quickly from a hearing about the patient to a mob-like inquisition and interrogation of the black analyst. In keeping his countertransference in check before his colleagues, throughout the interrogation, the analyst never breaks from his cool, professional demeanor. In fact, performed here using Poitier's classic blank stares, the doctor appears utterly bored by the patient's predictable deception. It is only when the analyst realizes that his colleagues do not believe him—that he has become an

outsider in the discourse that he has mastered—that he vows to quit and
storms out of the meeting to immediately pack up his office.

The visual composition of the next scene accentuates the black analyst's unique bind and limited options. As the patient, who has been
granted release by the review board, visits the doctor one final time, the
camera's angle and large depth of field create a visual confusion between
the cell across the hall and the doctor's doorway, giving the impression
that the doctor's professional space, the spatial terms of his influence, is
now contained. Psychoanalysis—the concretized tools of the interracial
psychological mission—has not worked up to this point in the treatment
of the antipsychological subject's supremacism. The patient directly dismisses black exceptionalism and expertise, taunting, "All those people
you've been working with, who'd they believe? The big black boy who's
supposed to be running this place or the white, Christian American?" The
scene's spatial composition offers an unobstructed view of the doctor's
countenance as he reacts to these words and finally transforms into a
much-less-measured version of his heated signification. The doctor's transformation is both verbal and physical. Immediately crossing the room to
slam the door, he erupts, "You crud, you vicious, slimy, rotten little crud!"
By closing the door, the doctor communicates that what he is about to say
comes from a private, not a professional, ambition. The closed door also
deemphasizes the bars across the hall and the way the professional setting
and tools have until now contained his agency and true desires.

In fact, up until this point, the black expert's direct use of psychological discourse has only compromised, rather than secured, his own authority. It follows, then, that neither transference nor the dramatization of
black object survival/recognition will suffice in this final confrontation.
Instead of continuing what the failed analysis has shown as the limits of
the language of psychology, the doctor instead rants using the related un-
disguised rhetoric of generic national dominance:

> Now let me tell you something! This is my country. This is where
> I've done what I've done. And if there were a million cruds like
> you, all sick, like you're sick, all shouting down, "destroy, degrade,"
> and if there were twenty million more sick enough to listen to

Systemic bias as imprisonment, *Pressure Point*

Analytic failure, *Pressure Point*

them, you are still gonna lose. You are going to lose, mister, because there's something in this country, something so big, so strong that you don't even know. Something big enough to take it from people like you. And come back and nail you into the

ground. You're walking out of here? You are going nowhere! Now
get out! GET OUT!"

Whereas in Poitier's most famous films American exceptionalist ambition
is disguised as an interracial culture of talking therapy that grants access
to a black exceptional other, in this speech, the ways in which psychological discourse functions as a governing national ideology is much more
apparent. If emotional healing will not work for what the script identifies
as an American identity that is too misguided and too damaged to change,
and if, as the doctor discovers about his colleagues' behavior, there is in
fact a structural system in place that can undermine this work, only the
wish of "something" in this country that is "so big" and "so strong" can
address this version of the psychiatric condition. Thus, the only thing that
can quell the disappointment of a clear and obvious failure of the intersubjective view of race is a nonspecific American essence, the personification of democratic greatness, that can take the country back from white
psychosis. While the doctor's speech nevertheless envisions an individual-
ized treatment for the potential "million cruds" like the patient who are
"all sick" and destructive, in no other cinematic moment is a Poitier character so closely aligned with the rhetoric of national exceptionalism and
its relationship to the protocols of analysis and black expertise.

Irrespective of the obvious failure of this particular course of treatment, black analytic expertise endures as a site of cultural meaning in
*Pressure Point*'s dramatic resolution. As it turns out, the doctor was right
about the patient's lack of readiness for democratic participation. In the
concluding moments of the film, the doctor rationalizes his experience
with systemic bias as a minor setback; he never quits his job, nor does
he permanently abandon psychoanalysis's potential for remaking the
national character one sick patient at a time. As the aged doctor explains
to his mentee in the final sequence, which takes place in the 1960s, he was
right all along: upon release, the patient remained a danger to society and
ended up being killed while committing a series of hate crimes. Despite
this notable failure in using psychoanalysis to treat racism and despite
the way the film evinces some of the institutional biases that have made
it difficult for black people to rely on the history, practice, and discourse

of analysis, the black analytical expert is represented as maintaining a blind faith in therapeutic intersubjectivity as the still-preferred, and possibly only, mechanism for dislodging white supremacy from the center of national consciousness. Further, in communicating the wishful optimism that the analytic impulse, despite all evidence to the contrary, will serve as a particularly useful tool for managing civil rights era race relations, the doctor is confident that psychotherapy *can* cure black rage and be used to create a successful instance of interracial transference between his white mentee and his "angry" black patient. When his colleague mentions that he will "get some burnt cork" and don blackface in order to create a stronger transference with his patient, the doctor's endorsement of this tactic ("Good idea, only don't let me down because you are a white man") only confirms the black analytic body's utility for bolstering the systematic cooptation, exploitation, and domination of oppressed people. So too does the popularized vision of black psychological expertise lack the ability to discern between what it construes as pathological anti-intersubjectivity and a possible justified social complaint—as the unnamed 1960s black patient may well have been demonstrating in his rejection of whiteness as a transferential object. Hence, while psychoanalysis did not work to repair and regulate the crazy white racist, it is upheld at the end of the film as a disciplinary tool that *can* "fix" and subjugate the racial other's civic discontent, which the narrative frames as a familiar form of psychotic pathology. Here, notably, the project of recognition, of learning to adequately "see" the black patient's humanity and interior logic, including the reasons he might hate white people, is cast aside as irrelevant and not as productive as the intentional cultivation of transference and countertransference or the deliberate use of fantasy.

Whether or not the psychotherapeutic project appeared as success or failure was not determined chronologically across the body of Sidney Poitier films from the 1950s into the early 1970s. The span of Poitier's career was not neatly split into intervals when he was inviting racial transference in one moment, signaling recognition and black survival in another, and tacitly criticizing a cultural reliance on psychology in the latter part of his career. Instead, he worked constantly shifting between these registers in many different and nuanced performances as an analytic expert. Any interpretation of his film career is complicated by these important subtleties and contradictions. It is difficult to argue, as I have here, that Poitier's characters functioned as both an object (idealized image) and as a "recognized," humanized, subject (surviving object), but this is precisely what the Poitier film vehicle does, however schizophrenic it may seem either to need to see as real and need to see as ideal or to appropriate psychological discourse only to undermine it at the same time.

# 3

# BAAADDD BLACK MAMAS
# AND THE CHRONIC FAILURE
# OF RECOGNITION

The literary and cultural theorist Hortense J. Spillers has tried to explain her understanding of the complicated role that she plays as a black woman in the American cultural imaginary. Spillers reflects, "Let's face it. I am a marked woman, but not everybody knows my name. . . . I describe a locus of confounded identities, a meeting ground of investments and privations in the national treasury of rhetorical wealth. My country needs me, and if I were not here, I would have to be invented."[1] As Spillers supposes, black women have played any number of roles as the mucilage that helps maintain our collective perceptions of a national identity. Our representational culture—film, television, fiction, autobiography, art—has been particularly good at inventing and reinventing the types of black women and mothers who best service our most basic national ideals. If Sidney Poitier's black male characters from the civil rights era represented a psychological expertise that was caught between transference and recognition, have black female characters functioned similarly in the dominant cultural appropriation of psychosocial themes? This chapter takes as a starting place that there is, in fact, a stubborn and captivating, obvious but often misunderstood, affective culture, or what Lauren Berlant calls sentimentality's "world of feeling politics,"[2] that has developed around the most negative and stereotypical representations of black women and, more specifically, black mothers.

This same calcification of intense feelings, fantasies, and politics informs even the most innocuous popular images of black women as mothers. Consider Diahann Carroll's civil rights era performance in *Julia* (1968–71) as a case in point. *Julia*, the first television sitcom to star a black woman in the lead role, did not rely on overtly negative imagery. In 1968, when the show debuted, Carroll's character, Julia Baker, much like Poitier's exceptional black men, was deliberately constructed *not* to resemble the other negatively associative images—from the mammy to the sapphire—that had dominated American pop-cultural depictions of black mothers. Treating the persistent negative imagery of black maternity as a thing of the past, Carroll's Julia was portrayed as an ambitious member of the professional class (she was fully employed as a nurse), and as a single mother, she provided a comfortable and loving home for her young son. Despite these attempts to distance the character from regressive depictions of black mothers, the historic comedy was roundly criticized for being out of touch with black political culture of the late 1960s and 1970s. As Donald Bogle recounts, summarizing some of the common critiques of the sitcom, "Julia Baker lived in a fantasy version of Los Angeles where the uprisings and disorders in ghettos around the country, including Watts, didn't appear to exist at all."[3] But the show's reflection of integrationist and middle-class ideals was not viewers' only concern. Although Carroll has said that everything about the show, from Julia's house to her clothes and her dating life, became the subject of intense criticism, the central complaint, Carroll says, the "heavy," "unkind," and "threatening" attacks levied directly at her, had to do with Julia's status as a single mother raising a black son.

Echoing Carroll's observations about the public outcry over Julia's role as a single parent, the pioneering television personality and *Julia*'s creator, Hal Kanter, tells a story about how even reactions to the show's title before it aired were political but also deeply emotional in nature. In explaining how the show came to be called *Julia* instead of its original title, *Mama's Man*, Kanter says, "When publicity came out about this new show, *Mama's Man*, Diahann had some friends in New York—Harry Belafonte and James Baldwin, among others—and they said, 'Now listen, that's a very bad title. It can't be *Mama's Man*. That's not the image we want to have about a little boy, a black little kid, being a mama's man. We're not mama's men. We're men!'"[4] Although Julia's son, Corey, was certainly not a man—he was only six years old when the series began and nine when it ended—Belafonte's and Baldwin's preemptory complaints reflected a broader social discomfort with, and stigmatization of, black maternal agency during the era. Their reaction to the show's original title consolidated public fears and frustrations with black women being cast and perceived as the central authority figures not only in the lives of their children but also in the black community in general. The objection endorsed the view that the emotional and political stakes were too high for anyone, particularly black men and boys, to be thought of as what the original title seemed to imply: black mama's possessive object.

Right at the margins of a show like *Julia* were concerns of a psychosocial and psychotherapeutic nature. For example, to deal with some of the affective politics that the show inevitably inflamed, the studio employed black psychological experts on *Julia*'s set. The principal reason for the use of psychiatric specialists was to ensure that the young actor playing Julia's son (Marc Copage) would not internalize the image of a black mother as the head of household as normative. Specifically, Carroll recalls, "We also hired black psychiatrists to guide us to make sure that our child, my son and his little playmate (both of them about five or six years old when they were hired), that they were involved in situations that made them aware of black males. . . . Also, mother dated and we brought the male into the house to say hello to the son, and usually it was another professional—black—that the son was exposed to."[5]

As Carroll explains here, the script included a decorated cast of black men (including Paul Winfield, Don Marshall, and Fred Williamson) to appear as Julia's love interests and also to serve as important role models for Corey. In the event that Marc Copage, the young actor, could not interpolate the appropriate lessons about black masculinity that Julia's on-screen dating life supposedly signified to the general audiences, the studio used direct psychiatric intervention to ensure that the real child's perceptions of black family life were not unduly influenced by Julia and Corey's fictional relationship. Despite the fact that by all accounts Julia was a good mother (she was patient, spent time playing with Corey, taught him valuable lessons about conflict resolution, and displayed an affectionate and compassionate parenting style), the affective politics surrounding black motherhood required clinical remediation and consultation. It is ironic that Carroll's Julia, who like Sidney Poitier's characters was critiqued for being unrealistically saint-like and banal, was nevertheless constructed alongside the intervening influence of psychological expertise.

*Julia* is something of an outlier when it comes to the most common depictions of black maternity, but I begin with this show as a way of demonstrating that as a single black mother, Julia's very existence was assumed to be negatively impactful to both on- and off-screen (no matter real or imagined) black children. The main stereotypes of black women as mothers have similarly participated in an affective culture that draws on conventions of excess as the images protract, exaggerate, and distort any real subjective experiences in order to create and sustain narrative tension and conflict, to communicate ethical or moral imperatives, and to encourage points of identification with certain characters instead of others. Full or excessive affect has defined nearly all of the dominant prototypes of black maternity we have seen in varied cultural contexts. For instance, "mammies" are effusive in their love, "matriarchs" are unmatched in their dominion, "jezebels" have unbridled sexual desire, and "sapphires" are unrestrained in their expression of anger. Throughout film and television history, these dominant characterizations of black mothers have appeared most consistently in family dramas, a form that also depends heavily on the aesthetics of excess, including conventions of melodrama and sentimentality. It is within this context, one where heightened affect fuses with political discourse in narrative accounts that are seemingly "psychoanalytic," "melodramatic," or "sentimental," that I encourage us to rethink the most enduring stereotypes of black motherhood.

In this chapter, I offer the turn of phrase *baaaddd black mama* as a way of emphasizing the times when all stereotypical ways of representing and discussing black maternity—the mammy, matriarch, sapphire, and jezebel but also the welfare queen, saint, and so forth—have in common an affective logic that presents them as subjects whose actions and desires, sometimes even just the fact of their existence, are experienced by others, especially their children, as physically or emotionally damaging. More closely examining the commonalities among the obviously stereotypical constructions of black mothers enables us to note that despite their excessive affect, black mothers in the wider cultural terrain have been consistently rendered as depressive figures. My use of the term *baaaddd black mama* also includes the shared cultural suspicion that black mothers are incapable of winning any part of the high returns attached to the game of recognition, a process that has been predicated on acknowledging the subjective independence of others. Depicted repeatedly as antipsychological subjects who fail to facilitate important rituals of mature psychological development, baaaddd black mothers have not only had an incredible ability to absorb common negative associations of black people and mothers in general, but their images and the stories about them have also incorporated problematic psychoanalytic constructions of "preoedipal" mothers.

As I argue here, there are varied narrative traditions and contexts that have conflated black maternity with psychoanalytic concepts, and mainstream civil rights era visual culture only compounded the tendency to link the intersubjective governed politics of recognition with the increase in the representation of black subjectivities in popular media. The first part of this chapter begins with a brief genealogy of the image problem surrounding black women and then situates this genealogy within the context of leading psychoanalytic themes that have been used to describe black mothers in literature and in black women's autobiography. Since black family dramas have been especially complicit in advancing tropes of the baaaddd black mama, the second half of the chapter is devoted exclusively to the ways in which these matters have been condensed in two civil rights era representative films, *Imitation of Life* (1959) and *Black Girl* (1972), and also how more contemporary works like *Precious* (2001) operate in a similar "world of feeling politics." Reading these texts as a part of an enduring conversation better establishes some of the ways in which the most common representations of black mothers, Diahann Carroll's Julia included, are all baaaddd black mamas—psychological beings who are measured by their destructive and depressive impact and by their assumed inability to embrace intersubjectivity within the home.

## Black Maternity's Image Problem as the Persistence of Stereotype

Why do contemporary films like *Antwone Fisher, Precious, Monster's Ball, Pariah, Mississippi Damned*, and nearly everything written and directed by Tyler Perry seem to revolve around stories about badly behaving black mothers? How is it that even a "good" black mother, like Diahann Carroll's Julia, could be accused of negatively impacting black children? The short answer to these questions is that black women have an image problem in American cultural life. The genealogy of this image problem, of black femininity's synonymy with problem laden, emerged well before the civil rights era and predates our many contemporary representations of dysfunctional bad mamas, angry black women, welfare queens, superwomen, and what Joan Morgan has called *strongblackwoman*.[6] Despite the fact that there have been a potentially endless assortment of such types or "controlling images,"[7] to use Patricia Hill Collins's instructive phrase, most of the distorted representations of black maternity continue to appear as some derivative or combination of the "classics," or the most enduring stereotypes of black women: mammy, matriarch, sapphire, jezebel.

As stereotypes of black people were created as serviceable fictions that could justify the dehumanization, enslavement, and continued exploitation of marginalized bodies, the mammy figure became known for what the literary historian Barbara Christian describes as her innately maternal, "kind," "loyal," and "sexless" attributes, a black woman often portrayed as a habitual domestic worker who willingly sacrifices her own well-being to care for her white employers.[8] Black women typified as matriarchs turn their penchant for caring for others into an ironclad rule of their own households as they perpetually fail to maintain and attract suitable romantic partners. Similarly, the sapphire, in contrast to the equally distorted but nonetheless pervasive cultural fiction of white feminine docility and soft-spokenness, has been characterized as verbally caustic and physically aggressive, the type of black woman and mother who administers the corporal punishment of others with ease. Meanwhile, the stereotypical jezebel, who served as a consistent projection of the psychosexual fantasies of slaveholders and was most notoriously signified in Sarah Baartman's image of Venus Hottentot, "branded" black women in historical memory "as sexually promiscuous and immoral."[9] In addition to working to create what Carolyn West describes as "a hierarchy of beauty and social status," these four basic stereotypes of black women and mothers have also been "updated" and reinvigorated in contemporary representations of black motherhood.[10]

While we might rightly resist organizing the entire history of mainstream black performances on film around the persistence of stereotypes as Donald Bogle does in *Toms, Coons, Mulattos, Mammies, and Bucks*, it is true that technologies of the moving image have been particularly adept at maintaining and compounding black maternity's image problem. For instance, we have seen mammies as early as 1903 in the various film renditions of Harriet Beecher Stowe's *Uncle Tom's Cabin* and as Hattie McDaniel playing Mammy in the film version of *Gone with the Wind* (1939). Black matriarchs have appeared as central figures in black family life in films like *Take a Giant Step* (1960), *A Raisin in the Sun* (1961), and *Sounder* (1972) and in television shows like *What's Happening!!* (1976–79) and *That's My Mama* (1974–75). We have heard and seen *Amos 'n' Andy*'s sharp-tongued character Sapphire, Kingfish's wife, on the radio and on television from the 1920s through the 1950s and listened to other sapphires' verbal rampages in films like *Black Girl* (1972), *Boyz n the Hood* (1991), and *Daddy's Little Girls* (2007). Meanwhile, the black jezebel in black and American popular culture has masqueraded as the tragic mulatta in films like *Pinky* (1949) and *Imitation of Life* (1959) while also informing Dorothy Dandridge's performance as Carmen Jones (1954). More recently, the black jezebel resurfaced in Halle Berry's Oscar-winning role in *Monster's Ball* (2001).

Of course, these stereotypes of black women and mothers have not been limited to fictional narrative representation. Sociological studies like Daniel Patrick Moynihan's *The Negro Family: The Case for National Action* (1965), a document that famously linked the "crisis in race relations" and black poverty to the gross absence of "a stable Negro family structure," have long been blamed for exacerbating the persistent image problem around black women in the civil rights and post–civil rights eras.[11] Specifically, in the section titled "Matriarchy," Moynihan linked the "tangle of pathology" of the black poor to the decline of two-parent households, to the lack of proper "socialization of children," and to the perceived centrality of black women in their families and communities.[12] American society "presumes male leadership in private and public affairs," wrote Moynihan, while black families "often reversed roles of husband and wife" in ways that were fundamentally incompatible with the preferred patriarchal order.[13] Even though the veracity of such claims has been widely contested since the report's publication, Moynihan and the U.S. Department of Policy and Labor have not been alone in faulting black women for nearly every problem facing the black community, including fewer employment and educational opportunities for black men and the ever-widening economic gaps between black and nonblack Americans. Other sociological approaches, like Franklin Frazier's *The Negro Family* and Kenneth Clark's *Dark Ghetto*, and some black nationalist discourses drew similar conclusions about black women and their complicity in the various crises affecting black families.[14]

While there are complex social, political, and economic reasons that better explain the ways in which structural biases have disproportionately impacted black communities, the way sociological studies tend to reduce problems of inequity to psychological or group behavioral factors has always spurred intense public discussion. Across disciplines, black feminist scholarship has been instrumental in debunking the constructed myths of black womanhood.[15] For example, Patricia Hill Collins's pioneering work has stressed the ideological purpose that stereotypes serve—to distort, divide, and distract.[16] Barbara Christian has concurred, arguing that stereotypes are "one of the vehicles through which racism tries to reduce the human being to a nonhuman level" because the stereotype "is the very opposite of humaneness."[17] Both of these critics, along with Hazel Carby, bell hooks, Evelyn Brooks Higginbotham, Dorothy E. Roberts, and Wahneema Lubiano, have historically contextualized and persuasively identified some of the social and political issues that motivate the persistence of the most familiar stereotypes.[18] Whereas Roberts analyzes the jezebel, mammy, matriarch, and the welfare-queen types in the context of reproductive policies and initiatives that have been designed to strategically control and vilify black women's bodies, Lubiano succinctly argues that framing the black mother as the welfare queen makes her an undisrupted "agent of destruction, the creator of the pathological, black, urban, poor family from which all ills flow."[19] Conversely, Kimberly Wallace-Sanders's rich account of a century of cultural representations of the mammy figure frames the mammy as a constellation of many things: as a stereotype and controlling image but also as a potentially subversive vehicle of political critique.[20] This now-extensive body of scholarship on black women and stereotypes has convincingly established, as Roberts reminds us, that stereotypes of black women, irrespective of their subversive potential, always reflect the complicated ways in which racism and patriarchy converge. The continued distorted imagery surrounding black women confirms that both interlocking systems of oppression are as invested as ever in the chronic "devaluation of Black motherhood."[21]

More recently, perhaps because of the discursive and methodological overlap between sociology and psychology, critics, theorists, and historians have begun to directly address and explore some of the ways in which the persistent stereotypes of black women have affected black women's self-esteem and self-perceptions. In this vein, the psychologist Carolyn West argues that popular stereotypes like mammy, matriarch, jezebel, and sapphire "influence the psychological functioning of many African American women" and have informed black women's attitudes about body image and other aspects of mental health.[22] Similarly, Sarita Davis connects the pervasive imagery of black women constructed as jezebels to harmful attitudes about sex and HIV among groups of young black women.[23] This aspect of psychological and sociological research that is primarily concerned with the *effects* of the dominant imagery, though invaluable to our broader discussions about black women in America, does little to interrogate how psychological discourses and psychoanalytic ideologies heavily informed the images, rhetoric, and representations surrounding black women in the first place. Only a few published works across disciplines have specifically explored the widespread denigration of black women and mothers in the context of psychoanalytic discursive histories. One exception to this omission is the edited volume *"Bad" Mothers: The Politics of Blame in Twentieth-Century America*. In the introduction to the collection, Molly Ladd-Taylor and Lauri Umansky chart out a brief but persuasive account of how the notion of "bad" (black and white) mothers has shifted over time by specifically arguing that the postwar American cultural appropriation of psychoanalytic models seemed to provide "'scientific' justification for mother-blaming" as psychologists set publicly embraced standards for a "course of normal development" for child rearing.[24] In the same collection, Ruth Feldstein posits that, "here and elsewhere, a centuries-old tradition of black women as quintessential maternal figures intersected with contemporary [psychoanalytic] theories about maternal rejection and overprotection."[25] Feldstein's work provocatively explores the way postwar American "liberal scholars melded preexisting ideas about black women's economic domination with the psychological terms and images that were circulating in so many arenas."[26]

These critical examinations notwithstanding, as media scholars, film spectators, and general fans of popular culture, we have become quite skilled at noting the persistence of stereotypes when it comes to representations of black women. We have been much less attentive, however, to the emotional and affective logic that informs such works. While it is tempting, for any number of reasons, to write black women out of the history of postwar America's vernacularization of psychological discourse, black women were and continue to be crucial to how race is psychologized. We certainly can continue, as others have already done, to theorize representations of the racial mother without engaging and problematizing the language and cultural logic of analysis, but to talk continually about these images, along with the countless personal accounts of dysfunctional black mothers, without connecting them to the postwar turn toward the psychological effectively writes black women out of the conversation and obscures the way the psychoanalytic so often gives traction to the stereotypical, the melodramatic, the sentimental, and the realist and to overtly social-political representations. If even a "good" black mother like Diahann Carroll's Julia needs a built-in measure of psychotherapy to masquerade as damage control, how else have the dominant themes of analysis overlapped with the basic stereotypes of black maternity? Further, if black women are consistently blamed for the failures of the race, and if they have continued to be represented stereotypically across media, how do these facts align with the equally persistent cultural focus on the psychological recognition of black humanity?

## The Cultural Life of Omnipotent Black Mothers

Although psychoanalysis has been critiqued since its inception for its blind spots, exclusionary practices, and intentional distortions when it comes to people of color, its disparate set of theories and perspectives have had significant cultural reach, especially in regard to popular perceptions about women and motherhood. In fact, some of the features of black maternity's image problem (mothers who are portrayed as godlike, for example) have had notable conceptual precedent in analytic discourse. To begin with, there is the issue of the mother's perceived dominion and uncompromising influence on her children, parental qualities that popular media depicts black mothers as deploying in excess. If there has been a cross-cultural concern that black mothers have an "unfeminine" propensity for being domineering or, like Diahann Carroll's Julia, are negatively impactful even when they have the best of intentions, how have the dominant analytical tropes of motherhood contributed to our popular understandings of black mothers' place in and beyond the home?

Disparate theorists, from Freud, Kohut, and Winnicott to Margaret Mahler, Melanie Klein, and Eric Fromm, have all written about maternal "omnipotence" in one context or another. While these often-warring branches of analysis differ greatly in their assessment of how much the desire to impact and control the environment outside the self falls within the range of normative or pathological behaviors, the concept of maternal omnipotence has generally been described as a fundamental lack of awareness of the boundaries between self and other. To that end, omnipotence often refers to an actual or fantasized control of other people. We can speak, then, both colloquially and analytically, about an individual's subjective view that includes the self but also expands to include a desire, wish, or fantasy to control the agency of others and the extent to which that view fails or maintains an association with reality. The surge of omnipotent feelings that are activated within the mother-child dyad have been described as particularly powerful, hallucinatory even, with both mothers and children in the early years of development being most susceptible to fantasies of controlling the other as self. Under ideal circumstances in developmental psychology, both mother and child outgrow this attachment and propensity for experiencing the other as an extension of the self's desires, actions, and private wishes.

Yet psychology as a discipline has concretized around the failure to progress in normative or ideal ways. As such, dread surfaces in the clinical literature as one of the more common reactions of a person who experiences the unresolved and unexpunged omnipotent fantasies of another. If Freud is remembered as pondering, "What does woman want?" popular and analytic discourses about women and mothers since Freud's time have answered that women dread becoming their mothers. While there have been many popular and cross-cultural confirmations of this sentiment, feminist psychoanalysts like Karen Horney have tried to figure out why dreading maternal influence and centrality has been such a strong cultural norm. Throughout her career, Horney used her clinical research with mothers and children to challenge Freudian drive and libido theory's emphasis on women's inferior and envious relationship to men. Specifically, in reimagining the dynamics of the preoedipal household and countering Freudian thought, Horney argued that young children experience mother as wonderfully everything—as the central agent in their lives, as having the singular ability to be nurturer and provider, as magically and instinctively aware of their needs, and as their most ideal agent and authority figure. Although the tendency to idealize mother's influence can be just as problematic as abjection, Horney's work has remained relevant since she was among the first to depathologize subjective interconnectedness and focus instead on how we came not only to mistrust the interdependence between mother and child but also to reject mother as a competent authority.[27]

At a crucial moment in the development of the mainstream psychoanalysis, Horney described a cultural rejection, fear, and dread of mother that developed as a response to the child's subjective experience of mother as positively omnipotent. In essays like "The Dread of Woman," "The Flight from Womanhood," and "The Denial of the Vagina," for instance, Horney argued that gendered hierarchies and the social domination of women stem from masculine frustrations with mother's inimical axis of reproductive power. The French Freudian psychoanalyst Janine Chasseguet-Smirgel and the social theorist Nancy Chodorow are a few among others who have continued to integrate and amplify some of what Horney saw as a cultural dread of woman that was not motivated by the Oedipal period's castration anxiety as Freud thought but instead emerged as a way to compete with the early experience of mother as the primary authority.[28] And so in redrawing the theoretical lines of analysis around the basic story of "preoedipal" experiences with mothers, post-Freudian feminist revisionists have taken a variety of approaches to concluding that Freud was wrong. The "father" and "his phallus" become powerful signifiers in the gendered social domain not because of instinct, nature, or drive but "because of their ability to stand for separation from the mother."[29] In time, children develop socially sanctioned but often-flawed ways of nullifying mother's perceived influence. These attempts to separate from mother include a pronounced gravitation toward the social norms of patriarchy and materialize as more general symbolic activities that can function as a "third agent" in what Chasseguet-Smirgel has theorized as destructive attempts to "beat back" mother's perceived centrality.[30]

When preoedipal mother is "beat back" or checked by patriarchal authority or other symbolic agents and activities, the "successful" outcome positions mother as a losing adversary in her child's fight for individualism and self-discovery. As the child participates in the larger social order and shifts idealization to other agents, mother becomes a figure of depressive clinginess in what is often culturally dramatized as a contest between the child's independence and mother's sense of purpose. In this context, theories of recognition have surfaced in contemporary psychoanalytic literature as a possible solution to the chronic dread and affective beat-back scenarios that stem from the pervasive fears and mistrust of maternal omnipotence. Writing about the practice of mutual recognition as a correction for the distorted cultural view of motherhood, Jessica Benjamin describes one of the primary aims of mutuality as the child's discovery of mother as neither a subject who controls nor an object who is to be controlled, dreaded, or destroyed.[31] Likewise, mother, by recognizing the child's independent will, grows to accept the child's desires as falling outside her jurisdiction, and the dialectic production of a shared reality that manages to keep the omnipotence of the self and other/mother in a constant tension can be used in the public sphere as the basic relational foundation for the advancement of other forms of gender and social equality.

In thinking about black women's relationship to some of these concepts, I am less concerned with the psychoanalytic theories of "maternal omnipotence" as biological or developmentally normative truths per se. It matters less in this regard if the Freudians or feminist revisionists were right about mother's actual role within the home. What matters more is the cultural life of the object, or the ways some mothers seem to represent an even more pronounced depiction of preoedipal mother's bind. But even if motherhood has been theorized and represented using concepts like omnipotence, dread, and recognition, why should we take for granted that the specific and complicated history of black maternal subjectivity has anything to do with these resulting cultural mythologies?

Surely we have good reason to use caution when applying psychoanalysis's discursive history to black women. Rita Felski, in *Literature after Feminism*, urges caution, for example, when applying dominant metaphors and ideologies to all women across race, class, and region. In this vein, the metaphor of the "madwoman in the attic," which is often used to describe the alienated white woman artist, does not work. In fact, Felski insists that it "fails dismally" when describing African American and Third World women artists.[32] Similarly, although Hortense Spillers has on several occasions used psychoanalysis to reframe American racial histories, Spillers, like Felski, rightly challenges some of the ways we are tempted to draw on dominant discourses to describe black women. Most famously, in her landmark essay "Mama's Baby, Papa's Maybe: An American Grammar Book," Spillers encourages us to think about the subjectivity of black mothers differently, for as she argues, it is the black mother's history of enslavement, along with the "banished" African father, that places her "*out* of the traditional symbolics of female gender."[33] I return to Spillers's provocation that we should claim what has been designated culturally as the "monstrosity" of black motherhood as an "insurgent," "female social subject" at this end of this chapter.[34] Before entertaining that possibility of insurgency, however, we cannot continue to discount the many and overdetermined ways black maternity's image problem, the "monstrosity" that appears as the static stream of stereotypes, continues to be created and rehearsed by both black and nonblack cultural producers as very much *in* line with the "traditional symbolics" of female subjectivity as outlined by psychoanalytic thought's emphasis on omnipotence, dread, and recognition.

We need not look far to confirm the ways in which black artists and public figures have constructed black mothers as "baaaddd," as toxic pre-oedipal mothers who need to be aggressively beaten back. For instance, although Michelle Wallace's *Black Macho and the Myth of the Superwoman* (1978) remains one of the lengthiest critical rebuttals to the accusation that black families and specifically black men during the civil rights era were being destroyed by angry, bossy black mothers, there are many times in her influential critical memoir when she articulates her mother's relationship to the prevailing psychodynamic theories of omnipotence, dread, and recognition. As an adult, Wallace seems to have discovered a more complex way of relating to her mother, but as a younger woman, she was keenly aware of the public scorn surrounding the image of the excessively strong, or super, black mother. She writes that her familiarity with the characterization of single black mothers as crushing emotional figures guaranteed that "by the time [she] was fifteen there was nothing [she] dreaded more than being like the women in [her] family."[35]

Not only did Wallace dread and fear becoming the scorned image of black maternity that she misrecognized as her mother, she complains explicitly about her mother's seemingly superhuman ability to know and control all aspects of her life. Writing of her many failed plans to distance herself from her mother's boundless reach and controlling gaze, Wallace explains that she wanted to "get a man, any man," so that she "would no longer have to answer to her mother."[36] From a daughter's perspective, it was much easier to accept the dominant conviction that the various crises in the black community were causally linked to black maternal dominance. It was easier, Wallace confesses, to accept the associative view of black maternity as pathogenic, not paradoxical. As she clarifies, "But at sixteen I had no use for paradoxes. The women in my family could not be both strong and weak, both victimizers and victimized. I could hardly see the point in pursuing such an obviously unrewarding line of contemplation. It was much easier just to believe these women were the bloodless monsters the Black Movement said they were, and to reckon with my share in that sin."[37]

Even though Wallace is critical of such characterizations, her reflections demonstrate the extent to which these stereotypes have had immense cultural staying power as shared transgenerational emotional realities. Her account also highlights some of the ways in which black nationalist and separatist discourses further perpetuated the preexisting assumptions about maternal omnipotence and imagined the image problem of black maternity as something that was best corrected by the competing, corrective actions of black fathers and sons, who needed only to exercise their patriarchal privileges.

With a similar fear and aversion of black maternal agency, in *A Taste of Power* (1993), Elaine Brown parallels her long, oftentimes exhilarating, oftentimes dehumanizing experiences with the Black Panther Party with her account of an unwanted emotional entanglement with her mother. Part of Brown's difficulty with her mother was that she felt that they were "virtually one person," prompting Brown to want to "leave her, to climb out of her or cast her out" of herself.[38] In her memoir, Brown describes the blurred subjective experience with her mother as something she felt limited her own psychological, social, and political development. As a result, Brown explains that she sought out affiliations with powerful Panther men (Bobby Seale, Huey Newton, Eldridge Cleaver) as the kind of connection that could disrupt what she was experiencing as a suffocating bind between mother and daughter. At one point, Brown recalls that she informed her mother of as much by saying, "Mom, today, I think we're going to have to cut the umbilical cord."[39] In moments like this, Brown, echoing Wallace, describes her black mother as a boundless and unyielding force who compromises her daughter's sense of distinctiveness and circumvents what dominant society has upheld as a healthy desire for separation.

As a woman trying to navigate the masculinist biases and sexism that Brown discovered were often a part of party rhetoric and her attendant relationships, she much later discovered that she was running from two things at once: her mother's excessive, superhuman reach *and* her mother's lack of real power and independent desire.

Brown describes an encounter that exemplifies the unique paradoxical nature of black female "omnipotence" when she recounts her memory of a time when the Panther Party chairman, Bobby Seale, urged a fifteen-year-old "sister" to explain her understanding of women's natural power and relationship to men. The fifteen-year-old girl proudly explained to Brown what she discovered as a personal truth, saying, "A Sister has to give up the pussy when the Brother is on his job and hold it back when he's not. 'Cause Sisters got pussy power!"[40] Brown reports being shocked by the comment, but the teenager's revelation offers a clever and precise analysis that describes black woman's agency in psychosexual terms. What Karen Horney theorized in "Dread of Woman" and "Denial of the Vagina" as predictable backlashes to the preoedipal mother's authority shows up, then, in "Nation time!" "Pussy Power!" and other intraracial hypersexualizations of black women as ways to mitigate the terrifying prospect of a truly insurgent black female subjectivity.

As other forms of black women's cultural production have demonstrated, depicting black femininity and maternity in these ways has never been limited to popular forms or to dominant (white) American culture. We know that accounts of "monstrous" and "engulfing" black mothers have had immense staying power and cross-cultural appeal. In this regard, the literary historian Trudier Harris has compared how black women writers from Lorraine Hansberry to Toni Morrison, from Dorothy West to Octavia Butler, have typified black women and mothers in their fiction in ways that replicate and mirror the leading controlling imagery, since black women writers have represented black mothers using a similarly narrow range of "saints, sinners, or saviors" as archetypal.[41] Although Harris does not include the influences of psychoanalytic ideology in her study of maternal stereotypes in black women's fiction, she does note that black mothers who appear in fiction written by some of the most canonical black women writers tend to share "an implied ideology of domination—emotional domination, though sometimes physical as well—in most of their interactions with their offspring."[42] With resignation, Harris concludes that black women writers "are *not* willing to give up the type," particularly the image of the strong black woman.[43]

Equally pervasive in the cultural archive of the "strong" or omnipotent black maternal figure is mother's emotional collapse as a reaction to her child's budding self-discovery or attempts at differentiation. Black mothers across type have been depicted as having predictable responses to conflicts, both obvious and symbolic, with their children. If the child's desire to "beat back" mother's influence is something that our popular American narratives represent as creating dire emotional consequences for the mother, African American literature has explored a similar type of responsiveness between black maternal figures and their charges. Like Wallace's and Brown's accounts of their experiences with their mothers during the 1960s and 1970s, fictional stories about black mothers have represented the daughters' desire for separation as something that might compromise their mothers' (or grandmothers') will to live. For instance, Paule Marshall's 1967 short story "To Da-Duh, a Memoriam" investigates the intergenerational contest of self-expression between a woman and her grandmother as something that will inevitably endanger the grandmother. Throughout the story, the granddaughter tells her grandmother fantastic tales about her budding independence and worldly experiences, eventually sharing that she has seen the Empire State Building, which is "taller than the highest hill she [the grandmother] knew."[44] Commenting on her grandmother's reaction to this news, the granddaughter says, "all the fight went out of her at that."[45] The grandmother, for her part, loses interest in the younger generation's emergent sense of grandiosity and feels her own sense of "bigness" fade before she retreats and dies.

Consistent with second-wave feminism's critiques of the cultural institution of motherhood, Alice Walker, in her early novels *The Third Life of Grange Copeland* (1970) and *Meridian* (1976), represented black mothers as caught in a bind where their desires are undermined by their responsibilities as primary caretakers. In exploring the emotional contours of black mothers, Walker uses some of the traditional symbolics of analysis to express the ways in which her characters feel a sense of hopelessness and entrapment. In *Meridian*, for example, the title character's mother remains keenly aware that her social status as black and as female produced the psychical conditions of her "frail independence" that caves beneath "the pressures of motherhood."[46] Meridian's mother comes to understand the scope of her influence and existence as depressive and believes that mothers like her feel internally "dead, living just enough for their children."[47] As a descendant of this conditional existence, Meridian mimics her mother's emotionally devitalized disposition and feels chronically guilty throughout her own journey of personal discovery, specifically "for stealing her mother's serenity, for shattering her mother's emerging self."[48] While Walker's novels critique overtly the call to motherhood as a social norm, her works also attempt to add some complexity to the psychological blueprint of omnipotent black mothers by representing them as grappling with the differences between how they are perceived (by their children, their communities, society at large) and their private desires and feelings.[49]

With a similar attentiveness to the emotional life of an obviously destructive or baaaddd black mother, Toni Morrison's *Sula* (1973) represents the issue of black mother's omnipotence as something that is a losing proposition for both mother and child. While it is more common for other narratives to represent the child's departure from the home as an action that compromises mother's interior solvency, Morrison's character Eva feels internally upended for the opposite reason: her son will not make the socially sanctioned move into the Oedipal phase and separate from her by moving out, falling in love, or pursuing other externalized ambitions. Plum, Eva's son, prefers to stay close to his mother even in adulthood. This proximity between mother and adult son creates for Eva the terrifying fantasy that he is trying to "crawl back" into her womb.[50] Instead of dreading his mother's preoedipal supremacy and vaginal signification, Plum idealizes her, prompting Eva to burn him to death in her desperate attempt to preemptively destroy what she construes as unnatural and regressive behavior. Eva explains, "I done everything I could to make him leave me and go on and live and be a man but he wouldn't and I had to keep him out so I just thought of a way he could die like a man not all scrunched up inside my womb, but like a man."[51] Eva's aversion to Plum acting "all scrunched up" inside her womb echoes, of course, the civil rights era cultural anxiety that black women could somehow emasculate and subsume their sons and other men. By burning Plum, Eva permanently releases him from her publicly and privately abjected presence while also freeing herself from the profound feelings of guilt that were produced by her experience of being stuck in an enduring preoedipal panic. Blackness "burns" not only literally, as Eva sets fire to her son to free him from her reach, but also metaphorically in all of these different types of narratives that naturalize black maternal destructiveness in order to tell stories about the private and collective dimensions of the image problem surrounding black mothers.

## The Psychoanalytic Mode of Black Family Dramas

If the psychoanalytic mode is evident in the sociological discourses that blamed a perceived black maternal omnipotence for quality-of-life disparities between the black poor and middle-class standards of living, and if some black women's autobiographies and literature have represented black mothers similarly, as casting shadowy, preoedipal prisms around their children, then film culture, as we might expect, has only reinforced these thematic and ideological persuasions. Yet, while American films have been widely critiqued for being particularly good at producing psychoanalytic white mothers and for liberally deploying common psychoanalytic metaphors to represent white femininity, we have never theorized filmic representations of black mothers as belonging to any part of these cultural and ideological traditions. Specifically, black women characters have been continually overlooked in film scholarship's long engagement with psychoanalytic theory, including in seminal texts like Laura Mulvey's 1975 essay "Visual Pleasure and Narrative Cinema," Mary Ann Doane's *The Desire to Desire: The Woman's Film of the 1940s* (1987), and E. Ann Kaplan's *Motherhood and Representation: The Mother in Popular Culture and Melodrama* (1992), an extensive study of maternity and psychoanalytic tropes.[52]

While these psychoanalytic studies of white women in film have necessarily included melodramas and other types of family dramas, black-cast dramas, many of them overtly "melodramatic," remain largely unaccounted for in our critical obsession with melodrama's place in film history. This is not to say that film scholars have been completely disinterested in films about blackness that engage overt questions about emotional health; it is simply that black films across genre, from *Within Our Gates* (1920) to *The Color Purple* (1985), remain absent in the "hardcore" psychoanalytic studies of related popular forms such as male weepies, women's films, and

family melodramas.[53] Most of the films featuring prominent black characters that we might consider in this vein were produced after the start
of the civil rights era—the historical period when by far more theatrical
releases were created for and starred black people than any time before
or since. Blaxploitation films were a major factor in the civil rights era's
boom in black film production, and dramatic films about black families,
some even mislabeled or marketed as Blaxploitation, were a significant
part of this cultural influx. These black family dramas, with their default
method of ensemble casting, presented unmatched opportunities for
black women actors to star in films as mothers, daughters, sisters, and lovers during that era—films that included *The Learning Tree* (1969), *Sounder*
(1972), *Claudine* (1974), *The Autobiography of Miss Jane Pitman* (1974), *The
River Niger* (1976), and *A Hero Ain't Nothing but a Sandwich* (1977).[54] Since
that time, black family dramas have been the most recognizable form for
presenting stories that are at once about racial identity, psychological welfare, and nationality.

As I argue here in closely reading *Imitation of Life* (a classic film melodrama) and *Black Girl* (a more conventional black family drama), the
baaaddd black mama is an enduring and compulsively reproducible figure
because psychological discourse "sticks" to the predominant themes and
stereotypes of black female subjectivity in compelling ways. The baaaddd
black mama's psychological makeup, her interiority, creates an adhesive
cultural imprint and a consistent through line that makes these images
coherent, recognizable, and more similar than dissimilar, despite changes
in time period, generic form, or intended audience. As these two films
construct it, the only way black daughters can move away from the emotional and political ramifications of being stuck with their mothers in a
depressive preoedipal hothouse is to move their bodies away from her in
order to create the psychic space deemed necessary to experiment with
self-differentiation. I have selected these two films because of the notable
differences in cultural perspective. For example, *Imitation* celebrates the
mammy construct, and the canonical film was created by and mostly stars
white cultural producers. Conversely, written by a black woman, directed
by a black man, and starring only black actors and actresses, *Black Girl*
negatively represents the sapphire archetype. Despite these differences

in production and the vastly different political contexts of the 1950s and 1970s, the dramas remain remarkably similar in their depiction of the psychological relationship between black mother and daughter. Highlighting the similarities between the two films helps us better understand the contemporary fixation on baaaddd black mothers.

## Mammy's Depressive Orientation in *Imitation of Life*

*Imitation of Life* is perhaps the one exception to the obvious omission of depictions of black women from the rich history of mostly feminist psychoanalytic approaches to cinema studies. For instance, E. Ann Kaplan analyzes *Imitation of Life* in her chapter on resisting mothers who discover that "motherhood may not be sufficient for woman's satisfaction,"[55] arguing that the white mother and daughter characters bond only in the post-Oedipal phase, after their shared engagement with the same male suitor. Although Kaplan notes that differing racial identifications prevent the black mother-daughter pair from bonding as the white characters eventually do, Kaplan's compelling psychoanalytic examination—her use and critique of specific psychoanalytic terms—does not extend to the black characters in each of the films. Instead, Kaplan casts the black relationships in nonpsychological terms that describe the nature of their conflict as primarily about the social construction of race. She writes, "In remaking *Imitation of Life* in 1959, Sirk allows us to gauge the distance travelled since 1934 in relation to the white mother, and to note the appalling lack of change in the situation of the black mother."[56] Yet *Imitation of Life*'s racial conflict between mother and daughter is also staged as one that occurs between psychoanalytically constructed women. Lost in Kaplan's and in the many other analyses of *Imitation of Life* (as it has been a popular subject of feminist inquiry) are the ways in which the psychoanalytic modalities of omnipotence, dread, and recognition create melodramatic realities for the two women who are inscribed as black.[57]

In fact, many of the attitudes surrounding the psychodynamic construct of the preoedipal mother have been conveniently reactivated around the stereotype of the black mother as mammy. The mammy is unique for being the only depiction of preoedipal black mothers that dominant American culture celebrates. To her white employers, the mammy is all "good breast"—she is a perfect fantasy of maternity who, as magically all things to everyone, never fails to solve the family's relational problems as she deftly, selflessly, anticipates the needs of others. To her own children, she is historically represented as all "bad breast," a maternal figure who can alternately be overbearing and domineering or indifferent, ineffectual, and out of touch. The psychoanalytic paradox of the mammy is that she signals the illusion of recognition and intersubjectivity to her employers because she is often hailed as just like them, as "one of the family," as a person who can be seen and valued as equal despite her terms of employment. The mammy's comparably poorer relationship with her own children, though, conveys the message that the same process of recognition and its resulting emphasis on intersubjectivity is impossible to achieve within black families. Between these two relational spaces, then, the mammy signifies both the fulfillment and the chronic failure of recognition.

Such is the case with *Imitation of Life*'s particularly resinous and canonical image of black maternity. In the 1959 remake of the film, Juanita Moore plays a civil rights era reinterpretation of the mammy figure in a representation of black maternity that is perhaps less ostensibly offensive than Louise Beavers's 1934 performance of the black mother in the original film. The 1959 version concentrates, much more so than the original, on the emotional clash between black mother and daughter. Moore's performance of Annie Johnson, a black domestic worker and single mother, crystallizes the competing messages about recognition with which the mammy stereotype is engaged. Annie's employers and friends revere her as selfless and unequivocally good; by the end of the film, she dies a martyr. Yet, since her daughter, Sarah Jane, rejects her mother's disempowered social status as her own fate, most of the film's action is driven by the conflict between black mother and daughter and their basic inability to achieve the type of recognition that Annie's relationship with her employers presumably reflects. Of course, the power imbalance between maid and employer challenges whether true, mutual recognition is possible in the main story line between the white and black characters.

When viewed in the context of the mammy's tenuous relationship to the protocols of recognition in her professional life, *Imitation of Life* becomes an instructive model for how some family dramas imagine the child's psychological relationship to a disempowered black maternity that is also experienced as far-reaching. In this case, the film translates Sarah Jane's desire to literally and figuratively move her body away from her mother's constricted social status and views about race as something that should be punished. At the heart of their conflict is Sarah Jane's wish to pass for white and leave behind the black maternal body's signification of unequal access to democratic ideals. Early in the film, one shot particularly well summarizes and visualizes the crux of their conflict. In the scene, Sarah Jane has just lost her boyfriend because he has discovered that she is not white. All of the women of the household—Annie and Sarah Jane along with Lora and Susie (the white mother-and-daughter pair)—stand in conflict on the family's staircase. The characters are visually stratified according to social position in a medium long shot, with Annie's two employers standing higher up on the staircase while Sarah Jane and Annie stand beneath them. The light-skinned, "nearly white" Sarah Jane (played by the Caucasian actress Susan Kohner) is positioned above her visibly much darker mother. When Annie tries to console Sarah Jane, Sarah Jane blurts out, "Everything you can spoil, you spoil!"

Sarah Jane's dialogue and the shot's mise-en-scène and spatial composition of its characters underscore the daughter's basic experience of the black mother as the proverbial bad breast or the classically to-be-dreaded maternal body. Her words create the impression of black preoedipal mother's "spoiled" milk as the fantastical negative projection of mother's reach from which daughter cannot escape. Black preoedipal mother's comparatively lower social position becomes indistinguishable (for her daughter) from a mother's lack of psychological complexity, humanity, and ability to properly nourish. As the story progresses, the civil rights era metanarrative of recognition gets hijacked by the daughter's quest to vilify and annihilate mother, on the one hand, and her employers' sanguine attempts to revere and martyr her, on the other.

To dramatize this contest between black preoedipal mother and daughter, *Imitation of Life* introduces the twin activities of racial passing and erotic dancing as the idealized "third agents" that Sarah Jane uses to combat her relationship to mammy's status as visibly black, emotionally devitalized, and physically desexualized. In pursuing these activities,

Staging female subjectivity, *Imitation of Life*

Sarah Jane becomes the jezebel or tragic mulatta to her mother's mammy. While the combination of dancing and passing has much potential to facilitate the transgression of rigid intra- and inter-psychic boundaries and to disrupt social hierarchies, this early civil rights era narrative construes the daughter's choice of actions as the primary reason mother and daughter remain subjective strangers. And, in this case, unlike more recent family narratives, the film empathizes *with* black mother's preoedipal predicament.

Sarah Jane's two on-screen dance performances illustrate both the potential and the consequences of daughter's attempt to move away from her black mother. Not only do the dance routines represent daughter's desirous movement away from the baaaddd maternal subjectivity, but her actions also work metaphorically to threaten and endanger mother's very existence. In each of the dance performances, Sarah Jane's cavorting body appears to upstage and dwarf her mother's. For example, in the first of two dance routines, the jezebel stereotype Sarah Jane racially passes and sings wantonly about emotional emptiness and her desire to be "filled up" in Harry's Club, a smoky nightclub occupied primarily by white men. As Sarah Jane performs onstage, Annie's face and her field of vision are impaired; she furtively watches her daughter from behind wooden blinds in an attempt to avoid being recognized. Sarah Jane's integration of this space populated by white men represents her attempt to force a corrective Oedipal alignment between herself and her mother, as the discovery of a romantic engagement with white masculinity is the same relational paradigm that is validated in the main story line between the white women and their romantic object. While it is not clear, by the black mother's logic, which is the more disappointing transgression—nightclub dancing or passing—there is little ambivalence about the fact that viewing Sarah Jane act in this way hastens Annie's demise, propelling her toward a martyred death of a broken heart.

In moments like these, director Douglas Sirk's use of film noir lighting techniques visually accentuates Annie's powerlessness and social imprisonment, and Sarah Jane's dancing decisively moves her away from these things. The fact that mother views her daughter's movement from an obscured, dimmed vantage point further stresses black mother and daughter's inability to "see" each other accurately. With this distorted way of relating as the norm, daughter remains unable to see or know her mother in any dynamic, subject-constituting way. In this context, pre-oedipal black mother functions as an overdetermined symbol of excess and lack. On the one hand, she is everywhere—Sarah Jane cannot escape her reach, as Annie is a relentless and disruptive agent who constantly threatens her daughter's chosen mode of separation. On the other hand, in this space as a black woman, Annie remains disempowered in the social world outside her employer's home, as the visual encoding of her arrival at the nightclub indicates (she appears small in a high-angle shot while awkwardly craning her neck beneath the nightclub's eclipsing billboard). Hence, after Sarah Jane's performance, a confrontation ensues between mother and daughter, and Annie falls to the ground outside the club, with her face once again framed behind bars as she collapses.

Sarah Jane's second dance performance, this time at the Moulin Rouge, a more established but also racially exclusive venue, functions as another opportunity for daughter to test her ability to migrate beyond black mother's tracking physical and emotional reach. This time Sarah Jane sings with an ensemble of white women, and the group of women rock and rotate around the stage, kicking their legs high in the air. Like the

Black mother's impeded recognitions, *Imitation of Life*

dance routine in Harry's Club, Sarah Jane's onstage performance is once again filmed with a succession of medium and long shots created by using a low-camera-angle perspective that makes her appear large as she teams with her chosen third agents. Meanwhile, as Annie approaches the performance in disbelief, her body appears comparatively smaller in frame. In contrast to her daughter's movements, Annie moves uncertainly, her body draped in drab, dark tones.

*Imitation of Life*'s only opportunity for recognition between black mother and daughter occurs immediately after this performance as the two meet for the final time backstage. For the first time, mother and daughter have an opportunity to realize the intersubjective ambition, to see each other, if only for a moment, as more than the dominantly constructed stereotypes of black mother as mammy and daughter as jezebel. During the exchange, Annie, who has fallen ill while Sarah Jane has been advancing her dance career, promises her daughter that she will stop monitoring her movements and chasing her down, confessing to having interfered only out of love. Upon Annie's departure, Sarah Jane, forlorn and in tears, confesses to a friend that she has had a mammy all her life. Just as Sarah Jane begins to entertain the possibility that black mother as mammy is not all bad breast and as Annie seems to acknowledge something of daughter's separate desire, this opportunity that might pave the way for a more substantive exchange dissipates, and mother and daughter do not appear on-screen together again because Annie dies in the next scene. In intersubjective exchanges when mother vanishes or dies, as Jessica Benjamin has observed about the mother-child dyad, "the child misses not only the encounter with mother's independent subjectivity (she goes away), but also the opportunity to work through the pain" of normal conflicts and turn their resolution into shared "emotional realities."[58]

*Imitation of Life*'s famous ending, then, with the return of jezebel as prodigal daughter to the stage of her mother's spectacular funeral, derives its bittersweet melodramatic ending from this missed opportunity for subjective recognition between black mother and daughter. By the end of the film, when Sarah Jane has completed the movement of the baaaddd mother in her mind from bad breast to good breast and interpolated those lessons about black femininity as her own, her public confession of killing her mother reflects her tacit acceptance of herself as the black feminine body who will replace her mother as caught between poles of excess and lack. Her concluding psychoanalytic revelation is that now it is *her*, not mother and her misplaced desire, who harms. While Sarah Jane is left with the painful and fantastical psychoanalytic revelation that her attempts at self-differentiation somehow killed her mother, in death Annie nevertheless manages to retaliate against the daughter who has foolishly averted her wishes; death becomes the definitive act of black preoedipal destruction. For only in death is the black mother as mammy capable of claiming divine supremacy and demonstrating her inextinguishable will's power to extract, at long last, her daughter's repentant compliance. As the emotional clash between Annie's carriage-driven funeral parade and Sarah Jane's sobbing repentance makes clear, the dying or dead black mother's emotional reach has the potential to be even greater from the grave— black mothers demand dominion over their children *and* die trying.

## The Sapphire's Emotional Demise in *Black Girl*

Many contemporary black films are less overtly melodramatic than *Imitation of Life*, and they also do not tend to represent the preoedipal baaaddd black mother as a sympathetic figure. Written by J. E. Franklin, *Black Girl* debuted as a television movie before it was adapted into a long-running play and then became a modestly budgeted, star-studded film directed by Ossie Davis.⁵⁹ The story revolves around Rosie (played by the actress Louise Stubbs) and her three daughters. One of these daughters, Billie Jean, aspires to become a professional dancer and to leave her impoverished neighborhood and her mother's crowded house to attend dance school. The conflicts of the film arise when Rosie and her other daughters violently attempt to dissuade Billie Jean from pursuing her dreams. As an early 1970s film produced during the wave of black action films that often portrayed violence as a necessary means to an end, *Black Girl* represents the baaaddd mother as an outspoken and short-tempered sapphire whose aggressive instincts appear to be a natural part of her personality. Compared to *Imitation of Life*'s Annie, black mother in this film appears as a much more transparently baaaddd mama who has a more demonstrable damaging influence on her children. The explosive physical interactions between mother and daughter reflect a common narrative tendency to create toxic black familial dynamics. In these stories, the younger generations of black characters either overcome these obstacles or succumb to them. As with the mammy, the matriarch, and other stereotypical representations of black maternity, the black sapphire's relationship to the preoedipal themes of omnipotence and dread is most apparent in her children's fearful responses to her.

While *Imitation of Life*'s plot thwarted Sarah Jane's sexual and other symbolic attempts to enter the Oedipal phase, *Black Girl* expresses Billie Jean's movement away from mother as raw, creative ambition, and dancing in this case becomes a way for the daughter to experiment with a nonsexualized expression of her desire to separate. While her mother and sisters dismiss her dancing as silly and "uppity" (white) "ballet," Billie Jean's actual performances reveal her command of an eclectic mix of dance styles. Evident in these brief reprieves from the tension within her mother's household is the way the actress Peggy Pettit uses her body to unify several discrete musical traditions and bring her own inventive sense of style to established genres as she integrates West African dance with funk music, dances ballet to rhythm and blues, and brings a freeform style of expressive movement to rock music. Billie Jean performs these routines both in public, at the Groovy Bar and Grill (a nightclub mostly populated by black men), and in private in the confines of her small bedroom, which serves as a throughway for other members of the household. When Billie Jean works at the Groovy Bar and Grill, a few black male spectators watch her approvingly, but the moment their remarks objectify her, the owner intervenes on Billie Jean's behalf. Once the men begin to recognize Billie Jean's style as distinctive and as a type of performance they have never seen before, all of the men support her enthusiastically and even pass around a collection plate. The owner's gaze is most telling. A medium close-up captures his mixture of awe, respect, and pride as he watches Billie Jean dance onstage. As in *Imitation of Life*, the on-screen audience that witnesses daughter's attempts at differentiation matters, and here again, even though men are not presented as potential love objects, they represent an alternative viewpoint to mother's dismissive evaluations of her daughter's deepest desires.

In addition to the brief introduction of black men who value Billie Jean's emergent self-expression, *Black Girl*'s plot conflates the middle-class valorization of educational achievement with the psychosocial work of beating back black mother's reach. Here, as in other contemporary films like *Pariah*, college becomes the main plan for permanently escaping life with black mother as Moynihan's "tangle of pathology." In this vein, other mentors like teachers or college-educated friends serve important roles in the black family drama's function as a parable for the need for therapeutic and democratic transcendence. Thus, while the mother, Rosie, reduces Billie Jean's dancing as shameful "shakin' her tail" and explicitly sexualizes daughter's actions, Billie Jean's friend and mentor, or "othermother,"[60] Netta, counters the sapphire's verbal attacks with direct praise. Instead of trivializing Billie Jean's eccentric dance styles and her integrative fusion of mind and body, Netta, who is studying to be a teacher, says to Billie Jean, "I sure wish *I* could teach someone to dance." Netta's words acknowledge Billie Jean as a like-but-distinct subject (as someone who has special talents to contribute) but also as independent from herself (Billie Jean's specific desires are hers alone).

Soon after Netta publicly supports Billie Jean by encouraging her to apply for a scholarship that would enable Billie Jean to immediately move out of her mother's house, the drama makes direct use of verbal and visual references to psychoanalysis to underscore just how much Netta's support compromises the authority and influence of preoedipal black mother and her other daughters. In two different scenes, both Netta and Billie Jean are threatened explicitly with castration because they appear to have an unnatural and unfeminine ability to transgress and transcend the boundaries of black maternal omnipotence. In these moments, the other characters use the threat of a violent physical castration as a desperate last attempt to preserve and defend what the narrative has already constructed as sapphire's dysfunctional and regressive household order. Or, as older sister Norma Fae assumes in the film's first reference, Netta is suspicious because she has achieved success in spite of her own baaaddd, crazy mama (played by Ruby Dee). And so Norma Fae pulls a knife on Netta to sever and dismember the "thing she must be hiding" under her dress. Nora Fae interprets Netta's strong affirmation of Billie Jean's independent will as a phallic intervention. The possession of an actual penis is the only "thing" that could make her bold and daring enough to oppose black mama's wishes.

Later, after Netta's near castration, once Billie Jean decides she will in fact pursue a degree in dancing and leave her mother's home, her older sisters pin Billie Jean down so that their mother can physically assault her. The two sisters position Billie Jean on the ground with her legs spread apart, creating the impression that they are exposing the same unnatural "thing" that Billie Jean, like Netta, must also possess now that she has insisted on claiming her own agency in her pursuit of nationalistic ideals (i.e., self-determination, individuality, middle-class status) and more normative social orders outside the home. The placement of the characters in the frame, the scene's props, and a slanted camera angle visually underscore *Black Girl*'s second reference to castration as a plausible option for severing daughter's disruptive pursuit of a third agent. Taken together, both scenes emphasize that in this household, real women are understood as not having any symbolic or real power outside their association and dependence on mother. Although the moral imperative of the film very much supports Billie Jean's physical and emotional separation from her mother, the story's construction of the other daughters' support of their mother draws clear lines between those who are fated to reproduce preoe-dipality and those who are fortunate enough to survive it.

Unlike *Imitation of Life*, the daughter's suffering in *Black Girl* can only end by rejecting an association to black mother. Despite Billie Jean's longing for recognition and the way dancing puts some creative distance between mother and daughter, the film ends depressively with a juxta-position between daughter's freedom and mother's emotional death. In the film's final sequence, as Billie Jean prepares to leave the house for an awaiting cab, her mother lies prone in a darkened bedroom, arms fold-ed across her chest. Although Rosie eventually rises from her emotional deathbed to say good-bye to her daughter, this image of the dying mother echoes the conclusion of *Imitation of Life*. *Black Girl* ends with a tight close-up of Rosie's mournful face while she watches Billie Jean's cab speed to-ward dance school. Without taking her eyes off her daughter's vanishing frame, Rosie talks to her own mother on the porch and provides the final dialogue of the film:

> Rosie: Mama? Billie Jean knows I didn't try to hurt her?
>
> Grandmother: She knows that now, honey.
>
> Rosie: Just seem like all my children were going to end up like me . . . just like me.

The film's final words are puzzling. Rosie's daughter has succeeded in using her creative ambition to transform herself into a national subject who has greater access to American democratic ideals. Yet Rosie's words fixate on what Billie Jean's departure means for her psychologically. Surely the film's concluding tone would be different had the narrative ended with the grandmother's words or with a medium shot of two generations of black mothers welcoming, reflecting, and holding in tension the third generation's successful psychic development and imminent class mobil-ity. Instead, the film ends with a close-up of Rosie's devastated expression and her complaint about her own lack of value. In this type of drama, the baaaddd mother stays bad (if somewhat repentant), and her conclud-ing remarks stress black maternity's uncontrollable destructiveness ("I didn't *try* to hurt her"). Rosie's reflection also emphasizes that mother's

Destructive black women, *Black Girl*

Black women and the threat of "castration," *Black Girl*

devaluation of her own subjectivity is a self-evaluation that she is bound to project onto others ("Just seem like all my children were going to end up like me"). This dialogue undermines any upbeat or celebratory affect that we might expect to find at the end of a film that has sympathized with

Black mother's depressive fate, *Black Girl*

daughter's quest for survival. If daughter has truly survived, why are the final moments of the film not shot from within the cab with Billie Jean, the subject/object who has successfully survived destruction en route to the achievement of democratic goals? Instead, the film's final words return us not only to how the emotional predicament of preoedipal black mother remains psychologically consequential for her but also to how it portends to impact and mitigate the survival odds of even the children who appear to leave.

## Melodrama and Sublime Survival in Other Black Family Dramas

In earlier family dramas like *Pinky*, *Lost Boundaries*, and *Imitation of Life*, the issue of passing and proper, socially sanctioned, racial identification functioned as the central moral dilemma around which clear demarcations of right and wrong were imposed. In later civil rights and post–civil rights era films, the lines of morality have less often been drawn around ideologies governing racial identification. Instead, dramatic conflict and questions about right and wrong have more often been generated around who has access to the American Dream. Baaaddd black mamas appear in this context as predictable villains who are often at the center of the families' deep cycle of dysfunction as central agents in family histories that routinely include everything from incest and rape to alcoholism, internalized rage, and self-destructive behaviors. In consistently representing family dynamics in this way, black family dramas that emphasize heavy emotionality and feature black mothers who are obstacles to the health or progress of their children are supposed to teach us something about the utility of trauma, suffering, and survival, particularly as these experiences relate to black humanity and recognition.

But what are "black family dramas," and how have dramas about black families since the civil rights era depended on modes of representation that, like other cultural works, continue to represent black mothers and children in psychoanalytic terms? Typically, black-cast family dramas visualize stories that cycle through scenarios of personal trial and triumph, suffering and survival. The films' most basic narrative conceits represent black families as habitually engaged in rituals of traumatic contest that often afflict multiple generations as black subjectivity becomes indistinguishable from persistent and essentialized efforts to overcome both external and internal, environmental and intrapsychic, obstacles. Some of these films are about the entire family unit and routinely identify one member as the lone survivor of a vast family web of dysfunction (like *Black Girl*, *Mississippi Damned*, *Precious*, and *Pariah*). The plots of other family dramas branch beyond the family unit but link an individual's struggle in society to that person's family's relational dynamics, generational strife, or history of shared (often secret) traumas (like *Antwone Fisher* and *Monster's Ball*). As a "genre,"[61] black family dramas continue to be produced partly because these stories, no matter how much they rely on manufactured realities and blatant stereotypes, nevertheless resonate with both the black and nonblack filmmakers who continue to produce them and with the audiences who voraciously consume and support such works.

Since black family dramas are often transparently about virtue, suffering, and survival, many of these works also reproduce much of what Linda Williams and Lauren Berlant have identified persuasively as "melodramatic" and "sentimental" narrative structures.[62] In Williams's and Berlant's analyses, melodrama and sentimentalism have been discussed as nearly synonymous modes of representation, especially when politically disenfranchised characters appear in texts intended for (and usually created by) liberal white audiences. We might say that it is the melodramatic text that produces a type of sentimental spectatorship. For example, although there are several narrative features of melodrama, like the sense that something happens "in the nick of time" or happens "too late," for Williams, melodramas are best characterized by their dialectical relationship between pathos and action. Plots like *Uncle Tom's Cabin* that are about moral rights and wrongs use this dialectic to arouse deep pity and empathy for individuals who suffer unjustly. Berlant's discussion of sentimentalism similarly pivots around the assumed affective and iden- tificatory responses that audiences have when watching or reading about someone else's pain and suffering. In representing extreme suffering and survival as spectacle, the narratives seem to identify the need for social change. Berlant explains that "the political tradition of sentimentality ultimately equates the vernacular with the human; in its imaginary, cri- ses of the heart and of the body's dignity produce events that, properly publicized, can topple great nations and other patriarchal institutions if an effective and redemptive linkage can be constructed between the privi- leged and the socially abject."[63] These "redemptive" links that narratives about trauma and suffering create between the privileged spectator and socially abject characters are specious associations that rarely, if ever, lead to demonstrable social change. The intense rise and fall of emotionality within such works creates and contains its own relief.

Though not always overtly about civil rights, many black family dra- mas since *Imitation of Life* and *Black Girl* saliently reflect both Williams's description of melodrama's investment in pathos and action and Berlant's insistence that sentimental stories will evoke strong emotional responses from audiences because they thematize and visualize assaults on a black person's physical and mental integrity. As I have shown with *Imitation of Life* and *Black Girl*, civil rights narratives about black families centralized the quest for recognition within the home as a way of commenting on an individual's desire and potential for recognition outside the home. Post– civil rights black family dramas often advance a similar ideological invest- ment in connecting black family dynamics within the home to a greater project of representing and recognizing black humanity in general. Even though a film like *Precious* seems to have nothing to do with "civil rights," we can consider the 2009 Oscar-nominated film about an obese, illiterate black teenager who is raped and impregnated by her father and sexually and verbally abused by her mother as having much in common with *Imitation* and *Black Girl*.

For starters, *Precious*'s spectacle of bodily and psychic suffering is immense, and the film's porously depressive mood and tone cohere around arguably the most exacting representation of a baaaddd black mama in cinematic history. Mo'Nique won an Academy Award for Best Supporting Actress for her performance of Precious's mother, Mary, a black mother who fails miserably and tragically at recognizing her daughter's humanity and subjective distinctness. Throughout the grim story, Mary treats Precious as a sexual rival for her husband's affections and also uses her daughter to satisfy her own sexual desires. At the film's emotional climax, with both Precious and a sympathetic social worker in tears, Mary explains to them her motivations for treating her daughter as less than human. She confesses, "I did not want him to do nothing to her. I wanted him to make love to me. That was my man. . . . And he wanted my daughter. And that's why I hated her. Because my man who was supposed to be loving me, who was supposed to be making love to me, was fucking my baby, and she made him leave." Mary continued to physically, emotionally, and sexually abuse her daughter as a way of externalizing her own deep sense of loss and rage. Still blaming Precious for compromising her happiness, Mary continues, "It's this bitch's fault because she let my man have her, and she didn't say nothing. She didn't scream, she didn't do nothing. And things she told you I did to her, who else was going to love me? Who was going to touch me and make me feel good late at night?"

In the context of other psychoanalytically rendered civil rights and post–civil rights era black mothers, Mary's speech explains why her household failed to adhere to an idealized Oedipal structure and instead fulfilled a cultural prophecy of a nightmarish black preoedipality. Author Sapphire, who wrote *Push: A Novel* (1996), from which the film was adapted, has spoken in detail about her motivations for constructing Mary and about her perception of how faithfully Mo'Nique portrayed her character in the film. Sapphire explains, "Rarely have I seen such a courageous exploration of the human psyche as the portrayal of Mary that Mo'Nique gave in *Precious*. She showed us the societal and individual effects of a narcissistic personality disorder on one level; on another level, she showed us a woman trapped within a patriarchal construct who feels she is faced with the choice: her man or her child."[64]

By envisioning Mary's baaaddd mama condition as one that is part "narcissistic personality disorder" and part "patriarchal construct," Sapphire understands her character as informed by both psychoanalytic and sociological factors.[65] Both the novel and the film try to navigate this uneasy ideological terrain of representing the psychological as the sociological (and vice versa), as the stories offer a dramatization of how external environmental factors affect the interior reality of black mothers and daughters. As Sapphire puts it, "Precious is traumatized to the point where she can no longer stay in her present reality and maintain psychic viability. . . . I wanted to convey a total break with reality, a psychosis, which if it wasn't so short-lived would be tragic."[66] Sapphire's emphasis on the pathological psychological relationship between Mary and Precious is further drawn out in the way the director, Lee Daniels, heavily uses dream sequences, flashbacks, and voice-over interior dialogue to capture the impact that trauma has had on Precious's interiority. In the film, long after black mother's totalizing destructiveness has taken its toll on Precious's mind, body, and spirit, only the desperate, late-plot actions of the teenager and a few angelic mentors create the tiny hope that empathetic and privileged outsiders, along with a system of barely functional social services, can do something to make the socially abject experiences of unseen and forgotten black girls like Precious a little more bearable.

Academic approaches to *Precious* have all focused, in one way or another, on the film's representation of Precious's trauma and hardships. For instance, Michelle Jarman notes that Precious's multiple "intersecting forces of oppression" (i.e., illiteracy, poverty, AIDS) motivate "the intense emotional reactions evoked by the film."[67] In exploring these intersecting forces, Jarman ultimately criticizes the film's narrow focus on familial abuse as something that displaces "a more productive exploration of social and systemic critiques."[68] Calling the film's imagery "some of the most provocative representations of black family life witnessed on screen," Charlene Regester advocates viewing the film in the context of classic horror films, particularly those about "monstrous" mothers, and she convincingly analyzes *Precious* as a pseudo horror film that is rooted in phallic symbolism and abjection.[69] As Jarman is concerned with the film's ability to evoke intense emotions and Regester is primarily concerned with how *Precious* works to "scare" its audiences, I am interested in how the film's depressive contours encourage viewers to empathetically and intersubjectively relate to the title character—precisely because it is so extreme in its representation of how Precious suffers.

The popular press and fan reactions to *Precious* more clearly demonstrate how the film connects black family trauma to an intersubjective view of race that so commonly surfaces in narratives about recognition. As one of the most spectacular popular fantasies of a baaaddd mama's complicity in crippling black familial dysfunction, *Precious* was praised roundly in the popular press. What the film's most outspoken fans have said about its central message further demonstrates some of the ways in which dramas about black families perpetuate a type of sentimental spectatorship that is ultimately about trying to recognize the racial other as human. For instance, Roger Ebert, an early champion of *Precious*, called it "a landscape of despair" that is nevertheless "a great American film" about a girl whom we may have recognized around us if only "we looked."[70] It is exactly the moral imperative of looking for those who suffer among us that the film preaches to liberal humanists and more privileged audiences, or as Ebert wrote of Gabourey Sidibe's performance as Precious, "The film is a tribute to Sidibe's ability to engage our empathy. . . . She so completely creates the Precious character that you rather wonder if she's very much like her."[71] Racial empathy, of course, buttresses the intersubjective view that marginalized others must be understood as psychological subjects in order to be recognized as "belonging" beside other state citizens. In making a similar claim about the film's most basic lessons about the humanity of black women—whom we come to know through their pain—the film's executive producer, Oprah Winfrey, argued that *Precious*'s story proves that, "behind every girl, every person who appears to be invisible, there is the visible pain. And everybody has a backstory": "And I thought, that will never happen again. I will never not see somebody and allow them to be invisible to me."[72] Precisely because the film defines black subjectivity through unimaginable suffering, *Precious*'s post–civil rights era narrative turns nihilistic psychosocial conditions into something purposeful, or as Winfrey saw it, the film eventually makes the "dire, dark space" of the character's plight "beautiful."[73]

If we read *Precious* as a part of a narrative tradition that includes earlier family dramas like *Imitation of Life* and *Black Girl*, then it is not surprising that in order to create spectators who can view the daughter's suffering and survival as beautiful, sublime resiliency, the film's ending refuses any enormous reversal of fate or fortune for Precious, who is a poor single mother to a second child by her father and has contracted AIDS from him at the story's end. That so many reviewers and spectators could be relieved by the tiny realization that at least Precious's infant son does not also have AIDS demonstrates how such dramatizations encourage viewers to settle for an immediate emotional catharsis created by circumstantial transformation in the absence of any articulation of larger systemic changes. In watching black children suffer the consequences of what has been narratively perfected as unchecked black maternal preoedipality, *empathizing* spectators can tell themselves that they are refusing to "allow" black invisibility by watching a film, and they can imagine themselves as called on to perform the psychological work that black mothers have been repeatedly represented as incapable of providing. This type of empathetic spectatorial response is consistent with how Sapphire wanted audiences to see (and read) her construction of Precious. As she explains, "A major focus of my art has been my determination to reconnect to the mainstream of human life a segment of humanity that has been cast off and made invisible. I have brought into the public gaze women who have been marginalized by sexual abuse, poverty, and their blackness."[74] Thus, through tears of compassion, empathizing spectators demonstrate to themselves, as Winfrey did, that they see a human subject in the story that has dared to visualize the invisible emotional pain of the underprivileged.

Yet the empathizing spectator who answers the filmic invitation to recognize black humanity achieved through suffering models only one, albeit problematic, type of spectatorship. Certainly, black family dramas about family trauma may be perceived differently by less socially privileged spectators than, say, Roger Ebert, Oprah Winfrey, or other vicarious sympathizers. Do such films serve the same social function for the audiences who are not just *empathizing with* but who actually *identify with* the on-screen characters' trials as remediations of their own lived experiences? Just as the critical interventions of Jacqueline Bobo, bell hooks, and Jacqueline Stewart have demonstrated that black spectators often have complicated spectatorial practices—particularly when navigating mainstream imagery—so too might we suspect that nonempathizing spectators might read *Precious* in different ways.[75] For instance, we can imagine, as I suggested in my discussion of *Antwone Fisher* in chapter 1, that narratives that pivot on the psychological task of recognizing black humanity will function reflexively for spectators who see some version of themselves—not a distinct Other—in the repetitive performances of black hardship and resiliency. These types of spectators are invited to perform the labored ontological work of creating a double recognition of sorts: they are able to recognize the humanity of the on-screen character partly because the scenes of trial (incest, abuse, neglect, discrimination, etc.) recall their own heroic survival of similar moments. While there is certainly room to further theorize the complex ways in which these two types of audiences might differently and similarly engage black family dramas, when it comes solely to the ideological function of psychological recognition, the distance between the empathetic and the identifying spectator is small. Both types of responsiveness facilitate a personalized, intersubjective, embrace of the black character who suffers. As the popular responses (and Sapphire's authorial motivations) indicate, *Precious* assures spectators that black humanity needs to be befriended and defended, identified with and understood, but these reassurances are only aroused in the face of extreme dehumanization or surface as a response to the grand spectacles of recognition failure. As we have seen time and time again in the psychoanalytic canon, in popular culture, and also in Berlant's and Williams's critiques, evoking empathy or marshaling tiny recognitions around a subject's demonstrative ability to endure and survive destruction is a generally fraught, ephemeral, and often dissatisfying practice for both subject and object, self and other.

But not all black family dramas are as melodramatic and sentimental or as overtly invested in the empathetic potential of black characters suffering and (barely surviving) as is *Precious*—for example, *A Raisin in the Sun* (1961), *Naked Acts* (1996), and *Soul Food* (1997).⁷⁶ Importantly, as I demonstrated with *Imitation of Life* and in my reading of the mammy figure, the baaaddd black mama is not always eruptive, obviously bad, or physically destructive like sapphire figures or *Precious's* Mary. What makes the black mother in family dramas "baaaddd" across so many different types of family dramas, though, is her excessive emotional reactivity and her overall depressive orientation toward her children—an affective logic that is often framed as a consequence of her limited opportunities to satisfy her own ambitions and desires. I do think that all family dramas are "melodramatic" to a degree and black family dramas perhaps more so because of the ways in which they use the family structure (and mother's depressive orientation) to analogously work through and represent social and systemic conditions. Though the film historian Thomas Schatz is not writing about black family dramas in his discussion of American film history and the family melodrama, he makes an even broader assertion—that "in a certain sense every Hollywood movie might be described as 'melodramatic.'"⁷⁷ Specifically, Schatz contends that social melodramas are "the inverse of social comedy. Whereas the characters of romantic or screwball comedies scoff at social decorum and propriety, in melodrama they are at the mercy of social conventions; whereas the comedies integrated the anarchic lovers into a self-sufficient marital unit distinct from their social milieu, the melodrama traces the ultimate *resignation* of the principals to the strictures of the social and familial tradition."⁷⁸

When the protagonists in black family dramas attempt to survive and overcome the "strictures" of their environment, they indeed labor emotionally to expose injustices in both familial and social systems. However, even if we take the broadest definitions of melodrama, some black family dramas still will not contain all of the conventions most often associated with the generic mode—including the melodramatic tendency to represent characters who are facing "life-altering moral choices"⁷⁹ or the story convention that "begin[s] and end[s] in a space of innocence."⁸⁰ For now, though, what remains most relevant in the scholarship on melodrama and sentimentality to black popular works is the way in which both concepts, like the general cultural life and image problem around black mothers, build on psychologized processes.[81]

Peter Brooks's classic definition serves us well here. In *The Melodramatic Imagination: Balzac, Henry James, Melodrama, and the Mode of Excess*, Brooks traces the evolution of melodrama to the "context of the French Revolution and its aftermath," a distinctive historical moment that marked "the final liquidation of the traditional Sacred and its representative institutions (Church and Monarch), the shattering of the myth of Christendom, the dissolution of an organic and hierarchically cohesive society, and the invalidation of the literary forms."[82] Melodrama became the representative space for expressing "intense emotions" and the "manichaeistic struggle of good and evil" in ways that always return to some of the "most fundamental psychic relations" and "ethical forces."[83] Brooks's definition of melodrama is also endemically psychoanalytic. For Brooks, even "political" and "realist" melodramas are obligatorily about psychology, and other forms of mass entertainment (like soap operas, police stories, westerns, hospital dramas, and dramas about families) become increasingly psychodynamic, not less so, as they are standardized and rise in popularity. Brooks explains, "That all these forms have become increasingly 'psychologized' . . . in no sense violates the melodramatic context. It is not that melodramatic conflict has been interiorized and refined to the vanishing point, but on the contrary that psychology has been externalized, made accessible and immediate through a full realization of its melodramatic possibilities."[84] Classifying melodrama as a psychoanalytic mode also exposes "our need for fully externalized, personalized, and enacted conflict, and for its clarifying resolution."[85] Like Antwone Fisher's discovery that psychiatry and a strong father figure's transference can heal him from the damage inflicted by Manichean baaaddd black foster mothers, "melodramatized realities" appear in black family dramas as grand, life-changing psychoanalytic epiphanies for some characters and as psychological paradoxes and dilemmas for others.

The persistence of baaaddd black mothers in popular culture is also the confirmation that "psychology has been externalized." Some of the same issues that Brooks outlined—such as stark ethical and moral concerns, the imagined and often personified value of Christianity, and both the advantageous and detrimental effects of hierarchies—are consolidated easily as external processes that black children must survive in their interactions with reliably destructive and depressive black mothers. In this regard, the popular dramas and public discourses about black families since the era have tended to externalize and personalize two things: our American cultural obligation to move from preoedipal to Oedipal orientations and our preference for suffering's ability to elicit empathy and recognition. In family dramas like *Imitation of Life*, *Black Girl*, and *Precious*, the externalization of these processes helps diagnose the race problem as a complicated set of psychological problems that exist both on the part of white audiences and as a part of what black people as a group must habitually overcome en route to claiming full participation in the democratic state. Yet, as the muted emotional victories for the daughters at the end of each of these films suggests, subjects who have to endure spectacularized suffering in order prove their humanity were perceived as barely human in the first place, making the fulfillment of the democratic wish on which this logic is predicated seem as illusive and unfulfilling as ever.

## Conclusion: The Value of Failed Recognition, or Lessons from Baaaddd Mama

If the countless representations of stereotypically baaaddd black mothers in the public sphere expose our collective anxieties about motherhood and also point squarely to the politics and value of recognition, it matters mightily that the stories we have watched, read, and celebrated are actually about the chronic failure of recognition within black families. Of what additional significance is it that black mothers are imagined so consistently across disparate cultural contexts as failing monumentally at what has been construed as a desired and important developmental task? Further, should the cultivation of psychological recognition within families function, even analogously, either as a correction for the predicament of the social misrecognition of women or as a model for civic participation and social interrelatedness?

Perhaps the most obvious problem of embracing mutual recognition or intersubjectivity as an antidote to pejorative attitudes about motherhood is that doing so charges mothers with solving the problem of their own oppression. The other problem with treating recognition as a corrective paradigm is that while the idea that subjects can get to know each other as equals is upheld as a major part of our collective values, the fact remains that successful moments of intersubjective recognition are rare. As I demonstrated with Sidney Poitier's therapeutic characters in chapter 2, not only is the magical potential of watching blackness "survive" object status ephemeral because the bob-and-weave dance of rituals of object destruction that help create mutual recognition often encourage actual violence, but that type of Winnicottian "hullo subject!" revelation is soon after hijacked by other relational demands, often of an overtly anti-intersubjective or antipsychological nature. At each juncture, then, there are innumerable opportunities for either self or other, mother or child, to fail at seeing the other's plurality, complexity, and subjective independence. As such, even though popular discourses and narratives uphold recognition as a desired goal, a failed or "false differentiation" is much more the norm, or as Jessica Benjamin describes it, "recognizing the other has been the exceptional moment, a moment of rare innocence, the recovery of a lost paradise."[86]

And so, although the popular representations of baaaddd mothers from *Imitation of Life* to *Precious* are very much consistent with the ways in which recognition appears as an exception rather than the rule in the clinical writings, black mothers are vilified like no one else for failing to meet this idealized standard of interrelatedness. The flight from recognition in these films is always packaged as pernicious dysfunction, while in other works across the cultural spectrum (from male buddy films to cartoons for children to hip hop), such breakdowns of recognition are permitted and used to creative ends. The fact that recognition failure has become such a major part of the image problem around black maternity, that we are all but guaranteed to see black women figured as the reason black people cannot see each other as mature psychological subjects, further demonstrates the way psychological concepts fuel a latent discourse of American exceptionalism. This inherent relationship between the protocols of recognition and

American exceptionalism creates a zero-sum game for black mothers and their children that only benefits the state of exclusion.[87] In mostly telling stories about the few who survive the spectacularized violence of living with baaaddd mothers, psychological dramas about dysfunctional black families turn failed recognition within the home into an important first test—a screening process—that proves a subject's true measure of democratic worthiness. Rather than uphold successful recognition between black mother and child as the goal, however, as we have seen, most black family dramas displace the exercise of successful recognition of a dynamic black subjectivity onto other characters, film audiences, or externalized third agents. Recognition's survival game as a rite of passage is most pronounced in films like *Precious* and *Antwone Fisher* where black maternity is coded overtly as a predatory agent and where representatives of the state (teachers and social workers in *Precious* and the navy in *Antwone Fisher*) function not only to offer respite for the immense suffering that recognition failure is imagined to have caused but also as the assurance that the saving grace of the state is prepared to do what black mothers tragically cannot.

For those who are fortunate enough to survive endemic recognition failure in the private sphere, the state (and pursuit of the American Dream) appears as the idealized third agent or "good father" to the baaaddd black mother. In this way, the myth of black preoedipality serves as a prerequisite for democratic citizenship. Because recognition failure helps dramatize, visualize, and make "real" the conditions of black hardship, abject suffering, and sublime survival, baaaddd mothers are, of course, very much needed in this cultural imaginary as a necessary component of the ideology of exceptionalism. They are necessary because we need to see these mothers fail, and do so repeatedly, in different social and cultural contexts. Characterized as innate, the far-reaching nature of their toxicity helps rationalize the state's ambivalence toward inclusion by illustrating why some will fall short in the attainment of national ideals—as we can see with Billie Jean's sisters in *Black Girl* and in the entire community of young men raised by destructive mothers in *Boyz n the Hood*, except Trey, the protagonist who escapes. If, as Allison Berg has argued, mother is responsible for birthing the race and if, as the cultural life around black mothers demonstrates, black women cannot recognize other people has human, then the race as a whole stays chronically unready and unprepared for full integration.[88] On the one hand, the state can always seem willing to incorporate the black subjects who have demonstrated their humanity and resiliency by surviving psychologized trials. On the other hand, the many who are assumed to be caught in the web of black maternal omnipotence justify the maintenance of social hierarchies, the prison industrial complex, and policies designed to contain the effects of a corrosive anti-Oedipal black subculture.

In post–civil rights era representations, each time we see the psychological blueprint of baaaddd black mothers on the screen, in print, or in memes and vines circulating on Twitter or Facebook, we do well to note the role these popular and personal accounts play in providing the cultural imagination with a convenient and dreaded symbol of dominant ideologies of oppression. As Laura Doyle has argued in her study of racialized trans-Atlantic maternal figures in modern literature, the additional burdens of motherhood charge women of color with the responsibility "for fixing, ranking, and subduing" their children so that they can be better classified into "a dominant or a subordinate group."[89] While the persistence of the image problem around black maternity functions as a hegemonic force, these portrayals of depressive and destructive black mothers also offer a damning critique of the politics of recognition's functionality on a metascale. As the predicament of both black mothers in *Imitation of Life* and *Black Girl* makes clear, part of the reason these mothers fail to succeed in playing the idealized maternal role in the survival game of successful recognition is that they have to perpetually survive and navigate the state's failure to recognize their own desire, autonomy, agency, and existence as anything other than stereotypically baaaddd. For example, in *Imitation of Life*, even when the destructive black mother appears to be harmless, she always maintains a fast and ready proximity to national ambivalence. The daughter's problem with the black preoedipal mother as mammy is that she represents and reinforces the state's reluctance to include either of them as equals. And so these black mothers, who exist at the site of a double failure of recognition, expose intersubjectivity's tenuous and inadequate potential to thrive fully in either the private and public spheres.

Narrative culture has become the battleground for where the politics of representation and the politics of recognition so predictably meet—in all those familiar moments when black subjectivities are rendered to either prove or disprove humanity and in all those moments that depict the precarious attainment of state inclusivity. As signifiers in this taxonomy, black mothers are the workhorses of the popular imagination, and their images bear the weight of the failed democratic mission. To return to Hortense Spillers's invocation that we claim the "monstrosity" of black motherhood as evidence that black women are social subjects who more accurately offer us "a radically different text for a female empowerment,"[90] I suggest that while we may never locate anything close to "the real" in popular depictions of black motherhood, we can best use the many images and narrative accounts of baaaddd mothers as frequent, sometimes daily, occasions to examine the political as well as the explicitly psychodynamic ideologies that always point back to the continued dysfunctionality of the state's treatment of black subjectivities. The steady production of baaaddd black mamas remains useful inasmuch as the representations better acquaint us with how this particular "monstrosity" is composed of both dominant cultural anxieties and aggressions toward black women *and* marginalized grievances about and critiques of a culture that emphasizes double standards, exceptionalities, and externalized emotional registries.

# 4

# PIMPING (REALLY) AIN'T EASY

## Black Pulp Masculinities and the Flight from Recognition

Like *Antwone Fisher*, the 2005 film *Hustle & Flow* does not seem overtly concerned either with the civil rights era or with its predominate cultural focus on the intersubjective view of race and the recognition of black humanity. One of the film's supporting actors (D. J. Qualls) explained that even though the story's events take place in the South decades after the civil rights movement, he was proud that it does not re-create any of the memorable scenes of violence, protest, or confirmations of racism that are so commonly dramatized in films about the South. Qualls joked, "Everything I see about the South is like a Cicely Tyson movie. You know what I mean? Somebody sitting at a lunch counter. Everybody has bad accents. And this [*Hustle & Flow*'s story] was real. It was really how I think things are down here."[1] While Qualls's comments may be unwarranted for any number of reasons, it is easy enough to conclude that *Hustle & Flow* does not appear to be cut from the same cloth of respectability as classic civil rights era dramas like *Imitation of Life* (1959), *In the Heat of the Night* (1967), or *Sounder* (1972)—the latter being Cicely Tyson's most enduring performance in a film about the region. Unlike these films,

*Hustle & Flow* features a completely different set of black subjectivities: pimps, prostitutes, hustlers, "street" men and women, people imagined to be from the most disenfranchised and disadvantaged socioeconomic group, the black underclass. Framed around underclass or underworld black subjectivities, *Hustle & Flow* tells a contemporary tale about a middle-aged pimp, DJay (played by Terrence Howard), who rediscovers his passion for rapping while he sells women's bodies and marijuana on the streets of Memphis, Tennessee.

In addition to the film's focus on "disreputable" black characters, another obvious way *Hustle & Flow* differs from civil rights era dramas is the central role that hip hop plays in communicating its post–civil rights story about urban black masculinity. Diegetic and nondiegetic rap music thematize both the brutality of the street scene and DJay's self-articulation. For instance, the lyrics of the film's Oscar-winning song, the pulsating "It's Hard Out Here for a Pimp," emphasize just that, as the words narrate DJay's quest to survive the harsh conditions of capitalism and the inevitable challenges he faces from the women he trades. Plaintively sung by one of DJay's prostitutes, Shug (Taraji P. Henson), the song's catchy hook articulates the grind of the pimp's survival hustle: "You know it's hard out here for a pimp / When he's tryin' to get this money for the rent / For the Cadillacs and gas money spent / Because a whole lot of bitches talkin' shit." Within the confines of DJay's cramped, humid apartment, he further clarifies in the verses he records for the track that his hustle (his job) and his flow (his creativity) are uniquely informed by his "duckin', dodgin' bullets every day," his need to "keep up" with his women, and his mission to "stay paid." As such, DJay's most prized objects in the opening segments of *Hustle & Flow* appear to be a battered Casio keyboard, his "whip" with its spotless spinners, and a spunky white prostitute, Nola (Taryn Manning), who canvases the streets for him in a halter top and taut yellow skirt.

Consistent with the soundtrack's focus on materiality and brute survival, the early plot actions of *Hustle & Flow* situate DJay as a pimp who will not hesitate to use force when managing his workers or when dealing with other hustlers, pimps, or underclass men. The character's "hardness," his visceral presence and physicality, are represented as just as essential to his constitution and motivations as are both his environment and the objects about which he raps. Despite this concentration on the exterior reality of the pimp's world, the film also manages to create a clear investment in representing DJay as an introspective pimp from the very start. This focus on his interiority is established formally and structurally in the opening seconds of the first scene, when after the initial fade-in, DJay's face appears on-screen in an extreme close-up of his lips, which part as his tongue glides across his teeth and pucker as he takes a protracted drag on a cigarette. In introducing DJay at first from this intimate proximity and only gradually widening the frame as he speaks, the camera's movement and distance creates an immediate focused attention on his mouth and his words, which are waxing, haltingly and philosophically, about man— humankind—not being like a dog. As DJay riffs in the opening segment about his purpose in life, about whether he and Nola should be sitting in his Cadillac waiting for potential customers, the tightness and closeness of the scene's cinematography establishes well that the story that is about to unfold will probe and represent DJay's interior logic as much as it portrays the spectacularity of his job, his hustle, and his ability to pimp and profit from women like Nola and Shug.

In addition to being introspective, DJay is also an intersubjective pimp. In fact, intersubjectivity—the articulation of a vested, if fantastical, relationship toward others—is an essential component of DJay's pimp game and general likability. For example, in one establishing scene, DJay awakens Shug in a cold panic with a pressing need to talk through his feelings. As he talks to Shug in the darkened apartment, he stresses that it is their intimate history and long-running business association that allows him to speak so freely with her regarding his private fears. He further confides in her about his current mental state, saying, "I just feel like I'm having one of them midlife crises, you know? I mean my daddy, you know, his heart gave out on him when he was like . . . shit, when I was twelve years old, when he was my age. And that shit has just been fucking with my mind."[2] DJay's midlife crisis, as he describes it here, and the way his circumstances are "fucking with" his mind, compel him to prioritize interpersonal exchanges with others despite the obviously dehumanizing nature of his job. In creating a pimp who can brag about his "bitches" in one song ("I got a snow bunny and a black girl too /You pay the right price and they'll both do you") and confess his psychic vulnerabilities in another ("Look, this is my life, and it's a battle within / I gotta survive, even if I'm sinning to win"), the filmmakers contrast the spectacularly dehumanizing realties of the pimp game with an emphasis on DJay's humanity, his psychology, and his emotions.[3] Rap becomes a way for the character to more fully express himself, and the raw, amateur music he records with the help of his women and a pair of middle-class hip hop enthusiasts expresses both the material and ontological aspects of his journey.

The decision to make a film about a pimp who is well versed in both the lingo and conventions of the street scene and in the rhetoric of interiority was deliberate. One of the film's producers, John Singleton, said that the production team did not want to make the film without Terrence Howard because they specifically knew he would bring "a lot of vulnerability to the role" of a struggling pimp who records a rap album in order to stave off a midlife crisis.[4] This combination of psychic vulnerability and desperate creative sublimation is exactly what another of the film's producers, Stephanie Allain, envisioned would distinguish DJay from how pimps have functioned in black popular culture since the 1960s and 1970s filmic portrayals of glamorous pimps in films like *Superfly* (1972), *The Mack* (1973), and *Dolemite* (1975). That is, as Allain argued, since pimps have been so "glorified in Blaxploitation films and music videos, this was a chance to set the record straight."[5] The film's writer and director, Craig Brewer, concurred, adding that he created the character with the explicit intention that DJay would be a corrective image. In other words, DJay would not resemble the other pimps in the pop-cultural imagination. Brewer stressed, "I don't want this character to be what we have seen in music videos. This is not your gold goblin, jewel-encrusted, covered in silk threads and the Kangols, and all that pageantry. I didn't want any of that! I wanted a guy who is really like three steps behind his girls on the track in Memphis."[6] Making DJay a less glamorous, more vulnerable pimp who struts "three steps behind his girls" gave him a particular circumstantial and emotional location on which to map blackness's twin themes of destruction and survival, or, as Allain put it, "the reason he is a pimp is that we wanted to take the lowest of the low and exalt him through creativity."[7]

The filmmakers' comments convey a conscious intention to use exploitative circumstances and actions, the theme of black dehumanization, as a precursor for redeeming black identity through the process of recognition. Their comments also mistakenly identify visual culture as setting the standard against which a contemporary pimp like DJay should be measured. As I argue in this chapter, however, both of these assumptions, the implicit one about the politics of recognition and the overt one about black pop-cultural histories, are tenuous. Civil rights era black popular print culture—pulpy novels and seamy autobiographies—are the more suitable establishing texts for understanding post–civil rights characters like DJay. As I argue here and throughout this book, the intersubjective view of race is an ideology that has communicated well across boundaries of form and time. Blackness burns, heavily laden, not only in what we have seen on television and in film but also in the live performances, novels, and autobiographies that share important intertextual relationships with the visual popular works.

In fact, two 1960s and 1970s black popular writers, Robert Beck and Donald Goines, have served as inspiration for many of the pimps we have seen in popular culture since the era. In the first part of this chapter, I engage the limited critical attention that Beck's and Goines's work has received by addressing the few academic works that hail these narratives as both "realist" and patently "postmodernist." In limiting the critical conversations about black pimps to realist or postmodernist claims, we have taken for granted that pimping and "macking" are first and foremost psychological games that are played out in an attempt to control black women's bodies and minds. As I argue here, derivatives of what I have called the baaaddd black mama crop up compulsively in the pimp archive, and the pimps' relationships to their baaaddd mamas shape their deliberate abjection of women and inform the ways in which they organize their emotions when they interact with other members of the underclass.

After presenting a set of psychoanalytic inquiries that give us some traction in untangling the pimp's overt fantasies for power and control from his most private "phantasies," or fears and anxieties, I devote a significant amount of attention in the second part of this chapter to closely examining Beck's and Goines's nonliterary or paratextual popular works.

Investigating the ways in which Beck and Goines crafted a tormented emotional script for this popular figure helps expose the many things in common that 1960s and 1970s pimps have with a character like *Hustle & Flow*'s DJay. Reading the print texts in conversation with the visual imagery makes clear that that the glossy exterior of the pimp man rarely, if ever, matches his chronically persecuted interior reality.

## Pimpology 101: Pimps and the Academy

The black pimp, with his legendary verbal acumen, stable of adoring women, and professed hypnotic prowess, has been a part of black folklore and popular culture since the late nineteenth-century songs about Stagolee.[8] More recently, black pimps have appeared across a varied landscape of popular works, including Blaxploitation film and hip hop music, documentaries like *Pimps Up, Ho's Down* (1998), *American Pimp* (1999), *Iceberg Slim: Portrait of a Pimp* (2012), and reality makeover shows such as MTV's *Pimp My Ride* (2004–7). In the current literary marketplace, stories about pimps thrive as popular writers like Nikki Turner, Terri Woods, James Patterson, Shannon Holmes, and Carl Weber tell new, imaginative stories about the black underclass. Throughout the steady production of pimp narratives in popular culture, both Robert Beck's *Pimp* and Donald Goines's *Whoreson* have been hailed for being particularly influential.[9] That there has been an extended engagement with pimp culture across forms and media attests to the fact that pimps have remained an easily commodifiable point of interest. Yet, even if black pimps have loomed large in the cultural imaginary, why would it seem so innovative to make a film about a pimp's midlife crisis, as we saw in *Hustle & Flow*? To best answer this question, we have to turn more squarely to some common themes that characterized Goines's and Beck's mass-marketed fiction and pulp autobiography while also considering some of the ways psychological perspectives have been deemphasized in the few scholarly considerations of these texts.

Goines's and Beck's pimp narratives belong to a broader tradition of black literary and print cultures that underwent several transitions and overt cultural renaissances during the long years of the civil rights era—including the production of "crime," "street," "pulp," or simply "popular" black fiction. Publication in this form increased dramatically in the early postwar years and peaked during the 1960s and 1970s. These novels, quickly written, cheaply printed, and widely circulated, have rarely been discussed in academic circles.[10] Chester Himes, perhaps the only critically acclaimed writer in this vein, wrote across genres and dabbled in pulp fiction during the late 1950s and 1960s, as he wrote novels like *The Crazy Kill* (1959), *All Shot Up* (1960), and *Cotton Comes to Harlem* (1965)—all detective stories that he crafted around his edgy, satirically named duo: Coffin Ed Johnson and Grave Digger Jones. Other black pulp fiction from the era included Herbert Simmons's novels about violence and economic hardship, *Corner Boy* (1957) and *Man Walking on Eggshells* (1962); Clarence Cooper Jr.'s novels about drug addiction, *The Scene* (1960) and *Weed* (1961); and Charles Perry's Oedipal thriller about a young black man's obsession with his mentally ill mother, *Portrait of a Young Man Drowning* (1962). The novels that make up this tradition of black pulp fiction were graphic in their depiction of key themes of a black urban underclass: drug dealing and sexual exploitation, pimping and hustling, prison culture and vigilante justice. Typically, the narratives were presented as "real," true-to-life experiences that the writers themselves lived or witnessed in their communities, and the pulpy and popular works functioned as the reportage of authentic representations of a large and disenfranchised group of people.

While the great majority of these writers have faded into obscurity as their works went out of print, only Beck and Goines have maintained their popularity beyond the era. Both writers were successful, in part, because of the emergence of Holloway House. Founded in 1959 by two white Hollywood publicists, Holloway House was the first publisher to target adult material and erotica to black audiences.[11] Answering Holloway's aggressive marketing campaign for writers who could appeal to the legions of black readers who had been largely ignored by other publishers, Robert Beck became Holloway's most successful author when he published *Pimp: The Story of My Life* in 1967. In its first printings, Beck's *Pimp* sold over a million copies and helped the house attract additional marketable stories about "pimps, prostitutes, hustlers, and junkies."[12] With Holloway, Beck published four novels and several autobiographical exposés throughout his career, including *Trick Baby* (1967), *Mama Black Widow* (1969), and *The*

*Naked Soul of Iceberg Slim* (1971). Donald Goines was inspired by the commercial success of *Pimp* and eventually became even more prolific than Beck. Goines wrote several of his sixteen plot-driven novels, such as *Dopefiend* (1971), *Whoreson* (1972), *Black Girl Lost* (1974), and *Inner City Hoodlum* (1975), either while serving time in prison or as a means to finance his heroin addiction.

Although Beck's and Goines's novels were best-sellers during the 1960s and 1970s and continue to be widely read in black communities across class lines today, there has never been an in-depth study of these works within the fields of African American studies, literary studies, cultural studies, or media studies.[13] That is not to say, however, that there has not been some scholarly provocation on the matter from scholars of African American culture and history. For instance, Mark Anthony Neal, dismayed that analyses of black literature continue to leave out popular fiction from the civil rights era, charges boldly that Donald Goines is "arguably the most influential chronicler of black urban life in the post–World War II era."[14] Speaking more directly about popular representations of "street culture" and pimp narratives in particular, Todd Boyd asks, "Why have I never read an intense study of the films of Rudy Ray Moore, the novels of Iceberg Slim or Donald Goines, the music of Tyrone Davis, etc.? Why?"[15] One of the motivations for drawing attention to Beck and Goines has been, as Robin D. G. Kelley puts it, a growing desire to "let the natives speak," that is, to explore works that move us away from the heavy reliance on social scientific studies of black urban life.[16] Relatedly, L. H. Stallings has argued that while the field of African American studies has been enormously attentive to hip hop music, to both its potentialities and its perils, these interests have chronically underappreciated and deemphasized black print culture's related significance. In order to draw more attention to the textual history, Stallings reads Goines's narratives in a realist vein, as ably documenting the "process of decolonization following enslavement" and as particularly vulnerable to "mainstream commodification" within the publishing industry because of the works' representational themes and influence on hip hop masculinities.[17]

Comments and analyses like the ones posed by Neal, Boyd, Stallings, and Kelley convey a hopefulness about black popular print culture. The hopefulness seems to be motivated in part by a desire to bring "real" and "folk," alternate and marginal, modes of expression to our discussions about representational politics. There is also the explicit hope that Beck's and Goines's novels have something to teach us about black experiences in postwar American culture that branch beyond what we have learned from the now-canonical triumvirate of Wright, Ellison, and Baldwin. This desire to more or less go to the source—to let the writers from postwar and late twentieth-century ghettos and urban communities speak for them- selves—has been further compounded by the various claims to authentic representation promoted by the opportunistic literary marketplace that brought Beck and Goines, and other black popular-fiction writers after them, to mass audiences. At every turn, the audiences for these works have been reminded that these are gritty and honest narratives that are based on lived experiences and are written by writers who have intimate knowledge of the urban poor.

While there has been some hope that these lost and critically over- looked popular narratives written by black men during the 1960s and 1970s might convey a more faithful account of the nihilistic conditions produced by the convergence of late capitalism and systemic racism, there has also been some reluctance to thinking about these works as literal translations. For example, since pimps continue to be the most consistent characters to appear in fictionalized representations of the underclass, some scholars have thought about pimps in popular culture as predomi- nantly figurative and as performative icons. In this vein, Eithne Quinn, in "Who's the Mack?," provides a capable genealogy of the constructed nature of the pimp's aesthetic and performativity as it has surfaced in gangsta rap. Quinn argues persuasively that we can better understand the heavily stylized and intentionally demonstrative nature of the black pimp in popular culture in nonliteral terms, specifically as an embodiment of the "signifying monkey" and "trickster" that has long appeared in black folk and urban traditions.[18] Similarly, Ronald L. Jackson's chapter on the pimp as a rich "hypertext" of black sexuality in *Scripting the Black Masculine Body* historicizes the many creative and even subversive ways black men have reinvigorated pimp imagery in music, Blaxploitation films, and more recent action films.[19]

The instructive but limited range of these essays and chapters demonstrates a need for continued examination of Beck's and Goines's work. In commencing the very difficult and tricky task of drawing attention to the masculinist works' resistant and disruptive potential, these ways of writing about popular culture have also created some critical blind spots. While there is an apparent tension between claims of authenticity and veracity, on the one hand, and claims about allusion and metatextuality, on the other hand, there remains, even in the more postmodernist engagements, a lack of attentiveness in these accounts to the role women play in the narratives' representational politics, be those politics literally or figuratively construed. Yet we know from the resistant and oppositional studies on hip hop and gender that women have been abjectly rendered in some of the most commercial and accessible, as well as in the "conscious" and more marginal, masculinist representational spaces. Black feminist contributions to hip hop studies by bell hooks, Tricia Rose, T. Denean Sharpley-Whiting, and Mireille Miller-Young, among others, have unsettled the scholarly temptation to dismiss the violent distortion of black female subjectivities in order to make important claims about "baaadddass niggas," shrewd trickster figures, and signifying monkeys.[20] In other words, the rich body of work on hip hop gender politics ably challenges celebratory analyses that would frame underclass black men as hard at work destabilizing norms and symbolically turning capitalism into a spectacle.

I mention feminist hip hop studies here because the spirit of these critiques works well as a guideline for devoting a similar kind of critical attentiveness to Beck's and Goines's works—a critical attentiveness that can be figuratively and literally interpretative and can also directly engage the popular works' through line of misogyny, sexism, and violence against women. In trying to make the popular representations of pimps relevant to our related fields of study, we run the risk of dislodging the imagery from other aspects of its social and cultural context. In trying not to take the pimps too literally, we have not thought enough about "pimpology," or the practice of controlling and exploiting a woman's mind, as a ritual that blends fantasy and reality around the abjection of black women. In trying to move the conversation about black urban life away from the social sciences (as Kelley, Stallings, Quinn, and

Jackson have encouraged us to do), we have also mistakenly deemphasized the role that psychology plays as the glue that holds the pimp and his cadre of exploited women to the wider conversations about black subjectivity and humanity that connect postwar, postmodern, and civil rights era American culture. If psychoanalytic metaphors were an influential discursive mode for representing race by the 1960s, and if pimping and macking are represented as the physical and psychological mastery over women, then the way these texts present psychologies of domination, the way they offer their own prescription for how to participate in and subvert the politics of recognition, continues to be a repressed and ignored part of this cultural history.

## The Pimp Game's Psychological Game

At this juncture, it becomes necessary to explore a few of the broad interpretative possibilities that become evident in even a cursory investigation of the ways in which the pimp game functions as a complex psychological game that casts black women as central to all the twists and turns of analysis. Two scenes, one from Beck's *The Naked Soul of Iceberg Slim* and one from Goines's *Whoreson*, illustrate some of the ways the pimp's psychosocial relationship to black women also revolves around some common tropes in psychoanalytic discourse. In Goines's novel, the title character, Whoreson Jones, sets out to "double-cross a woman he intends to 'con' and then 'flip'" in order to force her to become his first prostitute. Whoreson's motivation for selecting this particular woman, Ruby, is unclear—other than the fact that he seems both repulsed and aroused by her plump body. The way to become her pimp and effectively control her body, he reasons, is to use her body as the gateway for controlling her mind. During a protracted domination ritual that involves beating, kidnapping, and torturing her for an entire month in a dirty motel room, Whoreson tells Ruby, "a good whore always has respect for her man, and you definitely are going to be a good whore."[21] Rape becomes the most crucial part of Goines's lengthy explication of Whoreson's "transformation" of Ruby from a bad black woman into a good whore. As such, Whoreson describes in detail how he comes to possess and transform Ruby's body and mind:

When I got her pants off one leg, she opened her legs wide and
stared up at me. Her eyes were full of scorn as she coldly revealed
herself to me. But I had one hell of a surprise for her. Cunt was
the last thing on my mind. I moved to the head of the bed and
reached under my pillow. When my hand came out it was holding my pimp sticks, two coat hangers twisted together. . . . I had
lit into her with the coat hangers. Her screams fell on deaf ears
as I continued to beat her. . . . I beat her until her voice became
hoarse, then tossed her on the bed and stuck my jones in her big
wide butt.[22]

When Whoreson opts to rape Ruby anally instead of vaginally, only his
"pimp sticks" can brave the expansiveness of the large woman's vagina,
black femininity's pervasive signifier of engulfment. Several aspects of
this moment—the forced psychological submission, disregard for the
"bad" whore's pain ("her screams fell on deaf ears"), rape as a quotidian
part of disembodiment so that the body can be used as a tool of economic
production—are presented as commonplace features of the life of a pimp
and his sex workers. Most obviously, the physical violence against women
in moments like these signal a decisive departure from wanting to know
the other as human precisely because neither the pimp nor the prostitute
can see the other in that way—they can only see the fantasies and fears
of the other.

These rituals that are designed to punish, discipline, and possess the
body prepare the mind for participation in a patently anti-intersubjective
black cultural location. If the violence of the pimp scene signals a deliberate flight from recognition, the pimp's material culture—his style, tools of
the trade, other treasured objects—stand in for the fantasies of embodied, shared experiences. That is, the pimp notoriously relates to objects,
not people. Likewise, the women around him see only his pronounced
lack of humanity, and this valorized mutual dehumanization between
pimps and prostitutes enabled Goines and other street-fiction writers
to sensationalize the graphic scenes of violence that confirm this departure, not so unlike the way the film *Precious* depicts recognition failure
within black families. Yet, even as writers like Beck and Goines at times

demonstrate that intersubjectivity and mutual recognition have no place in the underclass economy, they nonetheless describe "the life" as imbricated in the language and metagame of psychology. For example, in The Rape of Ruby passages, Whoreson's subjective transformation of Ruby is not complete until he remakes her as a new psychological subject. After raping her with his "pimp sticks," sodomizing her, and then tormenting her for an extended period of time by making her work the streets day and night with no sleep and little food, Whoreson calls his newly reconditioned woman to stand with him before a mirror, saying to her, "What you see in the mirror, bitch . . . is my creation. Not something you did for yourself, but what I had to force you to do for yourself. . . . So from now on, when some bitch comes up to you and begins crying on your shoulder about how hard I work you, you laugh in her face, bitch, 'cause I ain't did nothing that didn't need doing."[23] After these instructions, Goines takes care to describe the pride that Ruby feels as a result of Whoreson's forced transformation of her. In rejecting the vaunted protocols of recognition where the two characters might see each other in the mirror as independent, desirous subjects, in these moments, Ruby and Whoreson enact a ritual that has more in common with Jacques Lacan's mirror stage and Julia Kristeva's notion of abjection. This aspect of the pimp game as psychological game confirms the Lacanian contention that identity is always externally formed (he argued that the "ego" or self is formed primarily by another person's image, the "mirror," of the self) and Kristeva's understanding of the abject other as a being who is radically excluded from the "symbolic" or intersubjective social order.[24]

Basic pimpology, then, aims to turn the self-constituted or "bad" (ugly, fat, autonomous, nonlaboring, etc.) whore into an other/pimp-constituted "good" whore in order to conform her into a purposeful, if still abjected, worker. Macking in this context is the practice and process of joining the domination of the body with the colonization of the mind into a cohesive and profitable new subjectivity. By the pimp's logic, changing the way Ruby thinks is the ultimate goal, and this is only possible after he has degraded, exhausted, and disciplined her body. The result is another compliant sex worker who will join his ranks as one of many who can cherish their collective abandonment of subjective equality. Pimping and macking in this context also carries with it some latent (disruptive) potential to "pimp" the more socially sanctioned value of intersubjectivity. Here again, around the bodies and minds of black women, we can see the glimmer of one type of critique of the intersubjective view of race that prioritizes recognition. Although it is not self-consciously represented in this way by Goines, we might begin to read pimp culture's flight from recognition as another cautionary tale about why the theme of recognition is raised around blackness only to fold. One reason, as pimpology teaches us, is that recognition is simply not profitable.

If The Rape of Ruby, with its emphasis on the subordination and "correction" of the mind and body of the prostitute, is somehow a scene that might predictably appear in the pimp canon since its pimpology proudly stresses and sensationalizes the failure of recognition, one example from Robert Beck's work is much harder to imagine as belonging to this foundational moment in genre writing about black masculinities. Published as a collection of short vignettes in 1971, Beck's autobiographical The Naked Soul of Iceberg Slim, a follow-up to Pimp, outlines some of the mental consequences the mack game produces for the pimp. In an event I refer to as The Tragedy of Shorty, Beck writes about one of the many times pimping and hustling landed him in prison. As an aging (and soon-to-be-former) pimp locked in the "steel box," Beck develops a compassionate, protective concern for Shorty, an inmate imprisoned in the cell next to his. Beck's interest in and concern for his younger neighbor is compromised, however, when he recalls,

> Again for the thousandth time I see and hear the likable little black con in the steel box next to mine, my only buddy, suddenly chanting freaky lyrics of a crazy frightening song about how God is a double-crossing cocksucker, and how he is going to sodomize and murder his crippled bitch mama.
>
> I cry out like a scalded child, leap off my straw mattress and stand on trembly legs peering into Shorty's cubicle through a ragged break in the weld of the sheet steel wall. He's buck naked and his soft black baby face is twisted hard and hideously old as he stands slobbery with his hands flying like frenzied bats up and down his long stiff penis.[25]

This moment in the "house of horrors" sends Beck into voyeuristic convulsions, as he leaps up and gets "scalded" like a child. The "freaky lyrics" of Shorty's song sing of a mother who is crippled and, like Ruby, is being sodomized. Beck is clearly aroused, his bodily and emotional reactions paralleling Shorty's "slobbery" stiffness, as he leaps into action and spies on his neighbor on his own "trembly legs." Beck says that he begged Shorty to stop "jeffing" until Beck himself became saturated by the "stink of emotion sweat."[26]

Contrary to the colder affect and emotionality that the pimp projects in the exterior domain of the street scene, both in isolation and in the company of other men, the pimp seems to be an entirely differently (de)composed subject. On the one hand, Beck's other numerous autobiographical confessions to both loving and abhorring his mother shed some light on the guilt that he feels after viewing Shorty masturbate to this song about rape, incest, and matricide, particularly as Beck folds himself into a fetal position after the guards beat and retrieve Shorty. On the other hand, there are any number of other, nonliteral associations that also seem to motivate Beck's response. For instance, the passage begins with his desire for intersubjective bonding with Shorty, his "buddy," but Shorty's own fantasy and actions (his singing and masturbating) as well as the actions of other external agents (the guards) impede on that wish. There is also the content of the song and the way Shorty's retaliation is directed not at the system, adversary, or oppressor (a "double-crossing cocksucker" God, in this case) but at his mother instead. The scene consolidates so many things at once: the desire for intersubjective connection caves around the threat of homoeroticism; prison culture or the law surfaces as complicit in facilitating black male anti-intersubjectivity (since the confinement drives Shorty crazy and destabilizes Beck as well); and the scene reactivates a vision of family dynamics in which black men are infantilized while the imprint of a baaaddd and punishable black mama looms large.

Like The Rape of Ruby, The Tragedy of Shorty proves to be a psychologically transformative experience. Beck tries to make some sense of the moment's impact on him, writing, "The tragedy of Shorty and its recurring long range misery for me is but one 'House' horror among many that haunt my new life."[27] What is perhaps most notable in Beck's account and in the way he views himself as a victim is the way the interior life of the pimp casts him as a figure who can persecute others with impunity but who also feels perpetually persecuted himself. Beck relates the chanting of "freaky lyrics" as evidence that prison, and by extension his life as a pimp, has continually subjected him to scenes like this one and to other games of mental trial. Beck's use of the word "horror" in this account and the intensity of his reaction again indicate the usefulness of Kristeva's notion of abjection for describing at least part of the emotional fallout of the pimp's quivery flight from recognition. Kristeva writes,

> Any crime, because it draws attention to the fragility of the law, is abject, but premeditated crime, cunning murder, hypocritical revenge are even more so because they heighten the display of such fragility. He who denies morality is not abject; there can be grandeur in amorality and even in crime that flaunts its disrespect for the law—rebellious, liberating, and suicidal crime. Abjection, on the other hand, is immoral, sinister, scheming, and shady: a terror that dissembles, a hatred that smiles, a passion that uses the body for barter instead of inflaming it, a debtor who sells you up, a friend who stabs you.[28]

Beck's experience with Shorty contains all of these aspects, from "premeditated crime" and "cunning murder" to "hypocritical revenge," but what sends Beck to prison in the first place is his "passion that uses the body for barter instead of inflaming it." If women are abjected, even when they are "good" whores, so too does the pimp feel similarly when he meditates on his proximity to them and to the other players and objects within his world. Eventually, as I explore in the next sections, it is exactly this discomfort, the horror-house effect, that pimping's psychological warfare produces that makes both Beck and Goines's character seek out people and relationships that can alleviate the stress caused by their celebrated rejection of recognition.

For now, though, apparent right at the surface of reading through the print culture's representation of "pimp psychology" are the ways in which such works may function in the cultural imaginary as scintillating "house horrors" in and of themselves, by providing funky, overdetermined spaces where prostitutes are disciplined with clothes hangers and the saving grace and intervention of the Christian God does little more than sentence black men to a long life of jacking off. Yet, as these two moments also demonstrate, the psychological blueprint that gets drawn onto representations of the black underclass frequently contains contours of desire and fear that we are not supposed to notice. More specifically, there are two types of psychological games going on here. The first type of game is the mind/body game of control that Whoreson plays with Ruby. He presents this process literally and self-consciously as an externalization that is predicated on real domination, as discrete and intentional actions that he fully understands. Yet, as Beck's reflections indicate, the way the pimp understands his ability to exercise control over others is a type of overt fantasy that is also inseparable from a host of surreptitious fears and "freakish" things. These two aspects of the psychological economy that informs the foundational pimp texts make it that much less surprising that *Hustle & Flow*'s DJay needs to produce a rap album in order to stave off a mental breakdown. As Beck's and Goines's foundational works make quite clear, the pimp always maintains a tenuous, fraught, and reflexive relationship to power, reality, and fantasy. At the very least, we can say that there is a fantastical relationship to power, domination, and persecution inherent in the pimp's interactions with others that displaces any process of recognition. But how might we begin to make clearer the element of fantasy that is a part of the pimp's psychological game, and is "fantasy" even the right word?

Since Freud, a number of cultural and social theorists have viewed fantasy as more than the opposite of reality, more than the psychical renderings—or mental work—of a desiring subject. There are, in fact, many types of fantasies, and most of them have little to do with what a person actually desires. One of the difficulties in talking about fantasy, as Anne Cheng proposes, is that "fantasy assumes that there is a stable and inviolate subject doing the fantasizing."[29] Yet the pimps in Beck's and Goines's accounts rarely, if ever, experience themselves as "stable and inviolate," because they have a much more symbiotic relationship to the people they are in the business of oppressing. To distinguish fantasy from the way it is associated with an identifiable subject, Cheng departs from Jean Laplanche and J.-B. Pontalis's dynamic definition of fantasy as she asks us to consider the distinguishing qualities of the "fantasmatic."[30] If fantasy implies an active or stable consciousness, the fantasmatic, "on the other hand, unclasps fantasy's securing of subject and object position and pinpoints the unstable interaction that goes into informing the making of the mythology of the 'object' or the fetish."[31] This distance between the overt fantasies of a consciously desiring subject and the fantasmatic thoughts and actions of the self when she or he is less stable, less aware, less coherent to the self and others opens up another set of possibilities for understanding the concept.

The object relations analyst Melanie Klein's theories offer additional ways of thinking about the role fantasy plays in relationships where there is an imbalance of power. For instance, Klein is concerned particularly with how "the phantasy of forcefully entering the object gives rise to anxieties relating to the dangers threatening the subject from within the object."[32] The subject or self who tries to control another, Klein argues, always runs the risk of absorbing and experiencing extreme feelings of persecution and of being controlled by others. The self's proximity to a colonized or dominated other creates an emotional process of "introjecting and reintrojecting the forcefully entered object" so that the self in turn feels plagued by "feelings of inner persecution."[33] Important to Klein is the way this process makes the self feel as if the dominated other actually represents "the dangerous aspects of the self."[34] Both what Cheng offers as the fantasmatic and what Klein emphasizes when she talks about a self that feels trapped in a cyclical process of persecution destabilize our familiarity with what we typically take fantasy to mean. Both interpretations raise the possibility that there is a relationship between the overt fantasy of domination and subversion and the internal feelings that make a person feel as if she or he occupies multiple, not singular, positions on the spectrum of subject/object, oppressor/oppressed, and pimp/whore.[35]

As scholars of black popular culture, we have focused more on the overt fantasies of the pimp game and less on the subtleties of feelings that lurk beneath those fantasies. While Cheng calls for expanding how we think about fantasy by insisting on the presence of the fantasmatic,

I situate the pimp's relationship to "phantasies" and the "phantasmatic" in making a similar lexical distinction and claim about a different set of mental activities. Since it is easy to overuse and dilute the word *fantasy* as we talk colloquially about sexual fantasies, racial fantasies, capitalist fantasies, and so forth, to more clearly establish what I mean, I use the British (and early object relations) spelling and its derivatives as a way of clarifying the type of mental process I intend to emphasize here in thinking more deeply about pimp culture. If fantasies represent the stage, frame, and narrative of conscious desires and wishes, phantasies represent the less obvious, often unwanted, unanticipated, and contradictory impulses, actions, and affect that are a by-product of the pursuit of those overt desires and wishes. Put another way, phantasies describe the interior experiences as the self interacts with the object world of her or his overt dreams. Shifting our attention in this way makes it more possible to peel back the layers of the pimp's overt fantasies (socially informed) and less pronounced phantasies (private experiences). In this context, phantasies are the emotional location for rituals of domination that inform the pimp's psychological game.

To return to Ruby and Shorty, in The Rape of Ruby, Whoreson tries to avoid contamination by the bad object by using the "pimp sticks" to rape her at first. Sodomizing Ruby becomes a way for him to manage the anxieties of "forcefully entering" the abject object (Ruby's terrifying, engulfing vagina) but nevertheless connects him to how he felt when his mother, using the same tools, disciplinarily whipped him as a child. In The Tragedy of Shorty, the sight of Shorty masturbating, much more so than Shorty's freaky song, causes Beck's sympathetic and homoerotic ejaculation—the ultimate "sickening" that sends him into a crumpled fetal position. When Beck collapses in a heap, he is both physiologically and emotionally emulating and appropriating a connection to Shorty, fag, God on his knees, and the "bitch" crippled mother. Despite the desire to remain wholly in control, the phantastical side of the pimp game always blurs the lines of emotional separation between pimp and prostitute, Mack Daddy and whore, just as Beck in this example internally feels no separation from what he imagines is happening in the cell next to his. If, as it is so commonly taken for granted, the pimp game is indeed a psychological game,

who are the key players, and why does the black family figure so prominently into the pimp's master design?

## Mothers Up, Pimps Down: Baaaddd Black Mamas Redux

As I argued in chapter 3, there are unique ways in which black mothers
appear in the popular imagination as familial villains and "preoedipal"
figures of engulfment; black women and mothers have been consistently
represented as undermining the intersubjective mission within the
black family either by failing to survive their children's normal attempts
to separate from them or by destroying their children's sense of psychic
independence. Pimp culture from the 1960s onward builds on this revul-
sion toward these women by configuring new spectacular stories about
her "power" and destructiveness. As a basic conceit, 1960s and 1970s
pimp narratives represent women and their bodies in general as con-
taminated, as sites of phantastical, abjected horror in ways that make
other black popular works that objectify women, from Blaxploitation
film to commercial rap videos and all points in between, look tame by
comparison. In *Pimp*, for instance, Beck describes vaginas as "gaping,
hairy magnet[s]" that possess the personified, superhuman strength to
lull and snare even the "squarest" of men or johns.[36] Beck also recalls a
particularly troubling memory of being molested by a woman and feeling as if he was going to be swallowed whole by the woman's "moist,
odorous darkness" while his small head was "wedged between her ebony
thighs" as he nearly suffocated in her dense, "hairy maw."[37] As one of
the first scenes in *Pimp*, this encounter with a black woman's body as
cavernous and animalistic makes Beck feel compromised, engulfed, and
terrified, and these feelings stay with him as he matures into a man who
maintains the overt and active fantasy of controlling women's bodies.
Once he becomes a pimp, he extends this affectively charged association to black maternal bodies to other black women and assumes that
all women possess the phantastical ability to destroy just like baaaddd
mamas and other predatory maternal figures. Later in *Pimp*, Beck
describes a moment when he tries to kill one of his prostitutes, but her
bodily excess, her matronly sustenance, saves her from a surefire death.
He explains, "When I shot her the only thing that saved her life was the

fact that she had a forty-six inch bust. The fatty tissue absorbed the bullet at almost point-blank range."[38] Figures who can chronically survive such purposeful attempts of destruction are that much less human in the pimp's experience.

Although Goines does not use molestation to frame the events that unfold in *Whoreson*, he does write about a moment when Whoreson is humiliated by a black woman's perceived and unnatural bodily ability. As Goines describes it, Whoreson's first sexual encounter includes a "freaky" vaginal ejaculation that shames and terrifies him tremendously. In the scene, Goines's character discovers himself in similar position to Beck in *Pimp*, as Whoreson's head gets stuck in a "lengthwise grip" between a black woman's thighs. From this ensnared position, Whoreson recalls that the woman "began to thrust her hips with a steady force until the continuous pressure produced a light discharge that seemed to spray" his face.[39] He responds to her seemingly freakish ability to ejaculate first with fear and then with unmitigated fury, or as he says, "anger and hate twisted inside my gut, as the notion ran through my mind that she had made a freak out of me."[40] This proximity to what he despises, being turned into a freak by a freak, is what shames Whoreson the most. In what ensues, the soon-to-be pimp uses his trademark clothes hangers to beat the woman into submission. In both narratives, the shaming and humiliation that the pimps feel in moments like these are always deliberately connected to their baaaddd mothers. To this end, Whoreson thinks of his mother, a prostitute, during some of his earliest sexual encounters with women, and Beck rationalizes that he was molested and emotionally tormented by his abuser because of his mother's willful neglect.

Pre– and post–Moynihan Report black pulp narratives describe the family life of the underclass boy and man as predictably locked into the dynamics of a preoedipal matriarchal household. Mothers, typed either as saints or whores, are consistently positioned atop the family power structure. "Fathers" in these narratives appear as any number of secondary figures—actual fathers, surrogate fathers, even patriarchal symbols of American wealth and prosperity like The (white) Man. The way the dominant cultural fantasy of the baaaddd black mother gets reworked in the pimps' backstories, as a part of their "shameful" and "freakish" relationship to other women, reactivates the culturally abhorred paradigm of black mothers at the top of bleak relational power dynamics.

It is helpful to visualize these family and relational dynamics in triangular form, in a deliberate engagement with and critique of the Freudian Oedipal contest. Thinking about the pimp's familial, social, and emotional life in triangular form is particularly compelling because, as Eve Kosofsky Sedgwick has argued in her pioneering work about homosociality, "the triangle is useful as a figure by which the 'commonsense' of our intellectual tradition schematizes erotic relations, and because it allows us to condense into a juxtaposition with that folk-perception" different theories and concerns.[41] With an interest in bringing a focus on race, gender, and class together here, I express this in the vernacular as "mothers up, pimps down," and the triangle in figure 1 represents the metadiscourse about black families that always includes the dominant cultural wish to overthrow the classically rendered baaaddd mama. This popular understanding of black family dynamics has many problems, as I discussed when thinking about the recognition battles that inform black family dramas on film in chapter 3. An additional problem with this cultural paradigm is that the overdetermined focus on the black mother's role as the head of the family structure obscures the ways other emotions beyond fear and dread may also coalesce around her. For example, although erotic desire between mother and son is taken for granted as fact in to our Oedipally obsessed and oriented culture, the dyad between black son and mother has been theorized and discussed socially as impervious to any axis of complicated physical or emotional desire.

Perhaps inadvertently but no doubt because of the violent eroticism that serves as a general frame and context for 1960s and 1970s pimp narratives, these works are much more explicit than other aspects of popular culture in establishing the psychosocial theme of erotic desire between black mother and son. In The Tragedy of Shorty, Shorty's overt wish to sexually possess and destroy his mother gets communicated as psychotically deranged; fantasizing about sodomizing and then murdering his mother renders Shorty mentally incompetent—he is immediately committed to an asylum for fantasizing publicly about these feelings. Two additional moments that crop up between these texts, one of a pimp

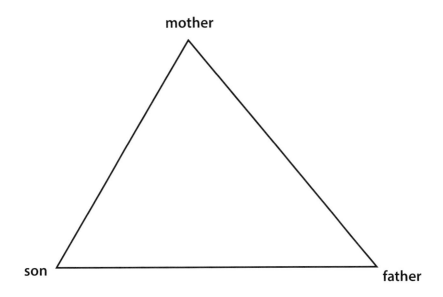

Figure 1: Fantasies of black mothers up, pimps down

being beaten and one of a mother being beaten, further make visible the baaaddd mother's proximity to erotic desire and sexual objectification. In the "pimp being beaten" example, a young Whoreson initially watches as Jessie, his mother, punishes his friend after the two boys have gotten into some mischief. Amazed and terrified, repulsed and stimulated, Whoreson watches the beating, recalling, "As I watched I began to shiver with fear. She struck with such brutal intensity. . . . I had never seen her like this before. . . . She stood there breathing hard with her hands on her hips. Her eyes seemed wild, her features were contorted by rage. . . . My mouth was dry, my legs trembled."[42] Nearly spent after beating Whoreson's friend, Jessie faces her son with a pair of twisted coat hangers in her hands. Whoreson remembers that his mother held him in an unflinching grip. In recounting this beating, he says, "the pain was inexpressible" as "the blows landed first on my back and shoulders, then moved down to my buttocks and legs, then back again." While Jessie beat him, Whoreson screams "from sheer pain, mingled with terror," and later confesses, "she beat me in such a cold fury, I thought she would kill me."[43]

In this account, Goines shares two details about Whoreson's mother that crystallize the son's erotic, albeit masochistic, connection to her. First, Goines is careful to note that Jessie is nearly nude when she begins beating her son. When the police bring Whoreson and his friend home, Jessie runs into the bedroom and reappears "swinging" the second important detail: her coat hangers. All eyes of the men and boys in the room are on her as "her large breasts strained to burst free from the sheer nightgown she wore. In her anger, she hadn't bothered to put on one of her housecoats, so the officers could see just about all they desired. They stared with open admiration."[44] Whoreson becomes an intermediary figure who is caught between what he recognizes as the white police officers' sexual desire of his mother and his own complicated mix of fascination, terror, and fearful desire as he watches his friend get whipped. Once Jessie turns on Whoreson, he becomes the object of attention in this primal scene of converging attractions and gazes. Further adding to the erotic contours of this scene, Goines places the "pimp sticks" in Jessie's hands long before her son uses them to rape Ruby and other women. About these hangers that represent his phantastic connection to mother, Whoreson recalls, "She even tried using coat hangers twisted together. She called them her 'pimp sticks' and used them only when I had been exceptionally bad."[45] Whoreson's very name sets up a complementary triadic impression that indicates the son's position to his mother, where the son is positioned between the mother in the dominant position and the father/phallus on the other side. That is, since the character's full name is Whoreson Jones or WhoreSonJones, the "Whore" in his name represents his mother and her occupation when she conceived him; "Son" is the signifier for the pimp-to-be; Jones, his surname, represents the missing father.[46] Hence, when Whoreson uses his mother's pimp sticks to vaginally rape women and then uses his "jones" to anally rape them, as he does in The Rape of Ruby, he experiments with the desirous eroticized split between mother, son, and father. The intertwined hangers visually render mother and son together, making tangible what the son later reconfigures as a phallic tool that remains ever connected to all that the baaaddd mother codifies.

In sharing autobiographical accounts of pimping, Beck finds that he, too, cannot shut off the steady stream of unwanted associations to his mother, and in *Pimp*, he describes a number of the shameful, "terrible" dreams he had about her. In one of these recurring nightmares, a white, "gargantuan" Christ with "blazing blue" eyes would shoot "white light" from his finger. The white Christ would then give Beck "a barbed leather whip" and say, "Punish this evil woman. Destroy the devil inside her. The Lord so directs thee."[47] In always following these instructions, Beck would feel a renewed excitement and intensity. He describes in detail how it felt to whip the unknown woman he assumed was a prostitute:

> Eagerly I would grab the heavy whip in both hands. I would bring it down with all my force on the woman's back. She would just stand there. The scarlet would drain down from her slashed back. She would be standing to her knees in a river of blood. . . . She would turn her brown agonized face toward me. It would be Mama. I would be shaking and screaming in my sweat. It was horrible. I could never cut the dream off until its end. It had to run its fearful course. The dreams about Mama came until her death.[48]

Strikingly similar to what Beck insists is Shorty's erotic wish when he recounts The Tragedy of Shorty in *Naked Soul*, here in Beck's dream, God is also a double-crosser who allows Beck to act out his own violent and erotic phantasy of whipping his mother. For Beck, these are embarrassing erotically charged dreams about his mother that haunt his life and work as a pimp. In spite of himself, these dreams about his barebacked mother are wet dreams that leave him hot and funky with "emotion sweat" and saturate him with what he describes as "the hot volley of the savage thrill" that rests "sticky wet" between his "trembling thighs."[49] Beck's emotional and physical response to his own dream also mimics his reactions to Shorty's song. In this version of the phantasy, the son's feared and longed-for wish for another agent to intervene in the toxically construed dyad between black mother and son is much clearer.

When examined together, these beating scenes in *Whoreson* and *Pimp* more fully reflect the range of emotions about guilt and sadomasochism that Freud famously theorized in the case history "A Child Is Being Beaten" (1919).[50] The case and its postmodern interpretations emphasize the unconscious feelings inherent in the responses of children witnessing others being beating. As these children typically watched siblings or other children being whipped by their parents, the child as spectator becomes psycho-sympathetically entangled with the child being beaten—the Kleinian "bad self"—and, as such, the child as spectator experiences some mixture of fascination, arousal, and guilt when watching the representation of himself being disciplined. In the pimp beating scenes, the pimps and their mothers play out a version of this. Whoreson's friend being beaten and Beck's belief that God is forcing him to whip an "evil" woman satisfy this aim of watching and vicariously participating in the discipline of a bad (abject) self who is represented simultaneously as both mother and son. Freud thought that the child would ultimately feel persecuted for having such shameful wishes. In the scenes from *Pimp* and *Whoreson*, Whoreson's mother turns on him, and Beck feels tricked and tormented for having participated in God's crooked plan. These are moments of confused or false identification that the child/pimp represses in order to minimize the event's significance. Fittingly then, Whoreson rationalizes that the woman beating him and exposing him to this complicated convergence of emotions could not really be his mother. He thinks, "I stared with fear at this dark angry woman, who I could hardly recognize as my mother."[51] Likewise, Beck is convinced that he dreams of lashing his mother only because he has spent so much time in the white man's prison. Prison, he rationalizes, wearies a pimp's soul and makes his psychological disposition more susceptible to identifying with overstimulating mental phantasies. In Beck's attempt to jokingly dismiss the uniqueness of his particular psychological fears and vulnerabilities, he alas admits that the pimp's plight is conventional psychoanalytic sadomasochism. He says, "I guess Freud was right. If it thrills you to give pain, you can get your jollies taking it."[52]

The revised diagram in figure 2 better expresses how the 1960s and 1970s pimp narratives tell a more complicated and phantastically experienced story about the dominant cultural representation of black mothers atop the nuclear-family power structure. Beck's and Goines's narratives help us rethink those dynamics because they represent more prominently the blend of fantasy and phantasy as an everyday part of pimps' scenes and schemes of oppression. Mother remains on top here because at the helm is the place she occupies in the metafantasy about black families, but the currents of desire, fear, and dread—the phantastical place that she occupies in son's mind—are more clearly established in the redesign in figure 2. Incidentally, in the formative stories that pimps tell about themselves, the father, that longed-for rival to mother's dominance, is experienced by the pimp/son as unimportant, as an illegitimate or untrustworthy third agent or rival to mother's power in moments such as these that occur early and often in the pimp's life. Although I find these narrative moments that detail the sons' relationships to their mothers to be powerfully evocative, they are treated in the pimp narratives as tangential, random, and aberrant tales about life in the 'hood. On the whole, both writers try to displace mother's centrality by raising and then denying her importance and by then focusing more deliberately on the other rules of the game, the "harder" fantasy side of the economic laws of macking.

Pimping, an activity that moves the pimps away from their mothers, allows both Whoreson and Beck to transform their erotic and fraught relationships to black maternity into direct capital. One moment in *Pimp* crudely transforms the phantastical relationship of the sublimated black

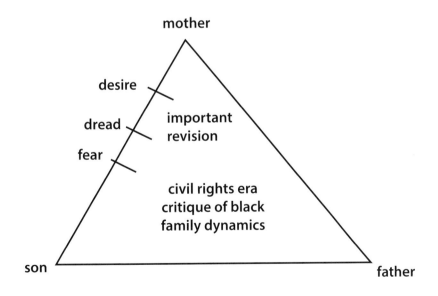

Figure 2: Phantasies of mothers up, pimps down

female (maternal) body into the auspicious search for money that is imagined to literally exist inside black women's abjected, but now made purposeful, engulfing vaginas. In the scene, Beck and his friends search a prostitute for her earnings from a john. Beck wonders, "Where did my street whores hide their scratch? In the 'cat!' In the 'cat,' where else? The clincher was this broad's wide-legged walk."[53] Fixated on her vagina as the natural vat of concealment, Beck explains, "We had to know if she had treasure up her 'cat.'"[54] As one of the men fists the woman in search of the pimp's loot, Beck, both amazed and disgusted, reports, "When he brought his mitt out it made a kissing sound. He had a long shinny plastic tube between his index and middle fingers. It stank like rotten fish."[55] As an occupation, pimping makes good on the dominant preoedipal fear of mothers and women by monetizing their feared and desired vagina, turning it into a treasure "cat" that participates in a sexual economy. As the pulp narratives depict a social transformation that finally places black woman in her proper place, the pimps' second-most-common overt fantasy imagines the ways in which men can finally top mother/woman/whore.

## Pimps Up, Ho's Down: Male Identificatory Love and Anality

In reappropriating and differently animating the dominant cultural fantasies about black women, the sons who grow up to become pimps, as I argue with the "mother on top" triangularization, harbor phantastic feelings that are rooted paradoxically in both the preoedipal fears *and* Oedipal-like erotic desires of mother. Both of these ways of relating stem from a lack of recognition between mother and son; and not only do the contradictory emotions help the pimps rationalize a general objectification and subordination of black women, but the feelings also motivate the pimps to use their occupation as a competitive economic subversion that draws them closer to other men. In a rereading of Freud's and the literary critic René Girard's theories that envision the levels of contest (Freud) and desire (Girard) between men, Sedgwick argues that homosocial interactions between men, those nonsexual patterns of "male friendship, mentorship, entitlement, [and] rivalry," cannot "be understood outside of [their] relation to women and the gender system as a whole."[56] Relatedly, Gayle Rubin theorizes that gender oppression can be summarized as cultural practices that are built around the deliberate and de facto "exchange of women," where men bond together as "exchangers" and women are "sexual semi-object-gifts."[57] Pimp culture literalizes the transactionary nature of the exchange of women by providing a context for men, even when they are adversaries, to come together as business partners who have a common, vested, interest in women's bodies. Predictably, then, both *Whoreson* and *Pimp* emphasize male bonding with various rivals, father figures, and community mentors. Both narratives devote lengthy passages to describing interactions with rival pimps or male friends (a pimp named New York and a friend named Tommy in *Whoreson*; two dominant pimps, Top Glass and Sweet, in *Pimp*). A major theme of these interactions is a pedagogical one, as there are lessons about prostitute acquisition, domination, and maintenance that the inexperienced pimp must learn from his male mentors.

While the impression of "mama" always vacillates for the men between either pole of the good breast / bad breast dichotomy of motherhood, in the underclass relationships between men, idealized fathers, even when they become rivals, benefit from much more consistent idealizations and transferences. That is, there are plenty of times in these works when other men become the central idealized figures, as Poitier's characters were for his buddies (see chapter 2). Pimps more freely express their homosocial affection for other men, or as Beck tells his mentor in one scene, "You know I love you like I loved Henry [his stepfather]." And then, to make explicit how this attachment to men relates to how he felt about his mother, Beck confesses to his rival/mentor, "Maybe I love you, 'Sweet,' more than I love Mama."[58] A lot of this male bonding occurs around the acquisition of women and material goods, but men of the underclass especially benefit from being in the solitary company of other men when in prison.

These scenes of male rivalry and bonding are a core experience in the pimp narrative, and they are motivated by a set of overt social desires—mainly, the hope that other men can interfere and help young black men navigate the social, political, and economic perils of the street. The triangle in figure 3 represents the desire men have to identify with other men and the way they privilege those interactions over their relationships to the women around them. Although each of the pimp narratives includes some version of a "son's" rivalry with a "father," I do not present the triangle in the more typical way showing father on top, as a traditional understanding of Freud's Oedipal triangle would frame it. Rather, I have inverted the typical relational triangle to stress that the sons/pimps are not on the same level as the women/mothers during these moments of contest and exploration of power with other men. "Pimps up, ho's down" represents a cultural logic of pimping that prioritizes masculinity in ways that Freud could not have imagined. For example, even though the pimps express wishes to eventually replace more established underclass men, this triangle emphasizes a quest for closeness, identification, and bonding through their competition. Here, as in other cases, black popular culture uniquely appropriates and modifies psychosocial themes.

Yet, as the pimps try to satisfy their needs for mentorship and camaraderie with other men, they also discover that these exchanges create an entirely new set of phantasies and anxieties that they must now manage. Once mother and women are in their proper place and patriarchy is restored, the constant disavowal of baaaddd mother's engulfing vagina and the search for an identificatory relationship with other men does not produce a simple Freudian Oedipal (genital) reordering of the underclass that would have us reading all about the pimps and their phallic power, or mighty "supercocks."[59] Instead, in the phantastical emotional hothouse of the pimp's scene, as Goines and Beck imagine it, men's anuses, not their penises, hold the most potential for reinventing power relations in the ghetto. In these narratives, the black supercock that is so common a signifier for black masculinity in popular culture does not rise to symbolic status in doing the overt fantasy work of subordinating women. Just as the men maintain a fearful and overdetermined relationship to "hairy maws" and terrifying vaginas, they also construct a set of complicated associations to the male anus as a phantastical signifier or embodied system of representation. As a competing signifier, the anus, along with references to defecation and bathrooms (called "crappers"), fill the relational void between men with additional psychodynamic value. Anality becomes such an important signifier in the economy of the underclass that there is even a telling colloquial expression that men share: good men, and this

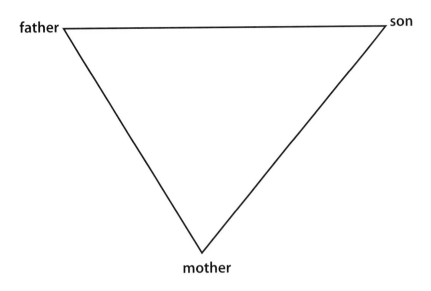

Figure 3: Fantasies of male bonding and identification

includes successful pimps, fall out of their mothers' butts, not out of her abject vagina, the place where men and their penises ("swipes") must stay clear. As one pimp puts it, "Pimping ain't no game of love. Prat 'em and keep your swipe outta 'em. Any sucker who believes a whore loves him shouldn't a fell outta his mammy's ass."[60]

The pimps' anal orientation, particularly when thought about in the context of their anti-intersubjective orientation to women, has some additional psychoanalytic significance. In "Defensive Anality and Anal Narcissism," Leonard Shengold describes anality as an intense focus on the ego-body that includes a fascination with anuses and feces. For Shengold, anality and anal narcissism become a metaphor for control, for the wish to put things in their place, and as an emotional strategy for containing situations, people, and feelings that have run amok.[61] This particular thematic conceit is less dominant in Goines's novel but is particularly salient in Beck's fiction and nonfiction. For instance, a good deal of the action in *Pimp* takes place in bathrooms—men talk to one another and confront idolatry and rivalrous feelings in the crapper. Beck is both jealous and intrigued, for example, when he notes that his mentor Sweet's crapper, where he previously learned valuable lessons about pimping while talking with his mentor, is now closed to him. In one moment, Sweet decides that his crapper is the safest place to both punish and contain a few women who have dared to defy his orders. As one man tells Beck when Beck wonders why he cannot get in to use Sweet's padlocked crapper himself, "Shit, ain't nothing wrong with the crapper. That cold bastard has his two whores locked in there for fucking with his scratch. They been in there for three days."[62] In this case, the crapper becomes the most reliable place to tuck away and punish bad objects at will. Of course, being locked in the crapper also reduces women to wasteful excess.[63]

There are other moments that pair the pimp's fantasy of control of the underclass with nonliteral phantastical feelings about containment. In one instance, while Beck is in prison (which he constantly refers to as the great "shit house"), he is attacked with crap and all that crap connotes as he becomes the subject of a smeary, bombing assault. He recalls, "Then I smelled it. I turned toward the door. I squinted through the soap on my eyelids. I had been bombed with crap. . . . It was oozing off the walls."[64] Being bombed with shit in this case presents Beck with a vastly important mental trial—he must survive the literal shit exchanged in papa's palace between men in order to prove his psychological durability. To survive the assault, he rehearses a mental exercise, repeating to himself on loop, "Watch out now, it's only crap, it's only crap. It's just crap. Watch out, it can't hurt you. It's only stinking crap."[65] Surviving the shit bombing and the other trials of incarceration, then, helps Beck psychically reconstitute, and wading through the shit of the underworld becomes an apt analogy for the themes of aggression and control that characterize how the narratives depict relationships among underclass men.

Other times in *Pimp* and *Naked Soul*, Beck's thematic references to anality present him as a loose young gun who does not yet possess the bodily control of more seasoned street icons. As such, Beck soils himself after being nearly raped by a woman, Red Cobra. A sympathetic bystander observes Beck's funky, faltering lack of control, saying, "Mary, mammy of Jesus, you stink. You musta shit in your pants. You sure getting funky breaks, Kid."[66] While Beck lacks the ability to control his own bodily responses, he learns to valorize what the waste of more established men symbolizes. As another hustler tells Beck when he dispassionately criticizes the top pimp, "You would gladly eat ten yards of 'Sweet's' crap. You think he's God."[67] It follows, then, that once Beck finally ascends to prominence in the ghetto and masters the metafantasy of controlling his own cadre of women, he becomes better able to use anal signification to his advantage, telling one prostitute that his excretions are golden. He explains to her, "You scurvy Bitch, if I shit in your face, you gotta love it and open your mouth wide."[68] Plainly stated, in the phantastical world of macking, pimp shit becomes worthy of consumption in a way that successfully rivals the value ("treasure" in the "cat") that mother's/whore's vagina represents.

Although the way anality surfaces as a theme in pimp culture mostly works to connect men to other men, the feelings that connect the pimps to the women of the underclass are never far from the surface. For example, in one telling moment in *Naked Soul*, Beck uses his feces to emotionally protect himself from his pervasive fear that his own body will be exploited by the people around him. As an aging pimp, Beck reasons that the best way to protect himself from becoming a nursemaid to the children that his prostitutes have accidentally mothered is to feign senility by defecating on himself. First, he expresses his fear in clear terms, saying, "And now in the funky autumn of my life I was apparently being set up for mamahood. . . . It was a treacherous and explosive situation."[69] Then, as he conjures a plan to tuck and contain those feelings, he asks, "What is usually most disgustingly flawful [sic] about the senile? No control of the plumbing, of course."[70] Sullying himself to mask his fear of being exploited by his objects of exploitation works, and Beck recalls that his prostitute "roughly diapered" him and "reeled away in disgust" when he "gurgled like a big black happy baby."[71] In the emotional life of the successful pimp, it makes perfect phantastical sense that self-defecation could protect a pimp from the threat of persecution and fear of being pimped himself. Tactical anality becomes a buffer to counter the Kleinian fear of the self becoming "the forcefully entered object."[72]

If anality becomes one way for pimps to transform their fears of disempowerment into a metafantasy of masculine order and control, this imagined power inversion also creates a surface text of homoeroti-cism. A similar type of homoerotic and homophobic "haunt" that Robert Reid-Pharr in *Black Gay Man*, E. Patrick Johnson in *Appropriating Black-ness*, and Marlon B. Ross in *Manning the Race* have identified as salient themes in some of the black masculinist discourses (letters, fiction, public exchanges) of the civil rights era also informs this aspect of pimp culture.[73] As The Tragedy of Shorty (with Robert Beck gazing at his friend mastur-bating) suggests, homoerotic desire and tensions work at every level here. This particular flight from the protocols of recognition and intersubjectiv-ity casts the rivalry between "father" and son as both identificatory *and* erotic. We can expand this discussion on the fantasies (desires for control and for male leadership) and phantasies (fears of persecution, unwanted erotic impulses, etc.) that are shared among criminal and underclass men by revising the "pimps up, ho's down" triangle to highlight the more complete nature of the interactions, including idealization, transference, rivalry, anality, and male-to-male erotic desire (see figure 4).

There are other ways in which homoeroticism becomes yet another phantastical consequence of the pimp game's psychological minefield. For starters, queer sexualities are quite visible in mass-marketed narratives about pimp culture. While men prefer the companionship of other men in these stories, so too do Beck and Goines describe the prostitutes as often preferring the intellectual and sexual attention of other women. Lesbian prostitutes are described as sabotaging rivals who convince other women in the pimp's stable to abandon him. The pimp's own homoerotic tenden-cies are justified in the narratives by the logic that if women are innately untrustworthy and they prefer to pleasure and desire each other, the pimp cannot direct his true erotic desires to these "freaky" and "funky" women.

Other times, the homoerotic impulses in pimp narratives are con-veyed through playfully coded sexual puns. For instance, when Beck goes to meet his father figure / rival, Sweet, for the first time, he describes himself as an excitable virgin who is about to lose his virginity as a result of being taken in by the other man. Of his excitement, Beck says, "I was trembling like maybe a hick virgin on a casting couch."[74] Another exchange in *Pimp* further evinces the poles of desire that also crop up in the reori-entation of the underclass around men and their bodies. As Beck stands

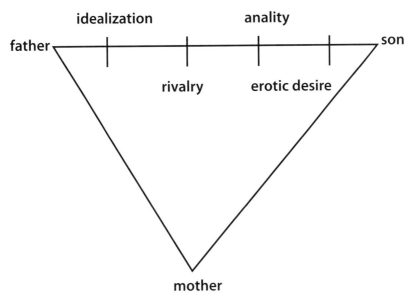

Figure 4: Phantasies of male bonding reconsidered

behind a man in a bar whom he has never met and prepares to touch him on the sleeve, Beck thinks, "He was sure a wrong doer all right. He frogged at least three inches off his stool. It was like I'd stabbed him in the butt with a red-hot poker."[75] Glass Top, another pimp, angered and already called out by Beck as a "wrong doer," responds, "You young studs sure ain't got no finesse. It drags me to get hit on like that. When somebody touches me I like to be digging it and facing the stud, you know?"[76] As they get better acquainted and shoot up cocaine together, Beck remarks how good the two "beautiful," "pretty" pimp boys look together as they strip down to their underwear. Beck is slightly embarrassed that his undergarments are shabby compared to "Top's" "candy-striped silk" shorts, and he experiences a "nerve-shredding climax" shooting up while Glass Top both attends to him and shares in his ecstasy.[77] At once, Top confides in Beck, "I love you, Blood. We gonna be tight."[78] Despite the fact that "tight" further stresses the ways in which anality functions as the dominant metaphor for this stage of relational reorientation, and despite Beck's obligatory denial of homoerotic tension in this moment ("Look man . . . I'm a pimp, not a faggot") and in others (as he does when he discovers that a beautiful white woman he is obsessed with is a transvestite), male-to-male erotic desire is as common as is the labored subordination of women in the black pimp's quest to rule the streets.[79]

The integration of homosociality, homoeroticism, and anality into the canon of pimp literature should not be surprising. Here again we are reminded of Sedgwick's conclusions about homoerotic impulses and desires, which are policed in homosocial interactions, and reactionary homophobic agendas, which are actively and violently encouraged in those same contexts. Discerning when a hug from another pimp is filial affection and when it is an erotic invitation is not always possible, or as Sedgwick argues, "for a man to be a man's man is separated only by an invisible, carefully blurred, always-already-crossed line from being 'interested in men.'"[80] The subsequent emotions and phantastic feelings that crop up within such spaces certainly resemble a "homosexual panic," which Sedgwick reads as "the most private, psychologized form in which many twentieth-century western men experience their vulnerability to the social pressure of homophobic blackmail."[81] As such, the adoration and love, but also the panic and terror, that the pimp feels as a result of getting closer to other men is represented as yet another psychological burden of the pimp game.

## Black Boundarylessness and Pimp Daddy Expansiveness

The final way the pimps' fantasy for control creates a set of charged emotional responses has to do with the way the pimp wishes to be all things for the women around him. This way of combining the social fantasies of masculine power with private fears and frustrations fuels the colloquial evocation of the pimp as "daddy" or "Mack Daddy." Once the pimp has mastered the set of tenuous strategies for containing mother and outpacing the success of other men, he then tries to embrace his role as daddy of the underclass. As Beck tells one of his women, "I take an oath to protect you for as long as you are my woman, Baby, I know that's for always. Now repeat after Daddy, baby."[82] And so while the pimp may refer to the women around him using any cluster of derogatory nicknames, the name for him is quite stable—he is daddy, and his women are his family. Both Beck and

Goines take care to cast themselves and their characters in this coveted position that represents profound social, economic, and cultural achievement for the urban pimp. As this move to Mack Daddy is an overtly filial one, I represent it in figure 5 as a more common triangle of household dynamics, with Pimp Daddy—father—alone on top. Once the pimp succeeds in becoming the daddy of his stable, his lead prostitute, the "bottom whore" or "boss bitch," becomes the central figure who rivals him for power and position; she occupies the position of the son in the typical Oedipal triad. The other women in the pimp's stable are called "sisters" and are at all times subordinated by the power struggle between Mack Daddy and bottom bitch, as they perform the traditional role of a disempowered mother in this new family.

It is not just that the pimp becomes daddy in a filial sense, however, for he becomes much more than that; and he fluctuates among any number of positions from father to mother, from fag to God. For instance, in *Pimp*, when Beck finally achieves Mack Daddy status, he rebirths the women around him, telling one that because of her proximity to him, she is now

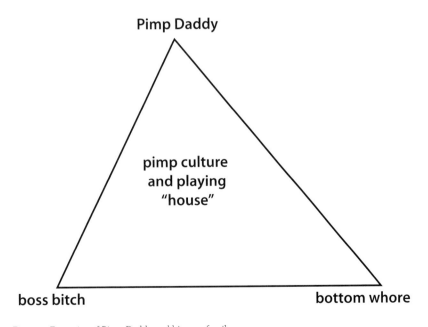

Figure 5: Fantasies of Pimp Daddy and his new family

"that great humping bitch reborn."[83] Beck as Mack Daddy grants her an entirely new subjectivity, or as he tells her, "You're gonna meet and work in the street tonight with your sisters. I'm gonna give you a rundown. Flap your horns and remember it. It will bring you into the family with some stardust on your tail."[84] As mother, Beck gives birth to this new prostitute, bringing her into the game of the underclass; as father, he offers her protection and guidance; as God, he gives her "stardust." Similarly, we can also recall Whoreson's purposeful rape of Ruby, which transforms and rebirths her into a new subject who can play her role in his family.

The pimp's fantasy of himself as Mack Daddy produces a host of new emotions that range from ecstasy to terror and fragmentation. As such, the successful pimp boasts frequently of feeling like Christ himself—like a black Jesus. In Beck's case, shooting and snorting "girl" (cocaine) and "boy" (heroin) exacerbate his feelings of omnipotent grandiosity, or the way he "thought and acted like a black God."[85] Yet, as God, the pimp is no less vulnerable to becoming all that he despises. Mentally, he feels frequently that he *is* mother/whore/fag just as much as he is Daddy/God/Mother. Beck describes himself in his most grandiose exhibitionist moments as a queer pretty boy: "Back in the joint I had dreamed almost nightly. They were cruel playets. They were fantastic. I would see myself gigantic and powerful like God Almighty. My clothes would glow. My underwear would be rainbow-hued silk petting my skin."[86] Not only is he a potentially fabulously queer God, as he tells one of his women, he is also so many other, competing personas at once. He says, "I'm gonna be your mother, your father, your brother, your friend, and your lover."[87] This subjective fluidity comes at a cost, though, and there is even a term, "georgiaed"—to be taken advantage of sexually without receiving any money—that describes the precarious roles that pimps play as potential whores themselves.[88] While it is common knowledge that a pimp receives money from the women who work for him, it is less commonly known that he rewards only the hardest working, highest paying women in his stable with *his* beautiful body. With his body reserved for just compensation for their hard work, he often feels himself to be a mirror of their labored bodily exchange, or as one of Beck's maxims puts it, "a pimp is really a whore who has reversed the game on whores."[89]

The psychodynamic contours of a pimp who is "really a whore who has reversed the game" is also an evidently postmodern logic and subjective orientation. To succeed at last in these stories is a no-win game for the pimp, who feels no separation from the objects he most despises. The triangularization in figure 6 represents a visualization of the way the pimp feels as he reigns atop his phantastically rendered new family. The postmodern convergence of these multiple subject positions grieves and punishes the underclass man so that even as he becomes a successful capitalist, the feelings of contamination, persecution, and abject fear are never easily managed. That is, the pimp, as Mack Daddy, as black, as boy desiring mother, as pretty man fixated on the anuses of other men, as king of the prison shit house, as one of the most celebrated and hunted icons of the ghetto, is a phantastic figure who performs his unique mode of excess while unraveling internally. Since the pimp resides on an emotional continuum where omnipotence is at times untrustworthy, being God or God-like only further wearies him as he tries to navigate the nearly infinite number of indeterminate identities that are at once stimulating and condemning, uncanny and emotionally unfulfilling. We might even say that as a figure of chronic indeterminacy, the successful pimp's mental state has much in common with the depressive psychological blueprint of the baaaddd black mama.

There is, of course, some precedent for thinking about blackness and indetermination, or blackness and various theories of postmodern identity. For example, bell hooks argues that postmodern theory, which claims such a liberatory embrace of "heterogeneity" and the "decentered subject," unfortunately "still directs its critical voice primarily to a specialized audience, one that shares a common language rooted in the very master narratives it claims to challenge."[90] While hooks explicitly wants to broaden the discussion about postmodernity to include race and nonesoteric forms of cultural production, Eithne Quinn seemingly answers hooks's call in his analysis of pimp culture and rap music, arguing that there is intentional spectacle and postmodern performativity inherent in the popular songs about black pimps—or as Quinn puts it, "macking is indeed the game that 'everybody's playing' in spectacle- and rhetoric-driven contemporary America."[91] Instead of hearing in rap's construction of the pimp a

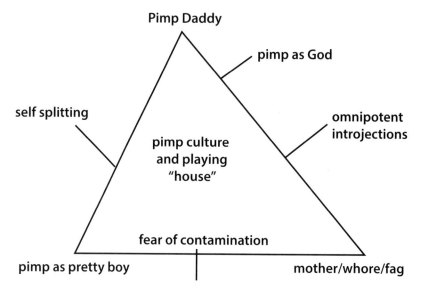

Figure 6: Phantasies of pimp as daddy, pimp as everywhere

kind of nihilistic determinism that only further essentializes contemporary notions of blackness, Quinn suggests reading the pimp as a figure of shifting signification. "Pimp poetics," he explains, "share affinities with post-structural notions not only of signification but also of subjectivity, whereby the mack serves as an emblem of ontological indeterminacy."[92] While Quinn rightly views the pimp personas of rappers like Ice Cube and Ice T as syntactical masters who are able to speak in one regard while signifying in another, as I have stressed in my reading of the civil rights era pimp narratives, indeterminacy is not always represented or emotionally experienced as playfully disruptive or subversively performative. That is, if macking is a game that everyone is playing, Robert Beck and Donald Goines make very clear that the game is a psychological one that has tremendous emotional and ontological consequences. Simply put, it does not feel good to be a tricky, shifty pimp.

Although not writing explicitly about postmodern culture, Robert Reid-Pharr's work on black masculinity addresses some similar themes and concerns about 1960s and 1970s work by black men. In "Tearing the Goat's Flesh," Reid-Pharr uses the term "boundarylessness" instead of "indeterminacy" to refer to the unstable and potentially disruptive personification of blackness that surfaces in some of the homophobic responses to black gay men during the civil rights era. He argues that gay men signal a unique kind of "boundarylessness" in the production of black masculinities. The reason gay men come to represent this site of instability is because, as Reid-Pharr explains, "the pathology that the homosexual must negotiate is precisely the specter of Black boundarylessness, the idea that there is no normal Blackness to which the Black subject, American, or otherwise, might refer."[93] The homophobic policing and violence in black masculinist discourses—as especially evident in the exchanges between Eldridge Cleaver and James Baldwin—turn the black gay male into a "scapegoat" whose flesh is metaphorically "torn" both in order to assault the communal disintegrationist dangers of boundarylessness and also, importantly, as a way of momentarily maintaining a connection to the radicalizing potential of that abject figure.[94] As an indeterminate subject, the pimp surely does play this role within black popular culture, but he feels as if everyone is tearing *his* flesh.

In many ways, the pimp's predicament is no different from how tropes of blackness function as boundarylessness in general. Psychological symbolism, usually packaged around some dramatization of the recognition of black humanity or the flight from it, is never far from narratives about black identity—which is why I argue that blackness "burns" as a signifier. The psychoanalytic mode and protocols work both to insist on recognition and to deny it, both to try to "fix" the meaning of blackness in place and to try to "free" it from familiar associations. In the pimps' case, the psychoanalytic impulse to stabilize their version of black masculinity comes from within the text. Both Beck and Goines wrote plaintively about what it felt like to live indeterminately, and both ultimately represent macking and pimping as emotional conditions that must be exchanged for more concrete and determinate experiences. That is, stories about the violence of failed recognition or the battle for successful black recognition, whether those moments occur in an interracial or intraracial context, often end up in the same place by the narratives' conclusion. This is precisely why pimp narratives often conclude by stressing an ethos of reform—both psychological and economic. The works end when the pimp is ready to embrace intersubjectivity. This readiness for inclusion is achieved not in spite of his past but, rather, as a direct result of his anti-intersubjective reign as Mack Daddy.

## "Keep Hustlin', Keep Flowin'": The Return of Recognition

In returning for a moment to the post–civil rights popular film *Hustle & Flow*, we can note that the contemporary film is replete with the same psychodynamic components of civil rights era pimpology as are evident in Beck's and Goines's texts, including baaaddd black mamas, sabotaging "bottom bitches," the constant threat of homoeroticism, tropes of anality that govern male bonding, and the pimp's sickening feelings about his own indeterminacy.[95] The more recent pimp narrative also features an arc of emotional redemption and intersubjective reform at the film's conclusion. Briefly, the ending of *Hustle & Flow* dramatizes DJay's precarious relationship to the American Dream. In the final sequences, the rap album has served its purpose as a creative vehicle that creates some separation between DJay, pimping, and the street scene that he so actively abhors. Yet, before his album can blow up and make him a local legend, DJay ends up in prison after a meeting between him and his idealized object (a local, successful rapper named Skinny Black) goes awry. DJay discovers, in coming to terms with the sobering realities of his failed idealization and transference, that Skinny Black will not mentor him or even listen to the product of his creativity. This painful, phantastical, revelation sends DJay into a violent rage; he pummels Skinny Black, calling him a sellout, and shoots one of his guards. The redemptive part of the film's ending, though, is in the way DJay connects romantically with Shug before going to prison (she becomes his woman, not his whore) and in the way that he establishes treasured intersubjective connections with his new middle-class male buddy, Key (Anthony Anderson), who has helped him produce the album. Hence, even though DJay is behind bars (a space so often represented as a rite of passage for underclass men turned rappers) at the end of the film, the narrative concludes by emphasizing the hopefulness and potential of the intersubjective view. The midlife crisis that stems from the wearied pimp's relationship to indeterminacy is neatly contained around the tiny promise that his life after he serves his five-year term will be much improved, perhaps materially but definitely relationally.

So too does *Hustle & Flow*'s ending resemble the narrative patterns established in the civil rights era print culture. Although Beck's and Goines's works graphically spectacularize a departure from the protocols of recognition, as the conclusions to both *Whoreson* and *Pimp* evince, even the popular works that seem most oppositional to the metanarrative of recognition gravitate toward ontologically "safer" and more traditional psychological orientations by the final pages. At the end of each work, the pimp trades his indeterminate and internally conflicted identity for the pursuit of a more integrated core self that he identifies as better suited to pursue middle-class, American ideals. Consistent with the narrative structure of other black pulp works, in both cases, the sensational lives and stories of underclass men are represented as a temporary departure from the desired norm; the confidence men, pimps, and hustlers are described as acting as they have only out of a sense of economic necessity and environmental factors such as personal trauma.[96] After the acts of violence, vigilante justice, and sexual escapades have been detailed extensively, the underclass man usually desires some sort of transformation that will enable him to give up the social and labor practices that have caused him so much internal and existential dissatisfaction. As such, activities like pimping and raping, hustling and murdering, either become behaviors that prematurely end the underclass man's life or become actions that get described as only a prelude to the "straight" and "square" American life of material success and improved mental health.

Following this pattern, Beck's and Goines's works end with the search for integration and healing, if not full intersubjectivity, and these ambitions replace the appeal of the pimp game and the messiness of pimpology in the end. For example, *Whoreson* ends with Goines's character incarcerated, where he is set to serve five years in prison because his former boss bitch has turned state's evidence against him. Weary of the emotional consequences of macking, Whoreson seeks to use prison as new opportunity to refabricate himself and deal with his mounting "bitterness and loneliness."[97] Removed from the material conditions of the street, for the first time in the narrative, the character reflects cerebrally on the lessons he has learned as a pimp, vowing to emerge from prison as a new man. Whoreson imagines that after serving his time, he will finally be able to shed the dehumanizing aspects of his personality that helped him thrive on the streets. The character recalls an old toast that brings together the material and the psychological components of his impeding transformation: "The jungle creed, said the strong must feed, on any prey at hand. I was branded a beast, and sat at the feast, before I was a man."[98] Relinquishing and destroying the "beast" within, he surmises, will free him to marry his childhood crush, Janet, the opposite of the mother/whore/fag construction that he has sought to so violently dismantle.

In Whoreson's beginning to see himself as different kind of psychological subject, he also imagines that he will have more of a future as a democratic subject. This particular turn toward bourgeois ambitions is articulated around his desire to live a middle-class life with Janet, a narrative move that reconstitutes his emotional relational orientation toward women as an important part of his vision of his life in the future. As Janet, pregnant with Whoreson's child, visits him in jail, their scenes together include each of them searching the other's face for awareness, understanding, and even something that approaches recognition that is grounded in attachment and vulnerability. About the new terms of their relationship, Whoreson reflects, "I had played the game and now I had to pay the dues. There were no more tears of frustration in the back of my eyes, because I knew I would not do this time alone. I had a woman who would be there right with me, writing and visiting until I came home. And now I knew there would be a real home somewhere in my future, a house full of love."[99]

The character's final wishes and vision indicate that the reformed pimp is not just changing occupations; he grows to valorize some of the standard tools and protocols of relating. Going forward, he wants not only middle-class material stability but also to forsake the trials and phantasies inherent in the game for a life of "truthfulness" between him and Janet, a life in which emotional deceit will be a "thing of the past."[100]

Similarly, although Robert Beck boasts throughout *Pimp* that "any good pimp is his own best company" because "his inner-life is so rich with cunning and scheming to out-think his whores," the tensions that characterize his solitary company by the end of his career aggrieves him so much that he wants nothing more than the simplicity of a "square" job selling insurance and marrying a saint-like woman.[101] While Goines tries to give his acclaimed pimp an ending that imagines a new material, emotional, and relational life that begins with newly constructed fantasies about black femininity as restorative, Beck's *Pimp* ends with a literal return to his baaaddd mother. If most of these narratives, as I have argued, implicitly or explicitly blame the black mother for her son's eventual career choice, it is fitting that in an attempt to shed the emotional traumas that have been further exacerbated by the oldest profession, Beck returns to his original figure of trauma. At the book's conclusion, Beck visits his mother as she lies dying and explains that for six months he and his mother rested "side by side on twin beds and talk[ed] far into the night."[102] During these conversations, his mother begs him to leave the street game (to "get married and have children"), and she apologizes for her role in his childhood sexual abuse.[103] With her last breath, his mother asks explicitly for his forgiveness, imploring, "Forgive me, Son, forgive me. Mama didn't know. I'm sorry."[104] At the moment of her death, Beck stands "watching her last tears rolling down her dead cheeks from the blank eyes."[105] This image of a dead but also crying black mother dislodges her in Beck's mind from the construct of the destructive baaaddd mother and gives him a new phantastic object to relate to, one that turns mother/woman from a figure of chronic abjection into an inspirational fantasy of eternal repentance.

What helps Beck the most, though, after his mother's cathartic departure is the former pimp's discovery of two new replacement maternal figures—his middle-class wife (he calls her "the perfect mother" who "always said the right things") and a woman whom he casts unambiguously in a psychoanalytic light.[106] Beck describes meeting "a charming, brilliant woman" who became an "indispensable source of help and courage during these hard times."[107] His relationship with this older woman resembles a patient/therapist dyad, or as Beck states explicitly, "She functioned as a kind of psycho-therapist. She explained and pointed out to me the mental phases I was passing through. She gave me insight to fight the battle."[108] Since the "battle" on the street has been consistently described by Beck as a mental and emotional one first and foremost, this verbal processing that he does with his new therapist better prepares him to make the move toward more socially sanctioned relational and material practices.

In relating to this older woman as his psychotherapist, Beck consolidates the dominant image of black maternity into a new but also familiar psychoanalytic frame—both analogously and directly bringing together black underclass cultural traditions and the pervasive discourse of analysis.

The problem with the narrative arc of *Pimp* and *Whoreson* and also with contemporary films about the black underclass like *Hustle & Flow* is not, of course, that it is somehow inherently specious for black characters to crave or cultivate friendships, romances, or other human connections. The problem has to do with the end that these dramatizations serve, or the reason the rituals of intersubjectivity are so heavily emphasized overall. In the case of popular pimp narratives and representations of the black underclass, the concluding relational aims are purposefully intended to separate the pimp from his dehumanizing actions and to specifically humanize him so that he might be more likable and can once again confirm that black humanity exists as purposeful, redeemable, and identifiable. This narrative pattern only promotes the myth that such characters need to be befriended and known in order to exist—before they can demonstrate democratic worthiness and suitability for inclusion. But the inverse or counternarrative of these stories would also have to be true: if the pimp is *not* psychologically transformable, then why would he ever matter, and how could the cultural lore and popular productions that stem from his (temporary) dislocation and disenfranchisement ever continue to both resonate in the mainstream and, importantly, turn profits? The challenge to the politics of recognition that such stories pose, then, whether they hail from the civil rights era proper or simply take up thematic inspiration from the time period, is consistent with bell hooks's broad but evocative claims about so many aspects of mass culture. In connecting the "flaws" in rap culture to larger systems of oppression, hooks argues that "the sexist, misogynist, patriarchal ways of thinking and behaving that are glorified in gangsta rap are a reflection of the prevailing values in our society, values created and sustained by white supremacist capitalist patriarchy."[109] That is, especially since hooks is quite aware that her critiques of gangsta rap might be used to condemn and vilify the form and individuals—instead of institutions—she is careful to connect her comments to systemic oppression.

I am similarly critiquing the system as a whole in highlighting under-class, underworld, and masculinist black identities' relationship to the intersubjective view of race. Rather than dismiss the misogynistic con-demnation of black women and mothers in pimp culture in order to make claims about disenfranchised subversiveness, I have argued that the por-trayal of black women in these works remains central to how we might better understand the social and cultural significance of this popular tra-dition. As foundational texts in the canon of American pimp literature, Beck's and Goines's 1960s and 1970s mass-marketed books depict and also sensationalize the economic and emotional consequences of failed recog-nition between black mothers and sons. In trying to represent black mas-culinity's flight from the disappointment and terror of failed recognition, their works endorse a cultural habit of prioritizing relationships among men only to unravel around the illusions they create of the pimp func-tioning as a fully empowered subject who can ably subsume multiple sub-ject positions at once. While the indeterminacy of this figure becomes yet another indication of the instability of blackness as a sign, the pimp feels this instability to be a tremendous and vexing emotional burden. In iden-tifying the various psychological conversations that have informed the pimp's stylized existence, I have stressed the many ways in which these narratives do not indicate a radical, poststructuralist, or entirely postmod-ernist departure from the regime of integration and the chronic wish for black mutuality and recognition. Reading (and viewing) the pimp game as a psychological game teaches us not only that blackness always promises to be redeemed by the discourse of analysis but also that there is ideologi-cal symmetry between overtly intersubjective narratives and overtly anti-intersubjective lore in popular culture—even when the style, content, or audiences for those works differ dramatically and insist otherwise.

# 5

# BILL COSBY AND THE RISE AND FALL OF BLACKNESS AT PLAY

Bill Cosby's current fall from grace is evident in the sharp criticism of his socially conservative views, the disdain over his vociferous attacks on the black poor, and the outrage surrounding the allegations that he drugged and sexually assaulted women throughout his career.[1] Only recently, however, has the wave of skepticism and suspicion about Cosby done anything to dislodge his popular image from the representation of an idealized image of contemporary American fatherhood: Cliff Huxtable of *The Cosby Show* (1984–92).[2] Why was it difficult for so many people to believe that Cosby could be anything less than the ideal father he famously represented on television? Was the image he projected through *The Cosby Show* and his various media enterprises ever stable in the first place? Unlike the popular-press appraisals of his contributions to American popular culture, academic considerations of Cosby have always been much more measured. In this regard, motivated by *The Cosby Show*'s unmatched significance in television history, Sut Jhally, Linda F. Fuller, Janet Staiger, Herman Gray, Michael Real, and other scholars of television and media have contributed insightful close analyses and reception-based research on *The Cosby Show*'s global cultural impact, including the show's complicity in projecting conservative Reagan-era ideologies about class and race.[3] However, when it comes to specifically examining how willful fabrication and strategic self-reinvention have always been a part of Cosby's career, as I argue here, we have been watching—and especially listening to—the *wrong* Bill Cosby.

While the most durable visual image of Cosby is intricately connected to his performance as Cliff Huxtable, we tend to overlook and outright forget Bill Cosby of the 1960s and 1970s—his comedy albums, numerous prime-time television comedy specials, and early television shows. And yet, more so than the Bill Cosby of *The Cosby Show* or the Bill Cosby in our current collective memory, Bill Cosby of the civil rights era crafted and presented an image to mainstream American audiences that was predicated on his relationship to an imagined, fantastical, and phantastical past that reflected his unique engagement with the civil rights era's fusion of racial politics to psychosocial themes. In part to destabilize the centrality of *The Cosby Show* in written accounts of Cosby's long career, in this chapter, I explore the humanizing rhetoric that informed his star persona of the 1960s and 1970s. In the first half of the chapter, I closely consider the recycled themes and autobiographical stories that defined Cosby's early career as a stand-up comic. By situating his deliberate construction of a black working-class boyhood pastoral in the larger context of how American culture has historically represented the inner lives of children, I remind us that Cosby used his routines to speak in parables about a past that he mostly invented. In the second part of the chapter, I exclusively examine Cosby's cartoon *Fat Albert* (1972–85)[4] as his most lasting contribution in this regard. Initially treating play as a redemptive and reparative tool (as something that existed despite the state's failure to recognize black humanity), Cosby's mythic creation of Fat Albert and the Cosby kids challenged popular constructions that imagined the interior life of black children as traumatized and depressive or as subjects whose humanity could be demonstrated through suffering. The cartoon in some ways radically participated in the culture of psychologizing blackness during its early run. Eventually, however, especially as Cosby became more synonymous with America's Dad, *Fat Albert* spiraled into a problematic cautionary tale, and its original focus on play, creativity, and the recognition of unique and indeterminate black youth morphed into a condemnation of those same subjectivities. Although there has been much public rumination in traditional media and over social media about Cosby's now fractured and controversial image, television and media scholarship has yet to rethink Cosby's career in a postscandal social and political climate. The arguments I make here about the intentional fabrication of his image from the very start of his career are intended to broaden our understandings of the star's lasting media contributions.

## Creating an Image: From Race Comic to Storyteller

Long before Bill Cosby became the most famous father in television history, and even before he became known for being a "race neutral," experiential, storytelling comedian, he developed his mass appeal and marketable image by first experimenting with a variety of comedic styles and themes during the earliest years of his career. Initially Cosby's performances in Philadelphia and New York nightclubs featured topical jokes about race relations and cutting commentary about race parody films like I Passed for White (1960). As Cosby recalls, "I was telling racial jokes then. You know, the biting, witty kind about the Negro's role in America. But pretty soon critics began to regard me as a sort of hip Nipsey Russell and a Philadelphia Dick Gregory. Well, I decided then and there that I had to be original if I wanted to fulfill my aspirations of becoming a big man in show business."[5] While Cosby thought about the era's other black performers as direct completion, the television and media historian Bambi Haggins considers the divergent civil rights era field of comedians as reflecting different political orientations. As she argues, "The style and content of [Dick] Gregory, Cosby, [Flip] Wilson, and [Richard] Pryor's stand-up acts (as well as the iterations of their comic personae across mediums) mark different positions on the comedic spectrum. Each comic persona represents a differing depiction of African American identity, which, in turn, is tied to changing notions of blackness during (and after) the civil rights era."[6]

Cosby's competitive awareness of how he differed from and measured up to these other comics prompted him to model the styles of comics who were known for telling stories on the stage. In this vein, Sam Levenson and Mort Sahl—modern Jewish comedians who were recognized for telling personal stories, not jokes—became his inspirational models. As a performance style, autobiographical storytelling allowed such comics to project a newly valued sense of intimacy that could satisfy postwar cultural preferences for popular narratives that communicated emotional accessibility and vulnerability. Humorous, exaggerated, autobiographical stories appealed to audiences who wanted to learn more about the experiences, life lessons, and

interior logic of the comedian on the stage so that they might in turn reciprocally recognize the mundanity of their lives as spectacular and meaningful. In making a calculated shift to this performative mode, Cosby honed his
craft by telling nostalgic stories about himself as a child. This early material,
as Haggins argues, always maintained an "amenable tone," and the routines
"simply did not threaten anyone."[7] It was specifically the "timeless" aspect of
Cosby's representation of childhood in these routines that "also served to
assuage late twentieth-century fears about social change in the dominant
culture, and most certainly, in the entertainment industry."[8]

While there are numerous examples, from Cosby's 1960s and 1970s
stand-up albums to his comedy specials and appearances on variety shows,
that reflect the nonoffensive thematic focus of his material, I want to use as an
illustrative example just one of these efforts—the now-forgotten one-hour
evening special *The Bill Cosby Show*. Airing on March 18, 1968, on NBC, this
Emmy-winning televised special exemplifies the basic framework of Cosby's
early material, and it also indicates some of the less obvious ways in which
his focus on childhood contributed to dominant media fixations on the psychological recognition of black humanity. The special begins with a montage
composed of slow pans and tracking shots of the sights and scenes of Philadelphia: industrial buildings, row houses, apartment buildings, and empty
streets. Over these images, Cosby comments, "I used to live there, and we used
to have a wonderful time." Suddenly, as the montage shifts seamlessly from
a reflection on his past to the action of the present, Cosby appears on-screen
in the pretaped footage of the city. While strolling through his hometown,
he discovers a group of school-age black boys playing games in the streets.
Against a musical backdrop of jaunty jazz, Cosby joins the boys in football and
tag and also in less structured play. "When we were kids, we played poverty
games," he says. "Now you don't have to be poor to play a poverty game. Just
as long as you have a friend who is." After playing "poverty games" with his
newfound friends, Cosby flees the neighborhood streets of North Philly and
runs to and through other areas of the vast, dense city, including some afflu-
ent neighborhoods, the countryside, and a golf course. At one point, he meditates on how he felt growing up, saying, "I never felt like I was hot stuff. . . .
I'm just happy to be here." On-screen Cosby continues to play and jostle with
one young boy who shadows him from the inner city to these other locales as

they move together through the new spaces that stretch beyond the confines of his old neighborhood. Eventually it becomes clear that Cosby and his companion are running together to a television studio, and the pretaped introduction to *The Bill Cosby Show* ends with both "the Cos" and the child running at full speed onto the brightly lit stage as a live studio audience welcomes them both in applause. The rest of the prime-time special features several vignettes about Cosby's life as a child who grew up in the 1930s and 1940s.

At one point, Cosby sits alone onstage and gazes fondly at a picture of himself as a young boy. "I love you, my fellow man," he says to his picture. This expression of love for himself as a child, along with the introduction's celebration of black children at play, is perhaps an odd affective register around which to construct an entire set of stand-up routines. Yet Cosby openly and nostalgically connects the story of his commercial and material successes to the way he lived, played, and felt when he was a poor black boy growing up in North Philly. Besides the familiar appropriation of a rags-to-riches ethos, how else did the thematic superimposition of the past onto the present, of the representation of a childhood characterized by "poverty games," increase Cosby's appeal and marketability during the civil rights era? In the case of *The Bill Cosby Show*, even before he performs a single comedy routine, the realist visual style and self-reflective narration of the opening montage establishes symmetry between the spirited playfulness of the young black boys and Cosby as the adult who can always return to the emotional and physical site of his youth. This particular ideological view of black childhood as exploratory and carefree serves as a flashpoint not only for the TV special but also for how Cosby's earliest performances endeared audiences to him. For instance, by publicly recognizing himself as a child and holding up an actual image of himself as a young black boy on the stage, Cosby could assure different audiences of different things. To middle-class or nonblack audiences who were presumably unfamiliar with "poverty games," Cosby could be the "friend" who introduced them to lessons (such as humility, inventiveness, and determination) that they could learn vicariously through him as he modeled the skill of playing freely, cheaply, and humbly. For black and lower-class audiences, Cosby could personify a resilient, essential self whose self-esteem never wavered despite any disheartening realities of American race relations and the state's continued failure to recognize black humanity. Thus, to multiple and diverse audiences, Cosby's 1960s and 1970s depiction of his child self, his inner "fellow man," could signify a personal readiness—an internal drive—for inclusion in the state. Strategically starting his career with a focus on childhood allowed him to reframe and personalize a story about black exceptionalism and class mobility that argued that blackness could thrive despite any gains and losses in the struggles for black equality.

By the time Cosby's intimate evening specials became commonplace programming across all three major networks, he had already released critically acclaimed albums like *Bill Cosby Is a Very Funny Fellow, Right!* (1963) (which features his much-praised Noah and God skits) and starred in the interracial espionage series *I Spy* (1965–68). The bulk of Cosby's public performances, however, as this special indicates, revolved around his fixation on the emotional truths of his upbringing and around his construction of his mischievous, resilient child within. As I discuss in the next sections, just as Sidney Poitier's characters became overladen with psychological referentially as directors tried to tell moody intersubjective stories about individuals rather than critique systemic bias, so too did Cosby's work absorb psychosocial ideologies as he avoided more direct participation in the era's most salient issues. That is, in order to nonoffensively restage scenes from his childhood while also *not* talking about race, Cosby sublimated his potentially subversive messages about black psychological well-being by playfully code switching and by rambling on about apparent nothingness.

## Performing Childhood: Significations, Parables, and (Over)determinations

After the debut of Cosby's first album, *Bill Cosby Is a Very Funny Fellow, Right!*, and its more general, parabolic meditation on what it feels like to be both ordinary and omniscient as he played both Noah and God interchangeably, his stand-up material began to prioritize almost exclusively stories about his childhood. This thematic reorientation paid off—as all of Cosby's albums about his upbringing became more publicly adored than the first, winning him an unprecedented six consecutive Grammys for Best Comedy Performance for each year between 1965 and 1970. The first of these albums about childhood, aptly named *I Started Out as a Child* (1964), served as a corrective thematic addendum to the beginning of his career. Additional material, including *Why Is There Air?* (1965), *Wonderfulness* (1966), *Revenge* (1967), *When I Was a Kid* (1971), and *Fat Albert* (1973), featured stories about Cosby's kindergarten escapades, drinking ink until his tongue went blue, playing with his navel, having his tonsils taken out, navigating the school playground, creating makeshift go-carts, having mysterious—spectacular—bowel movements at school, and conquering the personal-hygiene horrors of eighth graders. In offering a genealogy that connects economic depravity with playfulness and working-class sensibilities with creativity, these albums centralized Cosby's dramatization of himself as America's ordinary and ideal son. Specifically, his decision to turn to childhood as an alternative to talking openly about race tied his early narratives to a wider cultural dependence on the metadiscourses of psychology and analysis in three key ways.

First, it was a strategic choice for Cosby to design the majority of his stand-up albums around stories about himself as a child because children have long functioned as a loaded and slippery signifier in the popular American imaginary. For example, Mark Twain, whom Cosby adored and read often, wrote in the preface to *The Adventures of Tom Sawyer* that children had the potential to "pleasantly remind adults of what they once were themselves, and of how they felt and thought and talked, and what queer enterprises they sometimes engaged in."[9] Yet cultural theorists like Jacqueline Rose writing about Peter Pan and Lynn Spigel writing about American television history have been particularly skeptical of the "queer enterprises" that adults have assigned to children in popular narratives. Whereas Spigel argues that childhood has served referentially as "a fantasy world where the painful realities and social constraints of adult culture no longer exist," Rose implores us to pay attention to what the adult desires "in the very act of construing the child as the object of its speech."[10] Indeed, since the nineteenth century, depictions of American children, especially boys, have been created by adults to symbolize any number of things—from the simplicity of earlier times to free-spirited exploration and colonialism; from leisure time and the assurance of national prosperity to optimism and social progress. For the adult author, speaker, or performer, representations of childhood have intrinsically functioned as a complicated part of identity that includes "self, family, region, nation, and language."[11]

Cosby's production of comedy albums about his life as a child, then, served as his induction into well-established narrative traditions that conflated individual identity with representations of childhood and nation. Besides his creation of Fat Albert, the most memorable and instructive of all of Cosby's childhood segments are his reflections on sharing a room with his younger brother in a comedy sketch that makes up the entirety of the album *To Russell, My Brother, Whom I Slept With* (1968). At the start of his sixth album, Cosby reminds his audience that his family "lived in the projects" and that he and his brother were "the two Kool Aid lovers." Setting the tone and atmosphere for the skit, he says, "Now the scene is a bedroom, pitch black. There is a small bed with two brothers in it. They're both sleeping in what once was a crib." What ensues is a lengthy re-creation of Cosby and his brother playing tug-of-war with the covers, spitting water on each other, crying, and screaming late into night—all while they are supposed to be sleeping. Whenever their rambunctiousness reaches a crescendo, Cosby's father interjects, "What's going on in there?" In answering this refrain, young Cosby lies repeatedly, telling his father about a man who broke into their bedroom, jumped on the bed, threw water on them, and created all the commotion. About his father's frequent calls for order, Cosby recalls, "We had never seen the belt, but we had heard about it. The belt was nine feet long, eight feet wide. . . . It had hooks on it, and it would rip the meat off your body if it ever hit you." Eventually, at the end of the performance, both boys are punished by being sent to stand in the corner for the rest of the night, and as Cosby mumbles under his breath to his brother, "I don't want you touching me on my side of the floor either," the live audience erupts into peals of laughter.

The Russell skit demonstrates some of the ways Cosby represented his child self's personality as consistent with other popular images of an innocent boyish American mischievousness—best exemplified by characters with which his audiences were bound to be familiar, like Tom Sawyer and Dennis the Menace. With Cosby shifting between his child voice, his father's humorlessness, and the whiney squeals of his younger brother, Cosby's performance in *To Russell* also played with the distinctions between adult and child, father and son, as Cosby sonorously segregated the spirited world of boys from the unimaginative and contained world of men. While Spigel's and Rose's work suggests that the adult/child binary is falsely constructed in wishful narrative accounts of childhood written by adults, Cosby's performances only further confirm this suspicion. As the person who performed all of these subject positions at once, Cosby functioned in these early comedy routines as a friendly intermediary figure who could deftly embody and explore the interior logic of both children and adults and invite his audiences to vicariously do the same. For instance, in the Russell skit, he speaks using hyperbole as his child self who is terrified of his father's belt but who is also willful and noncompliant enough to assert his own agency. At the same time, the story resists full infantilization of his present-day subjectivity, lest he be *too* closely associated with immaturity and disruptiveness, because he also personifies the psyche of that wiser, rationale adult. Thus, as Cosby moves from boy to adult and back again, one of his evident "adult desires" is to be able to switch freely between the stubborn, curious child and the authoritarian adult who wants a child-free evening. This movement between child and adult consciousness is indeed "uncanny," a return of that which has been repressed, as Jacqueline Rose has argued, but the "return" to a constructed childhood also relies on a value-laden and often duplicitous embrace of an equally contrived notion of innocence. Specifically, Rose argues that "*Peter Pan* is a front—a cover not as a concealer but as a vehicle—for what is most unsettling and uncertain about the relationship between adult and child. It shows innocence not as a property of childhood but as a portion of adult desire."[12] In this regard, myths of innocence often masquerade as hypocritical and conservative agendas.[13] Likewise, although Cosby's social conservatism is implied but not celebrated outright in these early routines, his focus on his child self's innocence functioned as a similarly loaded vehicle that could carry with it intended and unintended meaning.

Second, in consolidating his tales around a sanitized image of himself as a poor child, Cosby repurposed an image of a working-class boyhood pastoral that has had enduring cultural significance since the nineteenth century. Often called the "Black Mark Twain" by comedy reviewers, Cosby was fastidious about integrating his material roots into the narrative architecture of how he "started out as a child" who may have been poor but who also had psychic and emotional freedom. By making his tales explicitly about a working-class identity, Cosby fueled a cultural appetite for the middle-class consumption of images of working-class children who are depicted as inspirational. As Karen Sánchez-Eppler claims in her analysis of narratives about street children from the 1850s through the 1870s, "with remarkable consistency it is the working child who is seen to embody play, and hence who teaches the middle class about fun."[14] Although eventually play and recreation became concretized around the privileges of the middle class, these ideals have historically been associated with poor children, who are often fantasized as being unencumbered by the sterility of affluence and unfettered by the pursuit of capitalistic achievements that might compromise their ability to take pleasure in raw, primitivistic play. If, as this work on the representations of poor children suggests, the middle class is viewed in these accounts as "an identity to be grown into" and childhood is interpolated as "a powerful site for such growth,"[15] then the many years that Cosby spent perfecting and performing the scenes from his childhood parallel his offstage "growth" and economic migration from one class to another.

Importantly, Cosby's construction of his childhood as a working-class boyhood pastoral was also built around the ideal of a two-parent household. In his early career stand-up routines, Cosby manufactured the lasting image of a two-parent household that maintained firm, but not overly strict, disciplinary practices that ostensibly permitted him and his brothers to be adventurous enough to explore and develop their own personalities and instincts. In doing so, however, Cosby deliberately obscured the harsher and more "painful realities" of his upbringing, like his father's alcoholism, absenteeism, and domestic abuse of his mother, as Cosby biographers have stressed.[16] Based more on a wishful fiction than fact, Cosby's embellished onstage retellings of his childhood also omitted other details, including his chronic struggles to succeed in school (he failed the tenth grade three times before dropping out), the untimely death of one of his younger brothers, and the family's extremely dire economic circumstances.[17] Cosby did allude to some of these somber truths in skits such as "The Giant," in which he re-creates pantomime games he and his brother played as they tried to avoid his father, who would "booze it up" every Saturday night. In these skits, Cosby jokes dismissively about the stress this created for the rest of the family, recalling that he would clownishly yell during his father's drunkest stampedes, "Dad, breathe so we can breathe!" For the most part, though, there is only the slightest suggestion of any phantastic affective responses in these skits; Cosby privileged the spectacularity of a working-class ethos of urban black survival over literal truth.

Evident here in Cosby's history of elision, in the mismatch between his actual lived experiences and what he represented publicly, are some of the ways in which we might link his commonsense understanding of boyish behavior to his own recuperative desires for an impossible and unattainable vision of childhood. In this vein, Spigel has argued persuasively that childhood has historically "been an unstable category, one that must be regulated and controlled constantly."[18] Not to be taken lightly, or literally, for that matter, narrative accounts of childhood are a site of immense cultural power because representations of children reflect "the difference against which adults define themselves."[19] For Cosby, though, perhaps there was much less distance between the child of his imagination and the adult he wanted audiences to embrace. Based on a series of partial truths, Cosby's comedic representation of his childhood served even more as a signifier for a past that, while never realized as living experience, could be redeemed in his stage performances as corrective fantasies, as emotional restitutions for not having the childhood he might have desired. Similar to how Rose uses Freudian theory to unravel the many layers of cultural repression surrounding the various Peter Pan renditions, we might also surmise that Cosby's compulsive and sentimental focus on his childhood indicated any number of delusions, dissociations, repressions, Oedipal traumas and daddy issues, or preoedipal haunts and mama issues—the possibilities for directly analyzing Cosby are endless. Why have we thought so little about Cosby's *actual* past when it comes to thinking about his lasting imprint on American cultural history? Certainly now, in a post–civil rights context, critics and fans have been more curious about Cosby's past and his personal experiences with trauma. As the writer and performer Aya de Leon discusses in her short reflection for an online feminist media collective on Cosby's current scandals, "What's clear now is Cosby's predatory behavior. But our association of him with the upper middle class character of Cliff Huxtable obliterates Cosby's real-life difficult childhood, which included racial and economic victimization and undoubtedly underlies his sexual violence. . . . When I think about the reality of Bill Cosby's life, I think of R. Kelly and Chris Brown—men who complete a cycle of violence inflicted on them by dishing it out them-selves."[20] While there are certainly many questions worth asking about Cosby's past, in noting here some of the personal as well as professional motivations for constructing idyllic untruths, I am inclined to pay closer attention to the cultural life of the fantasies he projected, particularly as they relate to the wider tendencies to psychologize families, childhood, *and* race. Further, as I will suggest with *Fat Albert*, it is possible that Cosby romanticized his childhood for personal phantastic reasons as well as in order to deliberately avoid pathologizing associations to black childhood.

This brings me to my third and final point about Cosby's early stand-up career: for the comic who would not talk about race, childhood func-tioned even more so as a signifier, parable, and proxy for many things at once, and these performances nonetheless played a role in the era's politics of race. Instead of talking explicitly about race as he performed embellished stories from his childhood, Cosby perfected a rhetorical style of speaking that relied on parables and code switching. For example, in the "T.V. Football" routine recorded on *I Started Out as a Child*, Cosby tells the story of playing football on television while at Temple University and being instructed by his coach not to do anything embarrassing on camera. From this advice, Cosby extrapolates that when he gets hit in "the worst place," his penis, he should cleverly substitute this site of pain for another, and so he grabs his head instead. "And to make it look good," Cosby says, "they bandaged up my head!" Similarly, instead of talking to his audience directly about cow feces, in "Frisbies [*sic*]" on the album *Bill's Best Friend* (1978), he jokes with them about "plastic cow chips you could never take to the beach" that served as the inspiration for the modern flying disc. Other times, like when his "slushball" melts and he cannot best another kid in an epic snowball fight, Cosby spits on him, replacing the biggest snow-ball in the world with saliva. While these particular examples may seem silly and inconsequential, that is partly the point. Even though Cosby code switched and played with trivial topics, he did so within the highly conse-quential framework of representing a particular vision of black childhood innocence. I also mention examples like these to draw our attention to Cosby's general willingness to play with meaning, both in what he said and in his heavy use of sound effects, metaphor, and metonymy.[21] These

different moments illustrate his participation in a patently figurative communication style.

Race "sticks" to these performances not only because Cosby was continually read and reviewed as a *black* comic whether he talked about race or
not but also because his figurative use of language left his routines open
for racially specific interpretation. For instance, when Cosby played both
Noah and God and placed them in a suburban American neighborhood,
he playfully and subtly created a parable for an embodied reframing of
American life that prioritized black masculinity as omniscient and as the
second father of humanity. The fact that Cosby does not call his Noah and
his God "black" does not take away from his stand-up's interpretive similarities to what the cultural historian and literary theorist Henry Louis
Gates Jr. has referred to as the revisionist "double-voiced" nature of the
African American vernacular and cultural production, or a text's ability to
include and consolidate multiple cultural traditions around black cultural
expressiveness.[22] In *The Signifying Monkey*, Gates explains,

> Black texts Signify upon other black texts in the tradition by
> engaging in what [Ralph] Ellison has defined as implicit formal
> critiques of language use, of rhetorical strategy. Literary Signifi-
> cation, then, is similar to parody and pastiche, wherein parody
> corresponds to what I am calling motivated Signification while
> pastiche would correspond roughly to unmotivated Signification.
> By motivation I do not mean to suggest the lack of intention, for
> parody and pastiche imply intention, ranging from severe critique
> to acknowledgment and placement within a literary tradition.
> Pastiche can imply either homage to an antecedent text or futility
> in the face of a seemingly indomitable mode of representation.[23]

In recasting Noah and God as black, Cosby modeled a form of "motivated" and "unmotivated" signification that moved seemingly innocu-
ously between parody and pastiche. Operating in this performative mode
gave his stories the interpretative potential to be experienced and read as
something significant and insignificant at the same time.

The ways in which Cosby's early performances reflected an unambiguously black cultural referentially are less pronounced than his general

use of figurative language but remain nonetheless significant to how he reframed his childhood. For instance, Fat Albert, Cosby's most famous "child" aside from himself, emerged in the stand-up performances from these years as a product of the same practice of seemingly benign shifty signification. For instance, when Cosby first introduced Fat Albert and the Gang in the "Buck, Buck" routine on his *Revenge* album (1967), he switched one intended signification for another and racially coded Fat Albert's voice as well as the implications of his large, black body. As Cosby has since explained, Fat Albert's famous "Hey, Hey, Hey" was inspired by his appreciation of The Temptations, and Cosby intended the character's voice to serve as an important melodic "signal," as a definitive "charge that he's coming."[24] If Fat Albert needed a particularly rhythmic voice in order to reference black musical and performance history as his voice punctuated his grand arrival, then the totality of what he represented was also inseparable from other racial associations. For Cosby, Albert's purpose was to challenge stereotypical associations, or as he notes, "In my time, fat people were stereotyped as clumsy, to laugh at, not particularly intelligent, low self-esteem."[25] In Cosby's imagination, his larger-than-life child character with the rhythm-and-blues voice performed meaningful cultural work because he took "a person like that" and turned "him into someone who is intelligent, compassionate," "wise and humorous," who has "feelings" and who is "a leader."[26] Although Cosby stopped there and did not complete the analogy, his conceptual emphasis on dehumanization and the terms he used to describe fat people (clumsy, unintelligent, low self-esteem) are the words that were much more commonly used as epithets against black people in the cultural milieu during the time when he created the central figure in his defining image of black boyhood.

Throughout Cosby's stand-up career, then, as the parabolic and didactic performer who submerged racial themes by turning them into generic life and cultural lessons, Cosby offered a vision of the 1960s and 1970s in which a black Noah could be a proxy for the humanity of the modern American man; a head could become a stand-in for a penis; poor black boys could remind the country of a newfound investment in play and creativity; gargantuan monsters like Chicken Heart could absorb the confusion and terror of small brothers who feared their drunken father; and a fat boy who sounded like The Temptations could encourage social tolerance and acceptance. While the stage became the place for Cosby to practice his process of chronic self-reinvention, one of the ironic consequences of Cosby's pretelevisual history as a race-neutral comic is that the basic themes he chose to work with—childhood, play, morality, family dynamics—were as steeped in psychological discourses as were the dominant public conversations about blackness and racial bias. That is, if childhood has long functioned as a signifier that is intricately connected to our understanding of self, family, and nation, and if blackness has been animated in the popular imagination in a similar capacity, Cosby's nonliteral treatment of identity and upbringing was equally primed to resonate psychosocially.

## Television and the "Inner Drama" of Childhood

Despite Cosby's penchant for using fabricated personal stories to attract a mass audience, his transition from stand-up comic to television star was far from seamless. In fact, the majority of Cosby's forays into television during the 1960s and 1970s were colossal commercial and critical failures (e.g., *Cos*, *The Bill Cosby Show*, and *The New Bill Cosby Show*). During the civil rights era, only Cosby's animated series *Fat Albert* thrived, precisely because of the ways in which his stand-up material, with its focus on childhood innocence and his playful use of analogy, was perceived to be so well suited for children's programming. In order to more completely understand why adaptations of Cosby's stand-up routines succeeded in the children's market when his efforts failed elsewhere, we have to also explore how and why it had become business as usual for the television industry to represent children and the family analogously, in quasi-psychological terms.

Evident in the postwar culture surrounding notions of an "American childhood," which included everything from the lively public discourses on "proper" parenting styles and the popularization of publications that offered a plethora of "commonsense" advice on child rearing (from the first publication of Dr. Spock's books in 1946 to journals like *Woman Today*, *Good Housekeeping*, and *Progressive Education*) was the steadfast belief that American households (and the country, in general) would rise and fall with the psychological well-being of its children.[27] Since Freud's influence on American culture, it has been taken for granted that parents need psychological experts to help them produce citizens who can protect the country's future. In the same vein, a catch-22 really, children's culture has become inseparable from psychology and developmental discourses, while discussions that are explicitly about analysis often end up as digressions about childhood. Or, as the "Wolf Man" in Freud's famous case once put it, "I believe that psychoanalysis takes you back to childhood, and that you then react more or less like a child."[28] The cultural lore around the child has become one of those sites of meaning that simultaneously requires and fuels a dependence on the psychoanalytic.

If, as Michelle A. Massé has argued, the United States and the field of psychoanalysis have both "narrated much of their stories through the structure of childhood development" to such an extent that it has become difficult for "us to imagine a time when there was not a psychoanalytic child," what is television's role in the collective treatment of the American child as a psychological subject?[29] Television programming from the late 1950s onward, including shows intended for crossover audiences of both adults and children like *Leave It to Beaver* (1957–63) and *The Andy Griffith Show* (1960–68), commercial material created for children like *Dennis the Menace* (1959–68) and *Davey and Goliath* (1960–77), and "educational" fair such as *Mister Rogers' Neighborhood* (1968–2001) and *Sesame Street* (1969–) continued the cultural pattern of representing the American child as a loaded and complex signifier that codified adult desires, fears, and anxieties much more so than the shows reflected anything about the lives of actual children.

In trying to account for these patterns of representation, most of the public discourse about children and the media has focused on either the harmful or beneficial effects of television viewing on children. Much less attention has been given to the ideological implications of the shows themselves. Yet, consistent with the dominant cultural turn toward the psychological, postwar televisual culture has taught us that America's child is introspective, is emotionally complicated, and above all has a rich and fantastical play life that makes good use of weird puppets, imaginary friends, repressed wishes, and the spectacularization of everyday living. While commercial television for children might integrate psychological perspectives into its content by way of allusion, educational programming has always been explicit about directly incorporating developmental psychology to reinforce the very need for such television. If, as the federally funded research conducted by the Children's Television Workshop (CTW) in 1968 has suggested, educational programming for children could facilitate intellectual growth, then so too, they argued, might televisual content help facilitate emotional development and maturity.[30] Unlike commercially developed material, educational programs were justified as supplements to child-rearing responsibilities that were previously ascribed only to parents and schools, or as the media historian Robert W. Morrow notes, shows like the CTW's *Sesame Street* were discussed as the "new bloom on the [television] wasteland."[31]

Another pioneering work in this regard, *Mister Rogers' Neighborhood*, debuted in 1968 on PBS. From its earliest episodes, as one of the most instructive models of educational programming for children, *Mister Rogers' Neighborhood* appropriated the rhetoric of a complex and essential child self as it valorized the developmental conceit that children must be carefully and respectfully taught how to acknowledge and explore a host of complicated feelings, from anger to sadness, from jealousy to regret. As Rogers famously sings in an early episode, "The things inside you—your thoughts and your feelings—are all yours, and you're the one to decide if you want to share them with anybody." Rogers distilled the show's dependence on the rhetoric of analysis most succinctly in 1969 when he appeared before the U.S. Senate Subcommittee on Communications to challenge the massive budget cuts aimed at public broadcasting. As he told the Senate,

> I'm very much concerned, as I know you are, about what's being delivered to our children in this country. And I've worked in the field of child development for six years now, trying to understand the inner needs of children. We deal with such things as—as the inner drama of childhood. We don't have to bop somebody over the head to make drama on the screen. We deal with such things as getting a haircut, or the feelings about brothers and sisters, and

the kind of anger that arises in simple family situations. And we speak to it constructively.[32]

In his remarks, which convinced the committee to fully fund the show and the network, Rogers took care to first identify himself not as an entertainer but as psychological expert. He then made it clear that educational children's programming, in this case the "drama on the screen," must be understood as something that is inseparable from "the inner drama of childhood." After speaking at length about feelings and how the right kind of television for children would ideally facilitate emotional growth and emotional intelligence, Rogers concluded, "And I feel that if we in public television can only make it clear that feelings are mentionable and manageable, we will have done a great service for mental health."[33]

Popular television programming like this helped further cement the vision of American children as complex psychological beings, but the ways in which the psychology of childhood became a dominant concern in postwar society certainly did not extend evenly to all children. While white children functioned as an analogy for America's future, mass-cultural representations of the mental health and well-being of black children became a fixture in the system of national fantasy in similar and dissimilar ways. Unlike the dominant depictions of white children, the mass-cultural representations of black children for the most part underscored trauma as a normative and defining part of their "inner drama." Black children's interiority was, of course, a focal point in the Supreme Court's rationale in *Brown v. Board of Education* (1954). The Court expressed an explicit concern that segregation created "a feeling of inferiority" in the psyche—in the "hearts and minds"—of black children, and Justice Earl Warren wrote at length in the majority opinion about the damaged inner motivations of black children in the Court's order to desegregate American schools.[34]

Aside from the Court's decision, throughout the civil rights era, the intimate logic of imagined young black minds was under constant consideration by sociologists, social psychologists, and clinical psychologists. Black self-esteem was the primary focus of these varying accounts. It is here that we can situate Kenneth and Mamie Clark's work with black children that sought to establish the causal relationship between segregation and black interior health. Beginning in the 1940s, the Clarks conducted social experiments on children with dolls and coloring books, and their research, which was used in the Court's decision, substantiated claims that black children suffered from confidence and self-worth complexes as a result of systemic racism.[35] Beyond the doll studies, Kenneth Clark's other research focused on the extent to which environmental factors like poverty and unequal access to social services compromised the psychological outlook of the black community as a whole.[36] Prior to this research but in a similar vein, social psychological works like Gunnar Myrdal's *An American Dilemma* (1944) and Abram Kardiner and Lionel Ovesey's *The Mark of Oppression* (1951) outlined social and economic oppression as the causes of depleted and seething black psyches.[37] These analyses insisted that the psychological costs of racism were unjustly taxing black people, especially children, since they were thought to be even more psychically vulnerable.

American mass and popular culture during the civil rights era further reinforced these dominant cultural impressions of black youth experiences, particularly in urban environments, as tragically endangered and devoid of playful spontaneity. The civil rights visual cultural archive that depicted black childhood in this way includes a range of works, from *The Quiet One* (1948), a documentary about an emotionally scarred black boy who is in residence at the infamous Wiltwyck School for Boys, to *A Hero Ain't Nothing but a Sandwich* (1978), a film adaptation of a novel about a black boy who becomes a junkie. The cinematic span includes lesser-known contributions like *A Bright Road* (1953), starring Harry Belafonte and Dorothy Dandridge as school workers who are called to action to intervene on behalf of one promising but emotionally neglected black student. Most obviously, these dominant media portrayals of black youth interiority veered toward depressiveness. Less obviously, the innocence, wonder, ability, and esteem of black childhood and important activities governed by fantasy, play, and joy were often defined through a prism of lack, as evinced in the conclusion of Clark's famous doll studies.

Bill Cosby participated in this culture both as a provocateur and as an opportunist. As an entertainer who did not want to talk openly about politics, Cosby did not hesitate to make overt statements about psychology and race. For example, when he hosted the 1968 television documentary *Black History: Lost, Stolen or Strayed*, Cosby provided narration over several long segments that spoke directly to the national tendency to conflate black youth interiority with low self-esteem. Throughout the documentary, psychological experts appeared on-screen to offer analyses of black life. In one crystallizing moment, a psychiatrist examines the drawings of black children. He observes that these images are—disturbingly—missing faces and that these drawings contrast with the drawings of white children. According to the psychiatrist, this represents a fundamentally flawed and lost sense of self. As the critically acclaimed program draws to a close, Cosby appears on camera to meditate on the overt esteem-building activities of preschool-age black children when they are encouraged to recite the black-nationalist affirmation that they are "black and beautiful." Cosby comments, "This is kind of like brainwashing . . . or is it? I mean, can you blame us for overcompensating, I mean, when you take the way black history got lost, stolen, or strayed? When you think about the kids drawing themselves without faces!" Cosby's outrage over black children drawing themselves without faces was not so unlike Kenneth Clark's objection to black children valorizing white dolls. Both responses dismissed the possibility of a black fantasy life that could involve a less obvious, less literal, engagement with the world. Both responses assumed a de facto pathology instead of prioritizing, as Cosby's stand-up did, an active fantasy life that might make productive, creative use of objects like Clark's dolls or the much-maligned faceless drawings.

## Fat Albert and the Politics of Black Recognition

In the context of the rest of Cosby's early career, his remarks in *Black History: Lost, Stolen or Strayed* represented an ideological aberration for the comedian who marketed himself as a purveyor of kid culture and play. Most of Cosby's pre–*Cosby Show* works on childhood, at least on the surface, were more consistent with the way his stand-up routines challenged and refuted the prevailing civil rights and post–civil rights tendency to pathologize black children's interiority. In fact, Cosby's successful adaptation of his stand-up routines about childhood into a televised cartoon became his most sustained engagement with the analytical culture of the times, and it was around the success of *Fat Albert and the Cosby Kids* that Cosby finally cohered his 1970s public image with the same kind of analytical expertise that Fred Rogers claimed on *Mister Rogers' Neighborhood*.

By the time the series premiered on CBS in 1972, the stars of *Fat Albert and the Cosby Kids*—Weird Harold, Dumb Donald, Fat Albert, Rudy, Mushmouth, Bucky, Russell, and Bill—were familiar and recognizable to American audiences as originating from Cosby's stand-up creation of a black working-class boyhood pastoral. During the twelve-year run of the series, it became a popular option for young viewers on Saturday mornings. But *Fat Albert* was atypical for many reasons: it starred animated black children; it was a cartoon, but it also included live-action segments of Cosby commenting on the boys' adventures; it made heavy use of stock and recycled imagery, which gave it a repetitive and predictable visual style.

In marketing the cartoon to networks, Cosby voiced his concern that the typical Saturday-morning lineup of *The Flintstones* (1960–66), *The New Casper Cartoon Show* (1963–69), *The Archie Comedy Hour* (1969–70), *The Hardy Boys* (1969–71), and *Scooby-Doo* (1969–72) did little to reflect the ethnic, racial, and economic diversity of American youth television audiences during the late 1960s and early 1970s. Utilizing the popular reclamatory speech around educational programming as a social service, Cosby claimed that *Sesame Street*, *The Electric Company* (1971–77), and especially *Fat Albert* could influence the beliefs and values of their child viewers. He argued that his cartoon would "establish in the minds of millions of television viewers and educators that black children are not by nature stupid or lazy; they are not hoodlums, they are not junkies. They are you. They are me. . . . Their problems are universal."[38] The animated show began as a remarkable programming initiative because, as Cosby hoped, "for the first time black children [would] have the opportunity to see themselves" in a televised cartoon.[39] The explicit desire to represent a positive, "universal" image of black children in the "minds of millions of television viewers" and to specifically mirror to black children something about their "nature" created a formula for success that could be measured in terms of social (instead of entertainment, artistic, or aesthetic) value. These goals helped *Fat Albert* outlast *The Harlem Globetrotters* (1970–71), *The Jackson*

*5ive* (1971–73), and *The Gary Coleman Show* (1982–83), the handful of other black cartoons with which Cosby's cartoon ran contemporaneously.

And yet *Fat Albert* was an odd mix of design imperatives right from the start. In an attempt to engage explicitly in the general discourse of psychology and child development, the cartoon's film editor, Rick Gehr, explains that Cosby and the cartoon's other creators "were trying very hard to involve a psychological slant to the show that was meant to instruct and move forward the viewer and guide the viewer in some form of instruction that was for betterment."[40] One early reviewer noted this effort, commenting on the way the cartoon represented a kind of therapeutic intervention: "The general thrust of the series does not focus on traditional curricular content but attempts to deal with issues related to values and value judgments, interpersonal relationships and the solutions of problems faced by children."[41] Like Fred Rogers of *Mister Rogers' Neighborhood*, Cosby saw himself as a key—if not the central—interlocutor in ensuring that *Fat Albert* used psychological expertise to prove its educational merit. For example, to demonstrate psychological credibility, the show's creator's employed an advisory board[42] to specifically assess the emotional impact the episodes were likely to make on young viewing audiences. "I wanted an educator or a psychologist," reported Cosby, "to look over these scripts."[43] At his insistence, then, the show's lead psychological consultant, Gordon L. Berry, scrutinized each episode of the series. His comments, along with Cosby's, influenced the final product.[44]

In addition to the inclusion of psychologists on the production team, *Fat Albert*'s episodes articulated complicated psychodynamic perspectives, more so than other children's programs of the time. In the next sections of this chapter, I look more closely at the cartoon's theoretical proximity to theories of play and postmodern psychoanalytic subjectivity as I explore why the cartoon does not maintain the same focus over time. Here, though, it is worth noting that there was a familiar concern about race and recognition that runs through the various iterations and narratives about Cosby and "the kids." By replacing his jokes with autobiographical stories and concentrating on childhood instead of race, Cosby created a personalized interpretation of the national tendency to link blackness and intersubjectivity. In the more than forty years since *Fat Albert*'s debut, Cosby has spoken about his boyhood creation in terms that reflect his investment in discourses that are ultimately about black psychological recognition. For example, when asked in an interview if he saw *Fat Albert* as an "authentic depiction of the world" or an idealization, Cosby answers at length:

> I saw it as a black, who's been rejected as a human being. In the eyes of some—capital letters—PEOPLE, this color causes an insanity in their minds. Their joy is in pulling the legs off, wrapping a rope around the neck of, denying any place, specifically attacking the mind of the brown-skinned person. All over, these crimes, these atrocities, placed on these people of color. I'm specifying where I lived, and who I am, to these people. It is not idealized at all. It is a continuation of the thought that, if what I'm saying happened to me and to my guys, and you are of a different culture, color, race, religion, and the same thing happened to you, where's the difference?[45]

A belief in human commonalities frames the beginning and end of Cosby's answer, but the middle of his remarks references discursively how he intended *Fat Albert* to demonstrate his humanity. While Cosby stresses here that "some people" have refused recognition and "rejected" him "as a human being," he processes that failure of recognition as an attempted attack on "the mind of the brown-skinned person." At stake in his interpretation is the emotional illness (the "insanity") of those who refuse to recognize the racial other as well as the mental health of people of color. *Fat Albert*, as Cosby explains it here, is a product of the failure of recognition. Speaking directly about the show's significance, Cosby argues for understanding the animated series not as wish fulfillment or as a straightforward idealization but instead as a corrective specification of his very essence, of who he was and where he lived.

Yet, just as other American cultural representations of childhood have worked as signifiers and fantasies, so too was Cosby's construction of himself as a child an idealization. As I discussed with his stand-up routines, his construction was idealized because his image of an essential black self necessarily obscured the biographical details of his upbringing. Mostly, though, Cosby constructed an idealized childhood because, in trying to argue a particular point about recognition, his narratives served a purpose other than telling a "true" story. Cosby's modus was to not demand the state's recognition of him as a black man living and performing during the civil rights era; rather, he called on his audiences to recognize his prehistory as a poor black boy who was every bit as relatable as other iconic American children. In placing his child self at the center of multiple narratives and brands throughout the better part of twenty years, Cosby repeatedly compelled mass audiences to "recognize" a cherished part of himself that they had refused to see in others. As I have demonstrated throughout this book in making clearer how closely tied representations of blackness are to psychological methodologies, the social and political climate of the 1960s and 1970s was particularly ripe for Cosby's articulation of a grievance on behalf of the poor black boy from the 1930s and 1940s who did not exist before the state as a psychological subject. As a civil rights era narrative solution that mapped the past onto the present and was predicated on using familiar tropes to establish Cosby's worthiness and readiness for retroactive integration, *Fat Albert* functioned as his barely allegorical response to his memory of "being rejected as a human being."

## *Fat Albert* and the Rise of Blackness at Play

If the demand for recognition served as the inspiration for *Fat Albert*, additional psychological themes further motivated, animated, and over-determined the cartoon's most unlikely of title characters—an obese black boy who lives in the ghetto and plays in a junkyard with his friends, many of whom are caricatures. *Fat Albert and the Cosby Kids* participated in the therapeutic culture of the time by emphasizing something that was rarely, if ever, associated with black children in the mass-cultural archive: the emotionally restorative potential of play. Playing has been widely valorized and thought about as "restorative" because many lay and clinical perspectives concur with the object relations theorist D. W. Winnicott's claim that "on the basis of playing is built the whole of man's experiential existence."[46] This cultural valuation of play rests on the notion that through play an individual can feel omnipotent, as though magically existing everywhere at once and as symbiotically connected to influential entities (such as mothers, other caretakers, idealized figures, powerful institutions). Consistent with the way childhood has been depicted in American mass culture, psychoanalytic theories of play have held that children need play to experiment with productive boundary transgression and destabilization in ways that inform a sense of one's own ability. When playing, the child creatively blends fact and fiction, reality and fantasy, in an "intermediate zone" or "potential space"—an often isolated play environment that permits and even encourages ambiguity, indeterminacy, and the exploration of aspects of identity that seem possible beyond objective reality and lived experience. Most importantly, unobstructed creative play helps the young child bolster self-esteem and experiment with feeling invincible as he or she controls and orchestrates all actions and narrative events within the protected space.

My point here is not to emphasize these theories as fact but instead to clarify how these ideas operate as "commonsense" assumptions about well-being. It has become a cultural truism that play is healthy, play is restorative, and play is something children and adults do to develop and substantiate aspects of their personality. Cosby's stand-up routines and his revisionist, autobiographical reclamation of black childhood took for granted this understanding of children's play as fundamental to mental health. As an example of how play and feelings of omnipotence correlate, the character Fat Albert emerged in the initial episodes of the cartoon as a visualization of black interior omnipotence. Meanwhile, the physical space of the junkyard where the boys played and were creative functioned as their transitional "potential space." The various members of the Junkyard Gang were remastered in this context as indeterminate possibilities of an expansive self (Cosby) who knows little psychic limitation.

In chapter 3, I argued that representations of black female omnipotence are often pathologized around the cultural myth of black maternal preoedipality. In the case of *Fat Albert*, however, dramatizations of omnipotent black male subjectivity emerged within the safer and differently regulated confines of children's programming, where omnipotent children were a norm. From a psychoanalytic perspective, it is not surprising that Cosby remembered his childhood friend Albert as abnormally large or that Fat Albert was drawn in the cartoon as spectacularly obese and as possessing a Herculean might.[47] Apparently, the most accessible way to imagine black omnipotence (a combination of agency and reach, hope and potential) is to do so visually. Hence, the psychic largeness of Fat Albert the character was translated (both in Cosby's onstage simulation of play and in the show's drawing and scripting of it) as girth, as physical largeness and visceral spread. The exaggeration of the character's physical size, aside from signaling psychological expansiveness, also works to remind us that playing is necessarily a *bodily* experience. Just as the physical fact of Fat Albert and his arrival in scenes was often punctuated by that reverberating "Hey, Hey, Hey!" that commands attention, he often seemed to be everywhere in the neighborhood at once because the scripts positioned him as the natural catalyst of conflict resolution, moral encoding, and problem solving. For young Bill and the rest of the Cosby gang, and more importantly for the imagined community of black and nonblack children viewing audiences, the character Fat Albert represented a normative view of individual agency as resourceful, as limitless.

During the early run of the series, Fat Albert's body and personality were complemented by the equally symbolic nature of the Junkyard Gang, who, like Albert, were all proxies for a boundless self. In this regard, one of the gang's main collaborative play activities was making music out of society's discarded objects—pipes, tin cans, mattress springs, broken washer boards—that they found and would imaginatively repurpose. Performing as the Junkyard Band in each episode, the boys sang songs about their recent experiences and lessons learned. The catchy music they created out of trash reinforced the way the cartoon animated the North Philadelphia ghetto as a Winnicottian intermediate zone where magical things can happen. As the boys played within this protected and nonliteral domain, we may also think of each of the characters (who at times seem to be caricatures or stereotypes) more rigorously.

For example, in the third episode of the series, "The Stranger," an outsider to the group, Betty (a young girl who wants to get to know the boys better), provides a contrapuntal analysis of the boys' personalities that is supposed to be effusive flattery. The bit of dialogue draws our attention to the ways in which the stereotyped constructions of who the boys appear to be (both visually and audibly) is actually of a much more complicated, contested nature and demonstrates a type of postmodern self-reconstitution. Accordingly, Betty interprets the stereotypical "cool man," Rudy, "as adventuresome, dashing, darling"; the typical "nerd," Weird Harold, becomes "intellectual, aloof, distinguished"; the "fat kid," Albert, is "mighty, powerful, magnificent, a monument of a man"; the "buck-toothed" Bucky is "that noble brow"; the inarticulate "buffoon," Mushmouth, is read as "rakish, debonair." When examined in isolation, each boy seems a gross stereotype that Betty's generous viewpoint cannot convincingly challenge. When examined together, however, the boys represent an interpretation of postmodern fragmentation in ways that may be transtherapeutic. Further, in these early episodes, many of the gang's activities, such as playing the dozens (which includes ruthlessly deriding each other), help establish important lines of difference in the junkyard, where self-knowledge is generated through a process of "othering" and "unothering." Ridiculing Albert for being fat or Dumb Donald for being dumb or Rudy for having "no class!" keeps the self and others in a comfortable, if productively destructive, tension. In this way, the gang offers weekly lessons in the Hegelian and Winnicottian paradoxes of the "Me/Not-me" processes of self-actualization.

Since Cosby created and voiced many of the characters on the cartoon, also evident in the program's mobilization of stock character types are postmodern and psychoanalytic theories of self-multiplicity, theories that have argued that a single person can contain and maintain an active tension of many competing, inconsistent self-identities. This is a vision of a postmodern indeterminate subjectively, much like the one I explored as a commonplace in pimp culture in chapter 4. The central difference here, however, is that the focus on the boundary-transgressive potential of children at play reconfigures black childhood identity as having some hopeful access to what has been perceived as a developmental rite of passage. In animating Cosby's response to a failure of recognition, *Fat Albert* aimed to open up the assumed-to-be-crushed metaphorical space of black boyhood and to redefine it as psychologically fluid, inquisitive, and creative. Both the cartoon and Cosby's stand-up routines necessarily simulate Fat Albert, Bill, and the Junkyard Gang as both real and unreal, as autobiography and

authentic but also as exaggeration and the stuff of phantastical mytho-
logical proportion.

## Things Fall Apart: *Fat Albert's* Sociological Turn

If the creation of *Fat Albert and the Cosby Kids* became a way for Bill Cosby
to insist that he, as a proxy for black children, developed a healthy subjectivity despite economic hardship, *Fat Albert* remained faithful to this
vision for only a brief while. The arguments I have made about play and
the intersubjective stakes inherent in *Fat Albert's* origins most convincingly apply to the fourteen episodes of the first season and to the first
two episodes of the subsequent season. Strange things began to happen
on the show after that. By 1973, three episodes into the series's second
season, the cartoon's thematic focus on play and its representation of the
junkyard as a psychically liberating space shifted, ever so slightly at first,
and became more pronounced throughout the 1970s and 1980s. By the
time the series was rebranded as *The Adventures of Fat Albert and the Cosby
Kids* in 1984–85 (the eighth and final season), it consistently paired its representation of a black working-class boyhood pastoral with the controlling
metaphor of the urban police state. As the cartoon became more engaged
with social issues, it began to communicate that there are grave consequences for black boys who experiment with multiple instantiations of
the self, for black subjectivities who attempt to play freely in a post–civil
rights America.

As I have argued, *Fat Albert* was already "postmodern" in a psychoanalytic sense because of Cosby's signature representation of blackness
as psychologically variable.[48] As the series progressed, however, many of
the cartoon's structural and thematic conceits changed in an attempt to
dramatize more literally and realistically the Cosby kids' relationship to
their North Philadelphia neighborhood. In trying to tackle topics such as
neighborhood crime, domestic violence, sexually transmitted diseases,
and drug and alcohol addiction, the cartoon departed significantly from
Cosby's stand-up material and forced his original insistence of blackness as creatively indeterminate into a sociological paradigm more concerned with "correct" and "incorrect" behaviors. To make more apparent
the cartoon's sociological turn and its departure from childhood play as

an imagined liberating force for black subjectivities, I conclude this chapter by considering some of the show's structural and thematic changes and the new problems of representation this shift in direction created. I examine closely two additional episodes, "Mister Big Timer" (1973) and "Busted" (1984), that well demonstrate the consequences of *Fat Albert's* departure from analysis and its project of psychological uplift.

## Breaking Up the Band: Structural and Thematic Changes to *Fat Albert*

Although Filmation (the cartoon's animation company) maintained a unique visual style that remained consistent throughout *Fat Albert's* long run, several changes to the show's form corresponded with a pronounced redirection of the cartoon's ideological focus. Most notably, the boys figuratively and literally stopped making music. As the series progressed, the musical interludes featuring the gang singing and playing with their found junkyard objects were mostly cut from the cartoon. The disappearance of these music-video-like segments means that after the first season, it also became rare for the kids to practice or perform on-screen together at all (although the "band" continues to exist in name). An additional, major change to the cartoon in the later seasons is the way *Fat Albert*, typical of many cartoons during the 1980s, got edited into multiple cartoons-within-a-cartoon. There was a direct trade-off, then, between the original representation of the boys as producers and their new roles as passive spectators and consumers. These production decisions limited their self-constituting and exploratory playtime in order to feature other cartoons that did not star the original cast of Cosby's kids.

This formal decision to replace on-screen playtime with passive television spectatorship is not problematic in and of itself. However, *Fat Albert's* two cartoons-within-a-cartoon, *The Brown Hornet* and *Legal Eagle*, replaced the boys' valuable on-screen time in their intermediate zone with a new set of tropes and conventions that heavily destabilized some of the fluidity of meaning and identity that was previously stressed in the main cartoon. Voice-acted by Cosby, the character the Brown Hornet bears a strong physical resemblance to Cosby of the 1970s and 1980s. The character sports a neat Afro, spry physique, and angular chin. He spends lengthy segments fighting the intergalactic, "world" problems of "vicious space hyenas," "destructo-vacs," and gigantic space fruit or "Jupiter juice." On the one hand, *The Brown Hornet* creates a new type of literal black superhero, something that was definitely missing from the annuals of mainstream comic books and cartoons. On the other hand, the Brown Hornet's battles have little to do with what the boys face in the main cartoon. Instead of emphasizing the ways in which the boys are in the process of becoming agents in their own lives while they continue to realize their own "superpowers," *The Brown Hornet* cartoon-within-a-cartoon casts the adult Cosby as the more literal hero—a formal move that redirects that important sense of grandiosity from black youth and maps it onto adult authority figures. Similarly, *Legal Eagle*, the other cartoon-within-a-cartoon that becomes a staple on *Fat Albert*, bizarrely uses "a southern-fried sheriff eagle and his squirrel sidekicks to teach kids the finer points of law."[49] *Legal Eagle*'s sheriff is coded visually (with a long white mane that covers his face) and audibly (voice-acted by the show's producer, Lou Scheimer) as a white authority figure, while his two diminutive sidekicks, Moe and Gabby, are brown squirrels who provide comic relief by being shiftless, idle, and always ineffectual and are coded as nonwhite. In every episode, the two squirrels jeopardize the eagle's shrewd detective work, endangering their southern, rural environment, only to have the more competent legal figure save the day. By introducing these new characters, *Legal Eagle* problematically dramatizes the boys' analogous relationship to the prison industrial complex.

If *Fat Albert*'s narrative integration of *The Brown Hornet* and *Legal Eagle* introduced new audio and visual tropes that associated adults with authority and black youth with a lack of productivity and competence, then *Fat Albert*'s scope also changed thematically in ways that deemphasized the boys' agency and indeterminate psychological makeup. From the mid-1970s forward, the cartoon began to feature prosocial story lines that gave more of the on-screen time to parents and teachers, adult community figures, and law-enforcement officials. There was an overt rationale for this change in direction, or as Gordon L. Berry explained, *Fat Albert*'s focus on contemporary social issues became a way for the production team to deal with "some very heavy topics for Saturday-morning programming."[50] The episodes in this part of the cartoon's production history further compromised the "intermediate zone" of the junkyard by empha-sizing the boys' difficult negotiation of new technologies and their uneasy existence in their local social environment. For instance, "Video Mania" (1984) explores Weird Harold's sudden video-game addiction, while the "Computer Caper" (1985) takes seriously the threat that computer hack-ers pose to the boys' community. Other episodes stress more directly the harmful potential of their neighborhood. In this regard, *Fat Albert* aired didactic "mature-content" episodes like "Soft Core" (1979), which features a story line about venereal disease; "The Gunslinger" (1980), which inves-tigates the rise of gun violence in the inner city; "Double or Nothing," in which the fan-favorite character Rudy develops a compulsive gambling addiction; "Teenage Mom" (1985), which tackled the trials of teen preg-nancy; and "Gang Wars" (1985), which included a sequence in which a young Latino boy dies in a gang shootout.

Bizarrely, *Fat Albert*'s thematic refocus was meant as a preemptive warning to its viewers. The show's producers knew that their young audi-ence might not have had any personal experience with social issues like teen pregnancy or gang violence, but, as Berry explained, the show's cre-ative team wanted "young people to reach for ideas and to try to under-stand things that may not be what they were engaged in at the present time."[51] In this regard, the show's ideological views became regressive by depicting the "inner drama" of black childhood as impinged by the imag-ined dramas of the streets. Despite Cosby's early career insistence to the contrary, these decisions locked the show into old cultural paradigms about black interiority.

## The Costs of Recognition: Lost in Space and Doing Time in *Fat Albert*

"Mister Big Timer" (1973) and "The Busted" (1984) crystallize some of the ways in which the cartoon's engagement with the protocols of recogni-tion and analysis proved unsustainable over time. Both episodes also sug-gest the way the symbolic nature of Fat Albert's body changed to match the boys' new, much more precarious relationship to the post–civil rights social world outside the junkyard.

In "Mister Big Timer," the episode that marks the series's most pro-nounced thematic turning point, the police force Fat Albert to help them arrest Muggles, his friend and the boys' favorite community "big spender." As Fat Albert unwittingly delivers a "secret package" for Muggles, the police take him into custody, interrogate him, and coerce him into entrapping his friend. In an interrogation scene more suitable for a prime-time drama than a Saturday-morning cartoon, the police inform Albert that he has been working as a drug mule carrying "hard narcotics" and that his friend Muggles is a "drug pusher." Until this moment in the series, the Junkyard Gang and Fat Albert mostly solved problems, both big and small, on their own. They handled conflicts either through creative play and the modeling of compassionate intuition or through Albert's signified omnipotence and fantastic might. In previous episodes, the gang never once relied on law-enforcement officials to restore a sense of order to their metaphorically dangerous play space. The plot of "Mister Big Timer," however, confuses the disruptive potential of play with a more literal relationship to corporal danger as it codes the environment (as opposed to the boys' subjectivities) as indeterminate and as a potentially overwhelming external agent in the boys' lives.

In this episode, the changing status of Albert's body is intricately tied to an object he paradoxically and compulsively cherishes: a golden compass. Just before he interacts with the police and Muggles, Albert finds the object in the junkyard and decides that it is a "genuine compass off an old Spanish gallon." While the rest of the gang cannot understand Fat Albert's interest in the relic, Albert is fixated on it. He rhymes about it, singing, "You can't get lost with a compass" and "Hey, Hey, Hey, I'm on my way." He constantly checks the compass while traveling through the familiar landscapes of the junkyard and his neighborhood; he even puts it to utilitarian use to help the boys set up an accurate baseball diamond. The compass gives him a concrete way to pinpoint his exact location, or as he explains to his friends, "if you know where north is, you know where you're at." The extended scenes of Albert and his compass (he has it in nearly every scene of the episode) convey an inexplicable new desire for him to "conquer" feelings of dislocation and dissociation.

Until this point in the series, none of Cosby's proxies had ever expressed any anxiety about their literal or metaphorical position in the world. Yet, in toying with the analogy of Fat Albert finding the "moral compass" that propels him to help entrap a drug dealer, the series also inadvertently emphasizes that which is lost in the show's thematic reorientation. For Albert, part of what is lost as he gains a sense of moral direction is dominion over his body once he is duped into working as a drug mule and then forced into becoming a police informant. After laboring his body in these unexpected ways, Albert feels ambivalent about the praise and attention he receives from the community. The episode ends rather depressively after Albert expresses a profound sense of guilt and uncertainty about the role he played in sending Muggles to prison. As a rebuttal to Albert's anxieties and reluctant heroism, Bill Cosby speaks the final words of the main story: "Dope pushers hurt a lot of people. Fat Albert and the gang think we all ought to be concerned about this drug problem." Cosby's comments about "this drug problem" that "we all ought to be concerned about" not only undermine his titular character's expression of guilt and confusion but also make clear the show's departure from his earlier celebration of a working-class boyhood pastoral that operated in a physically and psychically safe space.

Theoretically, there are some additional ways to think about why blackness at play began to fall, falter, and fail in a show that had been so committed to upholding it. For starters, playing (and its relationship to identity) often becomes increasingly associated with danger. This is because there is an inherently fine line between play and fear, safe exploration and terrifying discovery, because play "is always liable to become frightening" and "games and their organization" are only "part of an attempt to forestall the frightening aspect of playing."[52] That is, the kind of self-experimentation that children activate in play spaces has been thought about as potentially liberating mental and emotional work that children (and onlookers) will likely feel the need to control at some point. Mikhail Bakhtin's work on carnival emphasizes similarly that carnivalesque subversion is eventually met with outside attempts to contain, appropriate, and police it.[53] As such, when *Fat Albert* replaced the dream-like depictions of the boys' nonliteral, experimental activities (like making music out of junk) with didactic cartoons-within-a-cartoon and story lines about police raids, drug mules, "dope pushers," and venereal disease, the show began to reveal a similar discomfort with black bodies—even animated ones—at play.

The stakes in this regard only increased over time. In a surprising move for children's programming, *Fat Albert*'s "Busted" episode depicts visually the boys' move from subjective and bodily exploration to prison as Fat Albert and his friends are arrested, threatened with prison rape, and terrorized to the point of tears. Before the episode even begins, Cosby makes an unprecedented appearance on camera at the start of the show to warn children that in order to present this episode as "honestly" and "effectively" as possible, the creative team has "used some strong language in today's show." He continues, "While it's language you've probably heard before, it's not the type of language you've heard on the *Fat Albert* show, and it's not the kind of language I'd want you to use." The episode's language and dialogue are not the only aspects of its cautionary tale that are cause for alarm, however, since the basic story of the episode offers a justification for placing Albert and his friends into the city's "Scared Straight" program for at-risk youth. In "Busted," the boys once again interact with the police—this time because they were unknowingly riding in a stolen car on their way to a community swimming pool on a scorching summer day. As the police cruiser trails Fat Albert and his friends in the stolen vehicle, the episode's animators use shadowy silhouettes of the boys (instead of fully drawn character modules) to show them riding in the car from a distance. Represented here as lawbreakers, the boys look depersonified and dehumanized, depicted and framed in this context as one nondescript mass of black suspects who are predictably engaged with the penal system. Although the arresting officers are certain that Fat Albert, Bill, Russell, Weird Harold, and the rest of the gang are innocent, they decide that the boys need to be preemptively "scared straight" out of their naiveté.

In this context, the creative decision to scare the boys straight is indistinguishable from a societal discomfort with and desire to control black youthful indeterminacy. Faithful to the "Scared Straight" formula, this episode depicts a life behind bars as absolutely terrifying. Upon the boys' arrival at the "penitentiary," they reluctantly walk down a long corridor that is framed by inmates reaching for them and yelling various obscenities. The gang of prisoners taunt Fat Albert and his friends, threatening the children with both psychological damage and bodily harm, or as one inmate puts it, "There are men in here that are crazy, men who will kill you and not even know they did it. People die in here!" The inmates' frenetic speeches are also full of sexual innuendo and puns. For example, to Russell, the smallest Cosby kid, one inmate says, stroking and groping his bars, "Hey, little boy, you want a candy bar? Come in and get it." Mostly, though, the prisoners' pedophiliac gazes are concentrated on Albert's body, and each inmate comments directly on his size. To Fat Albert, the men say,

> Prisoner 1: Oh, you smell so good. Come closer. Let me sniff you.
>
> Prisoner 2: I want the big one. Give me the big one!
>
> Prisoner 3: We want the big one!
>
> Prisoner 2: He'll stop the drafts all winter, and in the summer, he can give me shade!

Depersonified animation, *Fat Albert*

After hearing these catcalls, Fat Albert, who rarely cries during the arc of the entire series, sheds large, silent tears and jumps trembling into Dumb Donald's arms. The implications of these words and Albert's actions are minimized, however, by the cartoon's laugh track, which plays as Fat Albert's resolve dissipates before the bigger and stronger men. The visual confirmation of Donald being able to carry Fat Albert when Albert's body has represented the boys' collective omnipotence and uncontainable expressiveness underscores how much Albert ceased to perform as that type of signifier as the series progressed.

The scene's most troubling subtext in this regard is conveyed equally through dialogue and visual cues. In one shot, Fat Albert and the gang are standing clustered in between a row of inmates who are behind bars on either side of them. All of the prisoners in the shot are black men. The prisoner who has been functioning as the boys' tour guide of "the life" takes this moment to give Fat Albert and the gang their sternest warning about what will happen to them should they find themselves on the other side of those bars: "You don't have any choice in here. When you're out in the yard or in the showers, you don't have any rights or any protection. If someone tougher tells you to do something, you have to do it no matter what it is." He emphasizes, eyes widening, "No matter what it is, you have to do it!" On cue, another inmate begs the officer to put one of Cosby's boys in his cell with him "just for a little while."

That these predatory jeers and direct references to prison rape would become the narrative response to the boys' departure from where they belonged (the junkyard and their neighborhood) conveys a palpable desire to violently check the relationship between indeterminate black subjectivities and social boundary transgression. If mischievous boys in television history like Dennis the Menace have been embraced as "the quintessential bad boy," where "misbehavior and disrespect for adult authority were often championed as a sign of unbridled curiosity, a natural and normal part of growing up in the free world," by this moment, the same cannot be said for black youth in narrative culture.[54] While the series initially began by humanizing—recognizing—the boys as complex psychological subjects in the post–civil rights "free world," the show's pairing of black youth with the prison industrial complex threatened to tear that all apart and, by

The Cosby kids behind bars, *Fat Albert*

Fat Albert's indeterminacy is "scared straight," *Fat Albert*

analogy, "rape" any complex subjectivity right out of them. Unlike Dennis
the Menace or Opie on *The Andy Griffith Show*, Cosby's kids are eventually
contained as subjects and as signifiers whenever they challenge the rules

Policing black masculinity of all ages, *Fat Albert*

of spatial, racial, and social logic—depicting once again the project of recognition as an untenable one.

If things eventually fell apart with *Fat Albert*'s focus on the interior
and relational dynamics of black boyhood, what can we say about Cosby's
role in all of these consequential changes? Like all television series, *Fat
Albert* was a result of a highly collaborative process that was influenced by
the educational board of psychological experts, producers, writers, the animation team, additional voice actors, and many others. With all of these
other creative agents contributing different aspects of the show's production throughout its long run, there is some indication that as Cosby's television career took off on a broader scale, he did indeed spend less time
overall on the set of *Fat Albert*.[55] Importantly, though, Cosby affirmatively
adapted to the show's changes by playing the new characters and deliv-
ering more and more didactic performances in his live-action segments.
From Cosby's perspective, the shift from an indeterminate representation
of black boyhood to one that focuses on psychically inhibiting environmental forces would not have to be perceived as an ideological departure
from his earlier interests or as a terribly inconsistent representation of
himself. It is quite possible that once he introduced the country to these

characters, gave some life to their spirited playfulness, and insisted on the existence of a working-class innocence and freedom, his attention naturally turned to the forces and social factors he saw as threatening that identity and inspiring self-fashioning. After all, most of the show's socially conservative changes in content and thematic focus are quite consistent with Cosby's personal beliefs, as the latter part of his career as a spokesperson for a conservative black social agenda indicates. As the star and name behind the brand, it is clear that Cosby retained veto power over the series, and given his widespread reputation for having a totalitarian presence on the sets of his other shows, it is unlikely that he would have endorsed any changes on *Fat Albert* that offended his sensibilities. As such, I think of his involvement during this phase of the series as a complicit form of creative agency.

## Conclusion: Pound Cakes and Tough Love as Psychological Nationalism

In the 1960s and 1970s, Cosby participated in (and capitalized on) well-established public discourses on civil rights healing and the traumas of racism by ultimately circumventing direct commentary about race. Without apology, his stage performances and televisual projects emphasized the restorative potential of play and fantasy, indeterminacy and creativity, as central not only to his personal story but also to his ambitious wish to depathologize the image of the interior and affective life of growing up black and poor in America. In this regard, Cosby's *Fat Albert* began as a personalized response to the chronic failure of recognition by insisting on the rich humanity of black youth only to become increasingly more of a socially conservative call for greater black accountability and behavioral reform.

By the series's end, *Fat Albert*'s thematic and ideological changes were consistent with some of the same ideas that have informed the rest of Cosby's career—especially his post–*Cosby Show* public appearances and speeches. If Cosby chronically reinvented and popularized stories about his childhood as the foundation for his demand for multiple levels of personal and public recognition, once mainstream audiences affirmed his psychological portrait of an essential self, he began to produce new autobiographical content like *Bill Cosby: Himself* (1982), *Fatherhood* (1986), and *Love and Marriage* (1989) that confirmed for those audiences his successful emotional and financial passage from his (and the country's) past to an updated realization of the American Dream. Most notably, Cosby created, through his success story from the 1980s onward, new narratives that outlined the relationship between his working-class boyhood pastoral and his successful maturation into an equally idealized American father. This more common perception of Cosby, his "maturation" into a fully participating national subject, though, is predicated on the metaphors of recognition that defined the part of his career that we have rarely examined.

I say we have been watching—and especially listening to—the wrong Bill Cosby because the image of Cosby from the 1960s and 1970s is vastly more interesting, contradictory, and psychologically complex than the scholarship that focuses on his *Cosby Show* or post–*Cosby Show* public image can reflect. But listen and respond is precisely what an onslaught of television pundits, former fans, black intellectuals, politicians, journalists, sociologists, and of course psychologists did when an aging and ornery Cosby spoke frankly before a live audience at the NAACP's 2004 commemoration of the fiftieth anniversary of *Brown v. Board of Education*. In the speech, Cosby identifies senseless crime, abject consumerism, and an epidemic of bad parenting as defining characteristics of black working-class and poor communities. Cosby makes explicit the connection between the *Brown* ruling and what he characterizes as a tragically unappreciative lower class, saying, "Well, *Brown v. Board of Education*, where are we today? It's there. They paved the way. What did we do with it? The white man, he's laughing, got to be laughing. Fifty percent drop out, rest of them in prison."[56] The speech immediately went viral and has since been referred to as the "Pound Cake Speech" because of a moment when Cosby complains that crime in black communities is often defined by nonsensical behavior—like stealing pound cakes or Coca-Cola. Perhaps predictably during such moments, Cosby always nostalgically references his boyhood as a counterexemplary lesson. He reminisces, "I wanted a piece of pound cake just as bad as anybody else. And I looked at it, and I had no money. And something called parenting said, 'If you get caught with it, you're going to embarrass your mother.' Not 'You're going to get your butt kicked.' No. 'You're going to embarrass your family.'"[57]

The Pound Cake Speech and Cosby's numerous subsequent public addendums to it (including television talk-show interviews, countless graduation keynote addresses, and the book *Come On, People: On the Path from Victims to Victors*) all reveal Cosby's disappointment that the black poor have apparently failed to learn the most important psychological lessons of the civil rights era. Cosby's speeches and call for a "tough love" form of activism within black communities take for granted that the legal victories of the civil rights era fully redressed the conditions that produce the chronic failure of recognition, and so he directs his ire at what he calls emotionally "sick black people" who have not taken enough personal responsibility to make good on the promises and social agendas of the era. Of course, Cosby's social conservatism in this regard echoes a strain of black nationalism that has had significant historical precedent in African American culture, as Booker T. Washington, Marcus Garvey, and Malcolm X, among others, have all made use of the rhetoric of personal accountability.[58] But as a part of the generation that that came of age during the era, Cosby, with his personal-accountability tour of Black America, also expresses a uniquely problematic commonsense psychology that diagnoses failure not in civic processes but instead in the black poor's inability to interpolate and introject what he continues to talk about as an essential self.

Just as John H. Bracey Jr. has written about the many different types of black nationalism, including cultural nationalism, religious nationalism, economic nationalism, and revolutionary nationalism,[59] I posit that Cosby's contemporary speeches and earlier representations of childhood are related in that they both express his vision of a black *psychological* nationalism. In continuing to draw on the language of analysis that was so readily available in 1960s discourses on race, Cosby's recent speeches advance the belief that post–civil rights black communities need emotional, behavioral, and psychological transformations to once and for all combat and transcend systemic bias and oppression. His psychological nationalism hinges on the idea that confidence- and esteem-building activities are best facilitated within black communities. For instance, in the Pound Cake Speech, he emphasizes the need for better cultural mirroring, saying, "Kenneth [Clark] said it straight. He said you have to strengthen yourselves. . . . And we've got to have that black doll."[60] In other public speeches and interviews, Cosby has continued to talk about a need to shore up and support internal fortitude, or as he tells his audiences, "We didn't pay attention to the dropout rate. We didn't pay attention to the fathers, to the self-esteem of our boys."[61] During this phase of his career, he has preached openly about his belief in psychological transformation as he offers unsolicited advice and shares his "thoughts on raising black children in the United States," encourages black people to remember that "we all start out as children," and advises black communities how to "face up to mental health issues."[62] Cosby is most explicit about his vision of a black psychological nationalism when he and Poussaint write in *Come On, People*, "People in the village work best to change their communities when they are educated, healthy, and mentally strong. We can change things we have control over if we accept personal responsibility and embrace self-help."[63]

While Cosby's comments are about the black poor and younger African Americans—especially men—his most receptive audience has been the men and women of his generation who witnessed firsthand the struggles for recognition during the civil rights era. Ta-Nehisi Coates persuasively describes this audience as "culturally conservative black Americans who are convinced that integration, and to some extent the entire liberal dream, robbed them of their natural defenses."[64] To this audience, Cosby's recent outspokenness about race advocates a call to action that can take place irrespective of the state or interpersonal and intersubjective recognition of black humanity. As Cosby clarifies, "I'm tired of losing to white people. When I say I don't care about white people, I mean let them say what they want to say. What can they say to me that's worse than what their grandfather said?"[65] In this vein, recognition functions as an unnecessary ambition that Cosby and his most ardent defenders view as now irrelevant to black progress and emotional health. The metadiscourse of analysis—particularly as it pertains to children—is revered here as something that can undermine white privilege but only when properly utilized by black people en route to becoming their best selves. "We are not a pitiful race of people," he tells his audiences. "We are a bright race, who can move with the best."[66]

Of course, Cosby's psychological nationalism is not completely independent of the responsiveness of other races, since he often speaks about white Americans "laughing" at the black poor's struggle to progress materially. Perhaps predictably, not only does Cosby's instructional evocation of his boyhood pastoral preach an idealized vision of a past that never was to contemporary black audiences, but as *Fat Albert*'s rise and fall of play demonstrates, the culture at large rarely tolerates black subjectivity rendered as vibrant, emotionally solvent, psychically indeterminate (in a good way), or riddled with contradiction. Just as Fat Albert and the gang end up behind bars, so too does the marriage between psychological perspective as a "treatment" for social or systemic issues tend to sway between hope and dread, possibility and doom. Additionally, what Cosby's psychosocial nationalist rhetoric most obviously produces is its own kind of misrecognition, as he reproduces the greater American cultural habit of relying on the discourses of analysis to lobby for measurable social change. The cultural tendency to map perceived wins and losses in the battle for recognition onto other aspirations (like economic achievement or human rights) is partly what has made the dependence on such discourses throughout American history specious and so often scorned.

Ultimately, a consideration of the more complete span of Cosby's career exposes some of the limitations in our reliance on psychology as anything that can work beyond the realm of individual, interpersonal relatedness. Like Sidney Poitier's conviction that psychoanalysis could make him a better man, Cosby's engagement with the protocols of analysis should always be thought about as a personal project that has been unevenly extrapolated outward. Even in his self-help crusade, his community-focused psychological nationalism that seems to challenge the politics of recognition only returns to him his singular obsession: the perfect childhood and chronic rediscovery of his ideal self. In telling homegrown stories instead of jokes in order to bring his "audience along" in the contemporary moment, Cosby has used his public visibility to project and revive the cultural myths he imagines black children need to hear today.[67] In answering a series of his own rhetorical questions about his current role in American popular culture, Cosby asks, referring to himself, "'Why is he doing this? Why right now?' You could probably say, 'He's having a resurgence of his childhood.' What do I need if I am a child today? I need people to guide me. I need the possibility of change. I need people to stop saying I can't pull myself up by my own bootstraps. They say that's a myth. But these other people have their mythical stories—why can't we have our own?"[68]

# 6

# "FIX MY LIFE!"

## Post–Civil Rights and the
## Problem of Recognition

The politics of recognition has functioned in popular and mass culture consistently since the civil rights era as inseparable from a cultural logic that psychologizes racial identity and emphasizes the democratic ideal of intersubjectivity. Instead of talking about representations of blackness in quasi-psychological terms, as we so often do, I have engaged psychoanalytic discourses directly in this project in order to better clarify how psychology works as the ideological glue that holds the politics of representation (increased black visibility in mass culture) and the politics of recognition (knowing the self/other as real) together.

The one thing that "hardcore" psychoanalytical theories have established across disparate clinical fields is that the process of recognizing equal psychological subjects who occupy the same relational space is a difficult, if not impossible, ambition to maintain. Leading object relations theorists—who all valued the project of intersubjectivity—have nonetheless established repeatedly that recognition is rare and that other emotional needs, fantasies, desires, and nonsensical, inarticulable, impulses and significations will always threaten and impede, hijack, and displace even successful moments of recognition. In these concluding reflections on race, popular culture, and the problems of representing recognition, I explore just a few ways in which the psychological continues to "stick" to blackness in the post–civil rights era.

## The Civil Rights Era as an Enduring Social Drama

I argued in chapter 2 that Sidney Poitier's career dramatized the pursuit of black recognition as a component of American exceptionalism that always led back to the metaproject of bolstering a dominant national self and national image. There have certainly been black actors and individual performers since Poitier who have functioned similarly (Michael Clarke Duncan's performance in *The Green Mile* [1999] and contemporary interracial buddy films, for example), but Barack Obama's popularity during the presidential races of 2008 and 2012 serves as the most significant instance of how the intersubjective view of race continues to function as an ideological extension of the doctrine of American exceptionalism in the post–civil rights era. Journalists and other politicians repeatedly referenced Poitier's movies when they talked about Obama. Some writers even argued that Poitier's image of dignified and humanized blackness "paved" the way for Obama, while others were more explicit about the therapeutic nature of an Obama-Poitier comparison. For example, in 2007, the *Los Angeles Times* ran an article titled "Obama the 'Magic Negro.'" Although it did not explicitly use the word "transference" as I did when I discussed Poitier's star persona, the article compared Obama's popularity to Poitier's characters and concluded that what was most attractive about then-senator Obama was his potential for "curative black benevolence" because "as with all Magic Negroes, the less real he seems, the more desirable he becomes. If he were real, white America couldn't project all its fantasies on him."[1] The "curative" is the therapeutic, of course, and as the comment suggested, black masculinity identified as such stresses the interpersonal benefit of maintaining a proximity to black exceptionality. But the comment also accurately conveyed the suspicion that fantasies of blackness (which preclude recognition) are ultimately more serviceable and democratically productive than "the real."

Once Obama became the United States' first African American president, other comparisons of Obama to Poitier surfaced as attempts to document the changes in social climate between the civil rights era and the time of his presidency. In this vein, in 2010, the mayor of Bridgeport, Connecticut, Bill Finch, introduced President Obama as his friend and then shouted, before Obama took the stage, "Guess who's coming to dinner?!" The Poitier reference in this case emphasized the personal connection to the racial other as something worth celebrating and also as something that could be directly connected to the civil rights era.

The affect of Poitier's characters, their compelling mix of emotional hotness and coolness, has so easily been mapped onto Obama's image precisely because the focus on emotionality and interiority continues to be a way to make a personal connection to an exemplary other seem both real and attainable. In this regard, Bill Clinton used pseudotherapeutic terms to introduce Obama at the 2012 Democratic National Convention. Clinton said, "I want to nominate a man who's cool on the outside but burns for America on the inside."[2] As a black man who seemed generally reserved and affectly cool in his outward presentation, Obama, like Poitier's characters in their moments of measured heated survival, could also, according to Clinton, "burn"—with passion, with indignation, with potential—or signify in just the right way. Obama, as Clinton continued, is "a man who believes we can build a new American Dream economy."[3] Newspapers and online blogs ran Clinton's quotes about blackness burning, paraphrasing the quotes into headlines, as in "Cool Obama Burns for America."[4]

Clinton's speech reframed Obama's cooler emotional register (which the national media construed as a fault in the debates with Mitt Romney, calling Obama "uninspired" and "flat") as cover for a deeper American ambition.[5] Meanwhile, in other social contexts, Obama's "Poitier-like" qualities were used to undermine his racial authenticity and emphasize the failure of recognition that such a comparison surely indicates. For example, the founder of BET, Robert L. Johnson, unfavorably compared Obama to the Hollywood film star, complaining, "That kind of campaign behavior does not resonate with me, for a guy who says, 'I want to be a reasonable, likable, Sidney Poitier 'Guess Who's Coming to Dinner.' And I'm thinking, I'm thinking to myself, this ain't a movie, Sidney. This is real life."[6] These overt and more subtle connections between the career of Hollywood's most successful black film star and the United States' first black president are uncanny and unsettling but not surprising because, as I have argued, in addition to celebrating the moments of the recognition of black humanity that Poitier's characters embodied, his films also always contained as much doubt and ambivalence about the psychological project of modeling racial transference and about the overall impact that "magical Negroes" or black surviving objects could have on more skeptical and reluctant subjects/citizens.

One reason the psychological culture around blackness persists as a feature of the politics of recognition is not only because the civil rights movement is constantly referenced in contemporary political culture but also because retrospective stories about the civil rights era continue to dominate mainstream popular culture. These nostalgic and endearing revisitations of the affective culture of the civil rights era reactivate and resolidify the previously established American cultural attachment to the intersubjective view of race. We need not look far to notice the unmistakable re-creation of the era's thematic emphasis on destruction, survival, and recognition that crop up in the contemporary films and television movies about the civil rights era that have been produced every few years, if not every year since—including *Driving Miss Daisy* (1989) starring Morgan Freeman, *The Long Walk Home* (1990) starring Whoopi Goldberg, *Remember the Titans* (2000) starring Denzel Washington, *The Rosa Parks Story* (2002) starring Angela Bassett, *Talk to Me* (2007) starring Don Cheadle, *The Help* (2011) starring Octavia Spencer and Viola Davis, *42* (2013) starring Chadwick Boeseman, and *The Butler* (2013) starring Oprah Winfrey and Forest Whitaker. As the retrospective narratives about civil rights continue to appear, they perpetuate and reproduce the two most consistent narrative conceits of recognition: personal transformation as a result of successful intersubjective rituals between whites and blacks, and humanized black resiliency proved through scenes of immense suffering and failed recognition, usually within a black social context. Incidentally, neo-slave narratives like *Django Unchained* (2012) and *12 Years a Slave* (2013), though not about the outright celebration of intersubjective achievement, operate in a similar affective mode that dramatizes black subjectivity's proximity to suffering and destruction in a way that continually lauds black psychic survival.

Just as we have seen with the mainstream culture from the 1950s, 1960s, and 1970s, stories about recognition in the post–civil rights era quickly become accounts that detail the (white) personal benefits of recognizing black humanity; or the works get caught in a downward spiral of spectacularizing violence as they attempt to document the consequences of recognition failure. As I demonstrated in chapters 3 and 4, it is the dramatization of failed recognition within black families that fuels representations of baaaddd, destructive black mothers, on the one hand, and justifies the dehumanization of black women in general, on the other hand. As evident in works as disparate as Tyler Perry's popular *Madea* films and the "binge-worthy" Netflix original television series *Orange Is the New Black* (2013–), the psychodynamically configured trope of the baaaddd black mama who perpetuates recognition failure as she tries to literally destroy her children has had immense cultural staying power.

One of the more recent and critically acclaimed black independent films, *Pariah* (2011), uses a baaaddd mama to create the audience's empathetic identification with a black queer character whose fight for social recognition is represented as starting in the home. In *Pariah*, Dee, like the daughters in *Imitation of Life* (1959) and *Black Girl* (1972), strives for autonomy and the recognition of her independent desire. While the original short film did not utilize the construction of a baaaddd black mother as it told the story of Dee's self-discovery and evolving queer identity, in the feature film, Dee's mother, Audrey, becomes threatened and disgusted by her daughter's sexuality. Audrey violently attacks Dee at the family drama's climax, and the film ends with a familiar dramatization of black mothers and daughters locked in conflict as subjective strangers. As *Pariah* made the transition from short film to feature, it needed the more socially recognizable trope and psychological blueprint of the baaaddd black mother to help dramatize and allegorize its queer black subject's fight for recognition and worthiness of inclusion. Like other contemporary black family dramas, *Pariah* uses family dysfunctionality and the spectacle of failed recognition as a training ground that can demonstrate the newly formed black subject's resiliency and preparation for inclusion and recognition outside the home. Like *Antwone Fisher*, contemporary films continue to advance the cultural logic that the exceptional few who are imagined to be able to survive the chronic recognition failure within black communities will be rewarded with recognition from the state (educational institutions, mentors, the armed forces) as an intervening third agent. Yet, as I noted in my analysis of the earlier black family dramas, often these works contain their own critique as they depressively indicate that the chronic failure of recognition within the black family may be only a dress rehearsal for what is to come.

## #TheStruggleIsReal or #FergusonSyllabus

If contemporary black family dramas about dysfunctionality, neo-slave narratives, and civil rights retrospectives continue to give us on-demand access to an affect-laden archive of trauma and pain and to reenactments of the never-ending quest for recognition and survival, does any of this—essentially watching blackness survive the proverbial fire time and time again—make black people seem more or less human in the end? Does a popular canon that is built around representations of blackness as perpetually enduring an inordinate amount of destruction only to be destroyed and rise again create a psychological portrait of black humanity that is actually *nonnormative*, especially since that representational canon stresses exceptionality and superhuman abilities over real human limitations?

Even though I have tried in this book to identify and destabilize our dependence on a view of recognition that hinges on an intersubjective view of race, I want to be clear that the fight for full inclusion and the equal protection of rights must never end until it is obtained. But I see this struggle as distinct from one that emphasizes the power of personal relationships and personal transformations. The problem with recognition is this: popular works that dramatize recognition and intersubjectivity might actually disrupt this aim or function as what Lauren Berlant has called "cruel optimism"—when "something you desire is actually an obstacle to your flourishing."[7] Tracking the ways in which the politics of recognition has fused with psychology in our representational spaces has convinced me that this combination produces "a confusion between survival and freedom, and between changed minds and changed worlds."[8]

I want to end with a brief examination of an instance of real, state-sanctioned violence and oppression—the misrecognition or failed recognition of black people—and consider one way this event became associated with personalized stories about the need for recognition within black communities. I hope to indicate where some of the harms reside in this swift transfer.

At the start of the school year in 2014, in addition to the Twitter hashtags #TheStruggleIsReal and #FergusonSyllabus, a *Chronicle of Higher Education* article titled "After Ferguson, Some Black Academics Wonder: 'Does Pursuing a Ph.D. Matter?'" made its way through my various social media networks. The article was about black doctoral students and their reactions to the events in Ferguson, Missouri (where a black, unarmed eighteen-year-old, Michael Brown, was killed by a white police officer, Darren Wilson). Maco L. Faniel, whom the article describes as the only black male in his Ph.D. program at Rutgers University, says he did not have the emotional energy to do his research because he was drained by the similarities between the scenes of police brutality and protest in Ferguson in 2014 and the state-sanctioned tactics of oppression during the 1960s and 1970s that impacted the lives of black political icons (like George Jackson and Angela Davis) that he writes about in his research. As Faniel put it bluntly, "I sat down to do my research but I didn't have the energy because I was so focused on the 'What the fuck? This is still happening?'"[9] The article validates responses like Faniel's and emphasizes that rage, depression, and burnout are all understandable reactions of academics of color who might have felt frustrated, helpless, uniquely isolated, and hypervisible on their college campuses.

As Faniel's frustration indicates, a lot of people made uncanny connections between the past and the present, as they drew quick and easy comparisons between 2014 and the civil rights era. In fact, from the very moment the civil disobedience erupted in Ferguson on the day Michael Brown was shot on August 9, 2014, news outlets, online bloggers, and social media users immediately compared the evident scene of recognition failure and the excessive police presence in the city to any number of moments from the 1950s and 1960s. The *New York Times*, for instance, compared perhaps the most circulated image from Ferguson (a young black man with dreadlocks raising his hands at gunpoint before an army of militarized police) with an iconic image from Birmingham, Alabama in 1963 (police dogs and officers attacking a black nonviolent protester).

These connections between the civil rights era and post–civil rights (or "postracial") era were talked about, among many people of color, as creating a sort of depressive historical hangover—as in not only does there seem to be a lack of systemic change, especially for working-class and black poor communities, that connects the two time periods, but there also seems to be an unfortunate lack of *affective* distance between the two moments. The imagery seemed to confirm that the circumstances and the emotions were very similar. As such, both the *Chronicle* article and respondents in the comments section mentioned the psychological impact of racism and the need students and scholars of color might have for culturally sensitive counselors and therapists. As the director of counseling services at Howard University, Ayana Watkins-Northern, explains, "To be an African American in an environment where there are few of you, while you're watching your folks being shot down like animals and people don't want to talk about it, leads you to hold in your feelings and be consumed by it," she says. "These students are experiencing normal depression and they have to remember that they are not unhealthy individuals. It's normal to feel like you might snap, say something destructive, or feel like you can hit somebody."[10]

Although social media (with its memes, vines, hashtags, and tweets) has played an unprecedented role in documenting, representing, and confirming gross spectacles of recognition failure in the post–civil rights era, traditional media outlets continue to participate in the politics of representation and recognition by blurring the boundaries between private and public, individual and communal. While there is a lot to say in this regard about the television news coverage of the events in Ferguson, what caught my attention at the time was a reality television show, *Iyanla: Fix My Life* (2012–). Iyanla Vanzant, who describes herself as an inspirational speaker, spiritual teacher, and life coach, hosts this weekly televised "therapy session" on Oprah Winfrey's OWN Network. Now in its fourth season, *Fix My Life* casts Vanzant as a black community therapist who travels to the homes of people who are facing some form of interpersonal crisis—bad marriages, familial traumas, a man who fathered thirty-four children. The majority of Vanzant's patients/guests are African American, and it is evident that the show aims to destigmatize the role of counseling and therapy within black communities. There is, of course, a good deal of melodrama and performativity (on the part of both Vanzant and her patients) and a weekly recasting of the motifs of destruction and survival. My point here, though, is that Vanzant's show and her relationship to Oprah (arguably the nation's original black female therapeutic expert) was well established in popular venues before the violence in Ferguson.

In the weeks after Michael Brown's death, Vanzant and her camera crew took to the streets of Ferguson to film a special episode of *Fix My Life*, titled "Special Report: Healing in Ferguson." In taking *Fix My Life* to Ferguson, Vanzant's actions became not so unlike Bill Cosby's model of what I identified in chapter 5 as a vision of psychological nationalism that emphasizes the restoration of an essential black self. Vanzant's exact language and her style are distinct from Cosby's, of course, but the message draws on a similar simulacrum of the survival of (self-)destruction. Cosby's response to the systemic failure of recognition? Stop stealing pound cakes and learn how to be better parents! Vanzant's response to the systemic failure of recognition? Create better opportunities for inter-subjectivity to flourish within black communities . . . and learn how to be better parents! Both responses repackage the flawed ideal of intersubjectivity as something that black people are uniquely failing to achieve. Both responses reproduce the misconception that somehow finally achieving and maintaining intersubjectivity in the private sphere will enable it to flow freely from the public sphere. For instance, during the *Fix My Life* episode, Vanzant organized prayer sessions and healing circles, led round-tables and community discussions, and created a group therapy session for members of local rival gangs. A big part of her trip was sharing her conviction that the community needed to get better at "seeing" each other and "being seen." During the group therapy, as Vanzant tried to help the young black men process their grief and outrage over the police shooting of Michael Brown, she capitalized on an opportunity to clarify for them the crux of her advice. She asked the men in circle, "When you kill each other, are you giving other people permission to kill you?" Or to put it another way, if you cannot recognize the humanity of other members of your racial group, why should the state? Unanimously, the men in the circle all answered in the affirmative to Vanzant's question. This logic is an insidious part of the psychologization of race because it erroneously implicates black behavior in the systemic problems with recognition.

While I do not intend to dismiss or disparage the inspiration here to create opportunities for open dialogue, I do encourage us to consider the times when the *representation* and chronic *remediation* of this type of interpersonal work (as captured on film, on television, on the Internet) masquerades as the therapeutic and impedes how effective such efforts can ultimately be. If psychoanalytic discourse teaches us anything, it is that once the specific relational actions travel beyond the initial primary context, as the Freudian dream about the burning child proves, those actions and what they mean, how they land and are felt, how they signify and what they really reference, become diluted and co-optable, distorted and fantastical. To return to the notion of blackness as burning, we cannot be done with psychoanalysis until we are done with the superdramas that represent race as a set of psychological challenges that can be overcome in interpersonal relationships. In essence, we cannot be done with psychoanalysis because psychoanalysis's ideological reverberations are not done with us.

# NOTES

## Introduction

1. Eve Kosofsky Sedgwick, *Between Men: English Literature and Male Homosocial Desire* (Columbia University Press, 1985), 18.

2. Part of the reason people I know call this film "The Black Man's *Color Purple*" is because both films emphasize trauma, hardship, and survival. Both of these films can also be easily satirized because of their use of melodrama; both can be embraced as "real" and also taken less seriously.

3. Sigmund Freud, *The Interpretation of Dreams*, in *The Standard Edition of the Complete Psychological Works or Sigmund Freud*, ed. James Strachey, vols. 4–5 (London: Hogarth, 1990), 509–11.

4. Ibid., 509.

5. Ibid.

6. See Leonard Shengold, *"Father, Don't You See I'm Burning?" Reflections on Sex, Narcissism, Symbolism, and Murder: From Everything to Nothing* (New Haven, CT: Yale University Press, 1991), 42–60. Shengold argues that although Freud claims that this dream was told to him by a female patient who learned of it from another lecturer, the dream may in fact be autobiographical for Freud. Hence, part of what Shengold does in his work on narcissism is locate this dream as a part of a larger collection of self-revealing moments for Freud. Shengold sees in this dream (and others) the fact that Freud was burning with sexual desire for his mother and forced to watch over his rival, his dying father.

7. Judith Butler, "Gender Is Burning: Questions of Appropriation and Subversion," in *Dangerous Liaisons: Gender, Nation, and Postcolonial Perspectives*, ed. Anne McClintock, Aamir Mufti, and Ella Shohat (Minneapolis: University of Minnesota Press, 1997), 388.

8. Ibid.

9. Freud, *Interpretation of Dreams*, 509.

10. I am appreciative of the anonymous reader who encouraged me to be more clear about the role that these types of fantasies play in reinforcing a politics of recognition. Additionally, about the sexual connotations of blackness "burning," in *Antwone Fisher* the way black women are cast as sexual predators while the black boy/man is framed as victim is a notable inversion of popularized racial and sexual politics. What

this inversion mostly demonstrates in this context is that at times stereotypes are used to signal that the black subject is tragically unrecognizable and at other times such associations are used to induct, discipline, and assist the project of recognition. Throughout this book, I discuss all stereotypes, sexual and otherwise, as fantasies that can be assistive or prohibitive when it comes to how recognition is dramatized. Chapter 3 of this book offers a more direct and extended exploration of how stereotypes work in the politics of recognition and representation as they relate to black women. Particularly useful to this discussion on how stereotypes might be thought of "burning" in their own right is Roderick Ferguson's "The Nightmares of the Heteronormative," *Cultural Values* 4, no. 4 (2000): 419–44, which I acknowledge in my reading of *The Defiant Ones*. Also see Evelynn Hammonds, "Black (W)holes and the Geometry of Black Female Sexuality," *Differences: A Journal of Feminist Cultural Studies* 6, nos. 2–3 (1994): 126–45.

11. See Magnificent Montague and Bob Baker, *Burn, Baby! BURN! The Autobiography of Magnificent Montague* (Urbana: University of Illinois Press, 2009).

12. Claudia Tate, *Psychoanalysis and Black Novels: Desire and the Protocols of Race* (New York: Oxford University Press, 1998), 198.

13. Hortense J. Spillers, "'All the Things You Could Be by Now, If Sigmund Freud's Wife Was Your Mother': Psychoanalysis and Race," *Boundary 2* 23, no. 3 (1996): 75–141; Anne Cheng, *The Melancholy of Race: Psychoanalysis, Assimilation, and Hidden Grief* (New York: Oxford University Press, 2001); Gwen Bergner, *Taboo Subjects: Race, Sex, and Psychoanalysis* (Minneapolis: University of Minnesota Press, 2005); Paul Gilroy, *Postcolonial Melancholia* (New York: Columbia University Press, 2005). I would add here that Christopher Lane's edited collection has also contributed greatly to these related studies of race and psychoanalysis—mostly about canonical African American literature. See Lane, ed., *The Psychoanalysis of Race* (New York: Columbia University Press, 1998). In the same collection, also see Gwen Bergner, "Myths of Masculinity: The Oedipus Complex and Douglass's 1845 Narrative," 241–60; Merrill Cole, "Nat Turner's Thing," 261–81.

14. Margo Natalie Crawford, *Dilution Anxiety and the Black Phallus*, 2nd ed. (Columbus: Ohio State University Press, 2008), 8.

15. Badia Sahar Ahad, *Freud Upside Down: African American Literature and Psychoanalytic Culture* (Urbana: University of Illinois Press, 2010).

16. Melissa V. Harris-Perry, *Sister Citizen: Shame, Stereotypes, and Black Women in America* (New Haven, CT: Yale University Press, 2011), 39.

## Chapter 1

1. Charles Taylor, "The Politics of Recognition," in *Multiculturalism: Examining the Politics of Recognition*, ed. Amy Gutmann (Princeton, NJ: Princeton University Press, 1994), 25.

2. Ibid., 38.

3. Nancy Fraser, "Rethinking Recognition," *New Left Review* 2, no. 3 (2000): 107.

4. While the scope of the theoretical discussion on recognition is vast, and the projects that are analogously concerned with recognition even more numerous, I mention here a few that have been particularly helpful in how I think about this topic. See Elizabeth Alexander, *The Black Interior: Essays* (Saint Paul, MN: Graywolf, 2004); K. Anthony

Appiah, "Identity, Authenticity, Survival: Multicultural Societies and Social Reproduction," in *Multiculturalism: Examining the Politics of Recognition*, ed. Amy Gutmann (Princeton, NJ: Princeton University Press, 1994), 149–64; Stuart Hall, "The Spectacle of the 'Other,'" in *Representation: Cultural Representation and Signifying Practice*, ed. Stuart Hall (London: Sage/Open University, 2009), 223–90; Patchen Markell, *Bound by Recognition* (Princeton, NJ: Princeton University Press, 2003); Kelly Oliver, *Witnessing: Beyond Recognition* (Albany: State University of New York Press, 2001); Greta Fowler Snyder, "Multivalent Recognition: Between Fixity and Fluidity in Identity Politics," *Journal of Politics* 74, no. 1 (2012): 249–61. Also useful are some of the many philosophical approaches to these questions. For instance, see Kay Young, "Kierkegaard's Claim of Mutuality and Its Problem of Representation," *Religion and Literature* 43, no. 3 (2011): 25–47.

5. Fraser, "Rethinking Recognition," 109.

6. Frantz Fanon, *Black Skin, White Masks* (New York: Grove, 1967), 109.

7. Ibid., 14.

8. Ibid., 216–17.

9. Ibid., 218.

10. See Kara Keeling, *The Witch's Flight: The Cinematic, the Black Femme, and the Image of Common Sense* (Durham, NC: Duke University Press, 2007), esp. 27–44; Glen Sean Coulthard, *Red Skin, White Masks: Rejecting the Colonial Politics of Recognition* (Minneapolis: University of Minnesota Press, 2014), esp. chaps. 4 and 5.

11. Fraser, "Rethinking Recognition," 109–10.

12. Ibid., 110.

13. As we can see, the politics of recognition and the politics of representation are closely tied; one hails from political theory and the other from cultural studies. As such, I treat these phrases synonymously throughout this book, but I use "the politics of recognition" more often in order to stress its psychoanalytic significance.

14. Stuart Hall, "What Is This 'Black' in Black Popular Culture?," in *Black Popular Culture: A Project by Michelle Wallace*, ed. Gina Dent (Seattle: Bay, 1992), 32.

15. Stuart Hall, "Cultural Identity and Cinematic Representation," in *Film and Theory: An Anthology*, ed. Robert Stam and Toby Miller (Malden, MA: Blackwell, 2000), 706.

16. Herman Gray, "Subject(ed) to Recognition," *American Quarterly* 65, no. 4 (2013): 781.

17. Ibid., 771.

18. Ibid., 771, 794n1.

19. Ibid., 794n1.

20. Ibid., 784.

21. Ibid.

22. Ibid., 771.

23. Gray writes, "This impossibility of achieving (and representing) black freedom within the liberal discourse of freedom and subjectivity forms the basis of my concern with the limits of representation and a politics of culture built on the quest for visibility and recognition within the context of market sovereignty and consumer choice organized by a logic of difference" (ibid., 775). Both Gray and Hartman propose that blackness cannot escape its degraded status through "the discourse of vision and visibility" (ibid., 776). Also see Saidiya V. Hartman, *Scenes of Subjection: Terror, Slavery, and Self-Making in Nineteenth-Century America* (New York: Oxford University Press, 1997).

24. Quoted in "Derek Luke: 'I Was Molested, and I Have My Own Personal Fight,'" CNN. com, December 19, 2002, http://edition.cnn.com/2002/SHOWBIZ/Movies/12/18/ sproject.cao2.luke.transcript/.

25. Both Lauren Berlant and Linda Williams, in discussing sentimentality and melodrama, respectively, make related arguments about the emotional and social impact that spectacular displays of suffering and pain often fail to make. Lauren Berlant, "Poor Eliza," *American Literature* 70, no. 3 (1998): 635–68; Linda Williams, *Playing the Race Card: Melodramas of Black and White from Uncle Tom to O. J. Simpson* (Princeton, NJ: Princeton University Press, 2001). I discuss both works more closely in chapters 2 and 3.

26. Aside from the two books Davenport gives Antwone to help him better excel through his analytic treatment, *Slave Community: Plantation Life in the Antebellum South* (1972) by John W. Blassingame and *The Philosophy and Opinions of Marcus Garvey* (1986), the diegesis of the film omits any direct references to the early time periods or political movements. The use of *Slave Community*, a book that explicitly uses Henry Stack Sullivan's psychological theories to understand how slaves emotionally dealt with slavery, is significant because it is up front about its analytical biases.

27. Antwone Fisher, interview with Rebecca Murray, "The Real Antwone Fisher Talks about the Movie, *Antwone Fisher*," About.com, http://movies.about.com/library/ weekly/aaantwonefisherintc.htm (accessed October 16, 2014).

28. James Baldwin, *The Devil Finds Work: An Essay* (New York: Dell, 1976), 65.

29. Fanon, *Black Skin, White Masks*, 222.

30. Baldwin, *Devil Finds Work*, 65.

31. Ibid., 67.

32. See Roderick Ferguson, "The Nightmares of the Heteronormative," *Cultural Values* 4, no. 4 (2000): 419–44.

33. Ed Guerrero, "The Black Image in Protective Custody: Hollywood's Biracial Buddy Films of the Eighties," in *Black American Cinema*, ed. Manthia Diawara (New York: Routledge, 1993), 237–46.

34. Benjamin DeMott, *The Trouble with Friendship: Why Americans Can't Think Straight about Race* (New York: Atlantic Monthly Press, 1995), 183, 3–4.

35. Ibid., 4.

36. James Baldwin, *Notes of a Native Son* (Boston: Beacon, 1955), 173–75.

37. Richard Iton, *In Search of the Black Fantastic: Politics and Popular Culture in the Post–Civil Rights Era* (Oxford: Oxford University Press, 2008), 19.

38. While there is no easy way to periodize here, I note that African American literary and mass-cultural representations that seem most overtly concerned with matters of a psychological nature spanned roughly from *Invisible Man* (1952) to the televised miniseries *Roots* (1977). When I refer to the "civil rights era," I am writing about this same block of time. But as I argue throughout the book, this way of thinking about race has stayed with us well beyond the era. Relatedly, in recent years, more than a few historians have argued that the way we think about the civil rights movement as from the *Brown* decision in 1954 to King's assassination in 1968 is limited and quite inadequate. See Jacquelyn Dowd Hall, "The Long Civil Rights Movement and the Political Uses of the Past," *Journal of American History* 91, no. 4 (2005): 1233–63.

39. Sidney Poitier, *This Life* (New York: Knopf, 1980), 268.

## Chapter 2

1. Thomas Cripps, *Making Movies Black: The Hollywood Message Movie from World War II to the Civil Rights Era*, 284, 287.

2. Aram Goudsouzian, *Sidney Poitier: Man, Actor, Icon* (Chapel Hill: University of North Carolina Press, 2004); Donald Bogle, *Toms, Coons, Mulattoes, Mammies, and Bucks: An Interpretive History of Blacks in American Films*, 4th ed. (New York: Bloomsbury Academic, 2001); Ed Guerrero, *Framing Blackness: The African American Image in Film* (Philadelphia: Temple University Press, 1993).

3. Peter Roffman and Jim Purdy, *The Hollywood Social Problem Film: Madness, Despair, and Politics from the Depression to the Fifties* (Bloomington: Indiana University Press, 1981), 252.

4. Ibid. The social problem film has also been described as "socially conscious films," the "prosocial film," or "message movies." It is possible to think of social problem films as a genre in its own right, as a hybrid genre, or as a production trend (not as a genre at all). Thomas Schatz identifies "prosocial fictions" as a narrative feature of other genres, 1950s melodramas in particular (for instance, the melodramas of Sirk, Minnelli, and Ray). As Schatz observes, films with prosocial messages were often found in genre films (melodrama, thriller, western) that used a familiar form to camouflage or soften social critiques. Hence, there are times when the social problem is the dominant "genre" of a film and times when a social problem project is added to a conventional form. See Schatz, *Hollywood Genres: Formulas, Filmmaking, and the Studio System* (New York: McGraw-Hill, 1981), 223–32. See also Tino Balio, *Grand Design: Hollywood as a Modern Business Enterprise, 1930–1939*, History of the American Cinema 5 (Berkeley: University of California Press, 1993); Roffman and Purdy, *Hollywood Social Problem Film*; Andrew Dowdy, *Films of the Fifties* (New York: William Morrow, 1973).

5. Additionally, the gangster, crime, or juvenile delinquency cycles were heavily represented in non–Warner Bros. productions such as MGM's *Manhattan Melodrama* (1934) and *Boys Town* (1938).

6. As Tino Balio notes, "Warners did not meet the social problems head on; instead, the studio typically sidestepped issues by narrowing the focus of the exposé to a specific case or by resolving problems at the personal level of the protagonist rather than at the societal level." See Balio, "Production Trends," in *Grand Design*, 281.

7. Roffman and Purdy, *Hollywood Social Problem Film*, 7.

8. Brian Neve, "HUAC, the Blacklist, and the Decline of Social Cinema," in *Transforming the Screen, 1950–1959*, by Peter Lev, History of American Cinema 7 (New York: Charles Scribner's Sons, 2003), 73. Also see Manny Farber, "Movies Aren't Movies Any More," *Commentary*, June 1952, quoted in ibid.

9. Schatz, *Hollywood Genres*, 226.

10. Stephen Farber and Marc Green, *Hollywood on the Couch: A Candid Look at the Overheated Love Affair between Psychiatrists and Moviemakers* (New York: William Morrow, 1993), 35. Also see Harvey R. Greenberg, *Screen Memories: Hollywood Cinema on the Psychoanalytic Couch* (New York: Columbia University Press, 1993).

11. See Farber and Green, *Hollywood on the Couch*.

12. Michelle Wallace, "Race, Gender, and Psychoanalysis in Forties Films: *Lost Boundaries*, *Home of the Brave*, and *The Quiet One*," in *Black American Cinema*, ed. Manthia Diawara

(New York: Routledge, 1993), 268. Also see Roffman and Purdy, who in analyzing this cycle of racialized social problem films note how the message of these films concludes that "blacks should be allowed to enter white society as equals, that is, as white black men. The barriers to this integration are found in blacks, with their inferiority complexes, and in some whites, with their patronizing view of blacks." Roffman and Purdy, *Hollywood Social Problem Film*, 247.

13. Sidney Poitier, *The Measure of a Man: A Spiritual Autobiography* (San Francisco: Harper-SanFrancisco, 2000), 91.

14. David Shipman, *The Story of Cinema: A Complete Narrative History from the Beginning to the Present* (New York: St. Martin's, 1982), 1175. Shipman may be right that although there were films before 1957 that featured interracial dyads, those narratives were not primarily about the friendship. In that regard, with films like this one, Poitier really began the tradition of the interracial buddy film.

15. Goudsouzian, *Sidney Poitier*, 118.

16. Christine Gledhill makes explicit the connection between method acting and the popularization of the Hollywood psychological drama. See Gledhill, "Signs of Melodrama," in *Stardom: Industry of Desire*, ed. Christine Gledhill (New York: Routledge, 1991), 207–232.

17. Poitier, *Measure of a Man*, 142.

18. Gledhill, "Signs of Melodrama," 224.

19. Linda Williams, *Playing the Race Card: Melodramas of Black and White from Uncle Tom to O. J. Simpson* (Princeton, NJ: Princeton University Press, 2001), 320n42.

20. Poitier, *Measure of a Man*, 139.

21. Heinz Kohut, *The Chicago Institute Lectures*, ed. Paul Tolpin and Marian Tolpin (Hillsdale, NJ: Analytic, 1996), 254.

22. Ibid., 257. This process of connecting with a perceived perfect other is ideally a short-term project. Eventually, as Kohut theorized, "once that reactivation of the early childhood wish for a merger with an idealized adult has begun to be accomplished, then a gradual, or at least a phase-appropriate, disillusionment can occur and ultimately will lead to the (simultaneous) setting up of internal structures, internal ideals" (ibid.).

23. *Time*, February 18, 1952, quoted in Goudsouzian, *Sidney Poitier*, 119.

24. E. Ann Kaplan, "The Couch Affair: Gender and Race in Hollywood Transference," *American Imago* 50, no. 4 (1993): 481.

25. This look might also be read as Cullen's dialectical exchange with the lynch mob. The look could be a bold inside joke shared between the mob and the racial other, and only Johnny misses the joke. The exchange adds some humor to the scene, even though it is delivered straightly. Along these lines, Poitier's/Cullen's look is throwing the aggression that Johnny exercises back at him because it is also a look of disowning (a perfect "fuck you" look). Now Cullen is confirming for Johnny that he really *is* alone. And so Cullen's look is as much of a survival of Johnny's destruction as is his subsequent spitting on the racist.

26. See Eve Kosofsky Sedgwick, *Between Men: English Literature and Male Homosocial Desire* (New York: Columbia University Press, 1985); Kaplan, "Couch Affair."

27. Robyn Wiegman, *American Anatomies: Theorizing Race and Gender* (Durham, NC: Duke University Press, 1995), 155. Although her work provides a rich and persuasive reading of interracial male bonding in literature and film, Wiegman, peculiarly, does not

discuss Poitier's classic buddy films. Instead she turns careful attention to interracial buddy films of the 1980s, arguing that "these films simultaneously assent to and resist Black Power analogies between masculinity and equality by defying the legacy of emasculation that attends black male representation, while recasting white masculinity as a disempowered and embattled marginality itself. In an ironic twist, incorporation of the black male into the reign of the visual that characterizes commodity culture becomes a mechanism through which the history of racism among men is revised and denied" (15). As I argue here, Poitier's film career certainly activated elements of what Wiegman argues here, but Poitier's characterizations wrap these dynamics around the therapeutic or psychoanalytic mode. Rethinking Poitier's career in this way only enlivens those readings of 1980s interracial buddy narratives that others have contributed in recent years. For example, see Manthia Diawara, "Black Spectatorship: Problems of Identification and Resistance," in *Black American Cinema*, ed. Manthia Diawara (New York: Routledge, 1993), 211–20; Ed Guerrero, "Black Image in Protective Custody," in Diawara, *Black American Cinema*, 237–46.

28. Wiegman, *American Anatomies*, 155.

29. With regard to gender, race, and the role of stereotypes in this film, I do find it productive to think a bit about how heterosexuality and femininity resonate within *The Defiant One*'s diegesis. White women in this story, as in other buddy films, are to be excluded from the hard work of intersubjective processes because they interfere with the work of subject forming and nation building that are the implied activities of men. Black women have no place whatsoever in the story, while white women are needed to make at least *some* appearance in order to both deflect and contain some of the homoerotic charge and also to help activate the stereotypes of black masculinity (which demarcate Cullen from Johnny in a way that still maintains the racial hierarchies). As such, after the duo's lengthiest fisticuffs battle, they meet a single white mother and her son. These characters exist solely to demonstrate Johnny's sexual attraction to women and latent interest in being a patriarchal head of household. Yet it is the white female's pronounced inability to truly know or care to know Johnny and respect the interracial dyad, her limited intersubjective capabilities, that Johnny uses as his reason for rejecting her in the end. Upon leaving her to go find Cullen in the swamp, Johnny retorts, "You don't even know me." Along these lines, Wiegman has it right, I believe, when she argues that narratives about interracial male bonding appear to forsake the "heterosexual romance as precondition to (and symbolic enactment of) the nostalgic dream of racial transcendence" (ibid., 172). Further, the historical stereotypes of black men are even more compulsively activated when Cullen and Johnny interact with the white female love object, particularly as she and her son are demonstratively terrified of Cullen and fear that he will attack them.

30. Georg Wilhelm Friedrich Hegel, "Lordship and Bondage," in *Hegel's Dialectic of Desire and Recognition: Texts and Commentary*, ed. John O'Neill (Albany: State University of New York Press, 1996), 29 (§ 179).

31. Ibid., 31 (§ 187).

32. For a brief and exceptionally clear summary of Hegel's notion of mutual recognition, see Stephen Hudson, "Intersubjectivity of Mutual Recognition and the I-Thou: A Comparative Analysis of Hegel and Buber," *Minerva—An Internet Journal of Philosophy* 14 (2010): 140–55.

33. See Toni Morrison, *Playing in the Dark* (New York: Vintage Books, 1992). Specifically, Morrison argues, "What became transparent were the self-evident ways that Americans choose to talk about themselves through and within a sometimes allegorical, sometimes metaphorical, but always choked representation of an Africanist presence" (17). Also see Kenneth Warren, *Black and White Strangers: Race and American Literary Realism* (Chicago: University of Chicago Press, 1993).

34. Morrison, *Playing in the Dark*, 57.

35. Victoria Burke, "Hegel's Concept of Mutual Recognition: The Limits of Self-Determination," *Philosophical Forum* 36, no. 2 (2005): 215.

36. See Georg Wilhelm Friedrich Hegel, "Lordship and Bondage," in *Hegel's Dialectic of Desire and Recognition*, 29–36.

37. The magical Negro is more often described as explicitly positive, lower class, and uneducated, and Poitier's characters are usually (but not always) positive, smart, and professionally decorated. I still argue, however, that the stereotype is relevant to his career (and that his career even set a standard for contemporary versions of the stereotype) because of the ways in which his characters serviced inept, wounded whiteness. But as I discuss here, the "magic" in the Poitier vehicle is psychological, and so his characters were also a combination of other popular stereotypes; the psychological expertise is the ideology that holds the different tropes and types together. For a longer discussion of magical Negroes in cinema, see Matthew W. Hughey, "Cinethetic Racism: White Redemption and Black Stereotypes in 'Magical Negro' Films," *Social Problems* 56, no. 3 (2009): 543–77.

38. D. W. Winnicott, *Playing and Reality* (London: Routledge, 1991), 90.

39. While there are a good number of post–civil rights era interracial fisticuffs narratives that restage the magical joy found in the spectacle of object survival (like *Rocky* [1976] and *An Officer and a Gentleman* [1982]), contemporary films offer a chance for new viewers to embrace the era's dominant story of interracial friendship. Films such as *Remember the Titans* (2000), *Radio* (2003), *Glory Road* (2006), and *The Help* (2011) reimagine the interpersonal conflicts and healing dynamics of the era.

40. Jessica Benjamin, *The Bonds of Love: Psychoanalysis, Feminism, and the Problem of Domination* (New York: Pantheon Books, 1988), 40.

41. Ibid., 45.

42. Quoted in Goudsouzian, *Sidney Poitier*, 264.

43. The quotation comes from the title of a bonus documentary included on the *In the Heat of the Night* DVD, 40th Anniversary Collector's Edition, 20th Century Fox Home Entertainment, 2008. Ironically, despite the title of the documentary, its interviewees do not speak directly about the significance of the slap-back scene.

44. Poitier, *Measure of a Man*, 136.

45. Ibid., 148.

46. Goudsouzian, *Sidney Poitier*, 1; Cripps, *Making Movies Black*, 287.

47. Martin Luther King Jr., "I Have a Dream," speech, Lincoln Memorial, Washington, DC, August 28, 1963.

48. Benjamin, *Bonds of Love*, 47.

49. Andrea Slane provides an excellent reading of the changes between the film and its source text, a case history written by the psychoanalyst Robert Lindner when he treated and "cured" an anti-Semitic prisoner. Importantly in the source text, the

original analyst was Jewish, but the film script changed that role to a black doctor. It is obvious that since blackness was a unique part of the national conversation in 1962, the change in the doctor's race was intended to make the work seem socially relevant to the era's racial politics. Slane ably destabilizes the film's tethering of black and Jewish identities in her reading. See Slane, "Pressure Points: Political Psychology, Screen Adaptation, and the Management of Racism in the Case-History Genre," *Camera Obscura* 15, no. 3 (2000): 70–113.

50. Ibid., 76–77.
51. Kaplan, "Couch Affair." Both Slane and Kaplan read the film as illustrative of transference, but neither reads it as connected to the broader contradictions in Poitier's stardom or as having any relevance to the politics of recognition. The fact that transference and countertransference exist, though, only makes more elusive any goal of recognizing black humanity as a psychological reality.

## Chapter 3

1. Hortense J. Spillers, "Mama's Baby, Papa's Maybe: An American Grammar Book," *Diacritics: A Review of Contemporary Criticism* 17, no. 2 (1987): 65.
2. Lauren Berlant, "Poor Eliza," *American Literature* 70, no. 3 (1998): 640.
3. Donald Bogle, *Primetime Blues: African Americans on Network Television* (New York: Farrar, Straus and Giroux, 2001), 150.
4. Hal Kanter, interview with Sam Denoff, Archive of American Television, May 22, 1997, http://emmytvlegends.org/interviews/people/hal-kanter.
5. Diahann Carroll, interview with Henry Coleman, Archive of American Television, March 3, 1998, http://emmytvlegends.org/interviews/people/diahann-carroll.
6. In this chapter, I do not offer a lengthy discussion of the dominant stereotypes of black women because there have already been several excellent summaries and discussions of these types. Rather than retread this discursive territory, I devote more time to interrogating the psychological life of the image since so little has been written in this vein. For more detailed discussions of mammy, matriarch, sapphire, jezebel, and other controlling or distorting images, see Patricia Hill Collins, *Black Feminist Thought: Knowledge, Consciousness, and the Politics of Empowerment*, 2nd ed. (New York: Routledge, 2000), 69–96; Ingrid Banks, "Women in Film," in *African Americans and Popular Culture*, ed. Todd Boyd (Westport, CT: Praeger, 2008), 67–88. Joan Morgan defines *strongblackwoman* in *When Chickenheads Come Home to Roost: My Life as a Hip Hop Feminist* (New York: Simon and Schuster, 1999).
7. Collins, *Black Feminist Thought*, 72.
8. Barbara Christian, *Black Women Novelists: The Development of a Tradition, 1892–1976* (Westport, CT: Greenwood, 1980), 12–13. Also see Carolyn M. West, "Mammy, Jezebel, Sapphire, and Their Homegirls: Developing an 'Oppositional Gaze' toward the Images of Black Women," in *Lectures on the Psychology of Women*, 4th ed., ed. Joan C. Chrisler, Carla Golden, and Patricia D. Rozee (New York: McGraw-Hill, 2012), 286–99.
9. West, "Mammy, Jezebel, Sapphire, and Their Homegirls," 294.
10. Ibid., 291.
11. Daniel P. Moynihan, *The Negro Family: The Case for National Action* (Washington, DC: Office of Policy Planning and Research, U.S. Department of Labor, 1965).

12. Ibid.

13. Ibid.

14. See Kenneth Clark, *Dark Ghetto: Dilemmas of Social Power* (New York: Harper and Row, 1965); E. Franklin Frazier, *The Negro Family in the United States* (Chicago: University of Chicago Press, 1966).

15. See Hazel V. Carby, *Reconstructing Womanhood: The Emergence of the Afro-American Woman Novelist* (New York: Oxford University Press, 1987); Lisa Dodson, *Don't Call Us Out of Name: The Untold Lives of Women and Girls in Poor America* (Boston: Beacon, 1999); bell hooks, *Ain't I a Woman: Black Women and Feminism* (Boston: South End, 1981); K. Sue Jewell, *From Mammy to Miss America and Beyond: Cultural Images and the Shaping of US Social Policy* (New York: Routledge, 1993); Patricia Morton, *Disfigured Images: The Historical Assault on Afro-American Women* (Westport, CT: Greenwood, 1991).

16. See Collins, *Black Feminist Thought*.

17. Barbara Christian, *Black Feminist Criticism: Perspectives on Black Women Writers* (New York: Pergamon, 1985), 3, 16.

18. See Carby, *Reconstructing Womanhood*; hooks, *Ain't I a Woman*; Evelyn Brooks Higginbotham, "African-American Women's History and the Metalanguage of Race," *Signs: Journal of Women in Culture & Society* 17, no. 2 (1992): 251–74; Dorothy E. Roberts, "Racism and Patriarchy in the Meaning of Motherhood," *American University Journal of Gender, Social Policy & the Law*, no. 1 (1992): 1–38. In addition to this establishing and influential body of scholarship, the 1990s saw a resurgence in critical assessments of stereotypes of black women. Also see Dodson, *Don't Call Us Out of Name*; Jewell, *From Mammy to Miss America and Beyond*; Morton, *Disfigured Images*; Dorothy E. Roberts, *Killing the Black Body: Race, Reproduction, and the Meaning of Liberty* (New York: Pantheon Books, 1997).

19. Wahneema Lubiano, "Black Ladies, Welfare Queens, and State Minstrels," in *Race-ing Justice, En-Gendering Power: Essays on Anita Hill, Clarence Thomas, and the Construction of Social Reality*, ed. Toni Morrison (New York: Pantheon, 1992), 323, 339.

20. Kimberly Wallace-Sanders, *Mammy: A Century of Race, Gender, and Southern Memory* (Ann Arbor: University of Michigan Press, 2008).

21. Roberts, "Racism and Patriarchy in the Meaning of Motherhood," 13.

22. West, "Mammy, Jezebel, Sapphire, and Their Homegirls," 297.

23. See Sarita Davis and Aisha Tucker-Brown, "Effects of Black Sexual Stereotypes on Sexual Decision Making Among African American Women," *Journal of Pan African Studies* 5, no. 9 (2013): 111–28; also see Wendy Ashley, "The Angry Black Woman: The Impact of Pejorative Stereotypes on Psychotherapy with Black Women," *Social Work in Public Health* 29, no. 1 (2014): 27–34.

24. Molly LaddTaylor and Lauri Umansky, introduction to *"Bad" Mothers: The Politics of Blame in Twentieth-Century America*, ed. Molly Ladd-Taylor and Lauri Umansky (New York: NYU Press, 1998), 13. While this collection includes a few essays on psychoanalysis and motherhood and some on race and motherhood, the works do not sustain discussion on the psychoanalytically constructed black mothers.

25. Feldstein, "Antiracism and Maternal Failure," in LaddTaylor and Umansky, *"Bad" Mothers*, 157.

26. Ibid. Also see Feldstein's more extended account on how notions of black and white motherhood intersected with liberal ideologies, both to the benefit and the detriment of feminist agendas: *Motherhood in Black and White: Race and Sex in American Liberalism, 1930–1965* (Ithaca, NY: Cornell University Press, 2000).

27. See Karen Horney, "The Flight from Womanhood," "The Dread of Woman," and "The Denial of the Vagina," all in *Feminine Psychology* (New York: Norton, 1967), 55–70, 133–46, 147–62.

28. Janine Chasseguet-Smirgel, "Feminine Guilt and the Oedipus Complex," in *Female Sexuality: New Psychoanalytic Views*, ed. Janine Chasseguet-Smirgel (Ann Arbor: University of Michigan Press, 1970), 94–134. Also see Chasseguet-Smirgel, *Creativity and Perversion* (New York: Norton, 1984); and Chasseguet-Smirgel, "Freud and Female Sexuality: The Consideration of Some Blind Spots in the Exploration of the 'Dark Continent,'" *International Journal of Psycho-Analysis* 57 (1976): 275–86. For Nancy Chodorow's interpretative retelling, I am specifically thinking of *The Reproduction of Mothering* (Berkeley: University of California Press, 1978).

29. Jessica Benjamin, *The Bonds of Love: Psychoanalysis, Feminism, and the Problem of Domination* (New York: Pantheon Books, 1988), 94–95.

30. Chasseguet-Smirgel, "Freud and Female Sexuality," 285.

31. Benjamin, *Bonds of Love*, 42–50.

32. For example, Felski writes, "The pressure of politics affects the clarifying power of metaphor. That the madwoman in the attic fails dismally as an allegory of the black female author has everything to do with differing social realities. African American women were not seen as delicate, helpless creatures in need of protection; they were not fettered by the constraining norms of genteel femininity or imprisoned and sentenced to inactivity in the middle-class home. Inevitably, the images of paralyzing anxiety and isolation that define [Sandra] Gilbert and [Susan] Gubar's portrayal of female authorship [in *The Madwoman in the Attic*] carries absolutely no resonance with black feminist critics." Rita Felski, *Literature after Feminism* (Chicago: University of Chicago Press, 2003), 80.

33. Spillers, "Mama's Baby, Papa's Maybe," 80.

34. Ibid.

35. Michele Wallace, *Black Macho and the Myth of the Superwoman* (1978; repr., London: Verso, 1999), 89.

36. Ibid., 96.

37. Ibid., 94.

38. Elaine Brown, *A Taste of Power: A Black Woman's Story* (New York: Anchor Books, 1994), 90.

39. Ibid., 89.

40. Ibid., 189.

41. Trudier Harris, *Saints, Sinners, Saviors: Strong Black Women in African American Literature* (New York: Palgrave Macmillan, 2002), 19.

42. Ibid., 11.

43. Ibid., 178.

44. Paule Marshall, "To Da-Duh, a Memoriam," in *Reena and Other Stories* (New York: Feminist Press, 1983), 104.

45. Ibid.

46. Alice Walker, *Meridian*, in *The Third Life of Grange Copeland, Meridian, The Color Purple* (New York: Quality Paperback Book Club, 1990), 40.

47. Ibid., 40–41.

48. Ibid., 41.

49. In other places, like *In Search of Our Mothers' Gardens: Womanist Prose*, Walker appears to celebrate a connection to black maternity, but her reclamatory praise of black mothers veers toward the type of idealization that reinforces the good breast / bad breast dichotomy. See Alice Walker, *In Search of Our Mothers' Gardens: Womanist Prose* (San Diego: Harcourt Brace Jovanovich, 1983).

50. Toni Morrison, *Sula* (New York: Penguin Books, 1973), 71.

51. Ibid., 72.

52. Laura Mulvey, "Visual Pleasure and Narrative Cinema," *Screen* 16 (Autumn 1975): 6–18; Mary Ann Doane, *The Desire to Desire: The Woman's Film of the 1940s*, 2nd ed. (Bloomington: Indiana University Press, 1987); E. Ann Kaplan, *Motherhood and Representation: The Mother in Popular Culture and Melodrama* (London: Routledge, 1992).

53. There is one exception here, Chuck Kleinhaus's short essay on Billy Woodberry's independent film *Bless Their Little Hearts* (1983). Kleinhaus, who is less concerned with how nonblack spectators might engage black melodramas, is correct, I believe, in asserting that the emotional dimensions of realist black melodramas might, for black communities, validate "the frequently experienced as well as what is emotionally desirable, but sometimes unattainable" and that realist melodramas "can speak profoundly about and to people struggling against capitalism's destruction of human values." Still, there has been little interest in melodramas and dramas about race that are not intended for mass audiences. Even Kleinhaus's approach, while persuasive, does not envision the black family drama's relationship to psychoanalytic film discourse. Chuck Kleinhaus, "Realist Melodrama and the African-American Family: Billy Woodberry's *Bless Their Little Hearts*," in *Melodrama: Stage, Picture, Screen*, ed. Jacky Bratton, Jim Cook, and Christine Gledhill (London: BFI, 1994), 163.

54. There are also scores of black dramas from the 1960s and 1970s that are lost or forgotten, swept up into the vault of "Blaxploitation" narratives. Because films could be made and distributed so cheaply, a lot were made that the scholarly community has lost track of. Fortunately, private collectors and fans have helped make many of these forgotten titles known again.

55. E. Ann Kaplan, "The 'Resisting' Maternal Woman's Film 1930–60," in *Motherhood and Representation*, 164.

56. Ibid., 175.

57. As I indicate here, there has been a good deal of scholarly interest in *Imitation of Life*. Although several critics spanning diverse fields, from cultural theory to feminist theory and film history, have contributed persuasive readings of the women characters in either version of the film, and some (like Marina Heung, Lauren Berlant, and Sandy Flitterman-Lewis) have specifically addressed the black mother-daughter relationship, that interest has not converged around the psychoanalytic interpretation of the black mother-daughter pair. See Lauren Berlant, "National Brands, National Bodies: *Imitation of Life*," in *The Female Complaint: The Unfinished Business of Sentimentality in American Culture* (Durham, NC: Duke University Press, 2008), 107–44; Marina Heung, "'What's the Matter with Sarah Jane?': Daughters and Mothers in Douglas

Sirk's *Imitation of Life*," in *Imitation of Life*, dir. Douglas Sirk, ed. Lucy Fischer (New Brunswick, NJ: Rutgers University Press, 1991), 302–24; Sandy Flitterman-Lewis, "*Imitation*(s) *of Life*: The Black Woman's Double Determination as Troubling 'Other,'" in Sirk and Fischer, *Imitation of Life*, 325–38.

58. Benjamin, *Bonds of Love*, 213.

59. This film should not be confused with the 1966 Senegalese film of the same title that was written and directed by Ousmane Sembène.

60. Patricia Hill Collins distinguishes "othermothers" from "bloodmothers" in the African American community. She identifies othermothers as black women within the community "who assist bloodmothers by sharing mothering responsibilities." See Collins, *Black Feminist Thought*, 178.

61. I think about these family-themed films as a genre with many subgenres in that sometimes they are action oriented, melodramatic, psycho-thrillers, etc. Mainly I use the term "family drama" to refer to films that centralize family dynamics even when the narrative branches to follow a singular character and even when there are other, secondary, generic influences present. It becomes a family drama to me if that character's relationship to the family is represented as foundational and if the dramatic tension around the family heavily motivates the rest of the story.

62. Berlant, "Poor Eliza"; Linda Williams, *Playing the Race Card: Melodramas of Black and White from Uncle Tom to O. J. Simpson* (Princeton, NJ: Princeton University Press, 2001).

63. Berlant, "Poor Eliza," 640.

64. Elizabeth A. McNeil, Neal A. Lester, DoVeanna S. Fulton, and Lynette D. Myles, "'Going after Something Else': Sapphire on the Evolution from *PUSH* to *Precious* and *The Kid*," *Callaloo* 37, no. 2 (2014): 354. Also interesting here is the fact that Sapphire is actually the pen name of Ramona Lofton. The author, in taking that name, is perhaps interested in implicitly creating new associations to the loaded historical reference to black femininity.

65. From my reading of Poitier's characters in chapter 2, we can recall that for Heinz Kohut, narcissistic disorders evolve because a person fails at internalizing a healthy transference. That is, "narcissistic" individuals are thought never to have learned to modulate the grandiosity and esteem of others with their own self-impression. Sapphire's rendering of baaaddd mama Mary is consistent with this analytic framework.

66. McNeil et al., "Going after Something Else," 355.

67. Michelle Jarman, "Cultural Consumption and Rejection of Precious Jones: Pushing Disability into the Discussion of Sapphire's *Push* and Lee Daniels's *Precious*," *Feminist Formations* 24, no. 2 (2012): 164.

68. Ibid., 166.

69. Charlene Regester, "Monstrous Mother, Incestuous Father, and Terrorized Teen: Reading *Precious* as a Horror Film," *Journal of Film and Video* 67, no. 1 (2015): 30–45.

70. Roger Ebert, "*Precious: Based on the Novel Push by Sapphire*," RogerEbert.com, November 4, 2009, www.rogerebert.com/reviews/precious-based-on-the-novel-push-by-sapphire-2009.

71. Ibid.

72. Knopfdoubleday, "Precious: Based on the Novel Push—Oprah Winfrey Interview," YouTube, November 9, 2009, www.youtube.com/watch?v=de_dggP-pHE.

73. Ibid.

74. McNeil et al., "Going after Something Else,'" 356.

75. See Jacqueline Bobo, *Black Women as Cultural Readers* (New York: Columbia University Press), 1995; bell hooks, "The Oppositional Gaze: Black Female Spectators," in *Black Looks: Race and Representation* (Boston: South End, 1992), 115–31; Jacqueline Najuma Stewart, *Migrating to the Movies: Cinema and Black Urban Modernity* (Berkeley: University of California Press, 2005).

76. Written and directed by Bridgett M. Davis, a black woman independent filmmaker, *Naked Acts* (1996) is a great film to think about here. The film's central character, Cicely, was molested while her mother, a famous Blaxploitation film star, was advancing her career in the 1970s. As daughter tells her mother, "My problem is that you were hardly ever home, and I needed you." Most of the action of the film takes place in the present day, as Cicely tries to begin her own acting career by starring in an independently produced art film. *Naked Acts* overtly tackles the history of exploitation and stereotype when it comes to representing black women in film. While the film is not exactly a family drama, it does mobilize the trope of the baaaddd black mother to create dramatic tension and give Cicely a personal grievance and trauma that she has to overcome en route to becoming a film star. From a plot standpoint, one of the things this film does differently, however, is include a powerful, melodramatic scene of reconciliation between black mother and daughter—something that is not often depicted on-screen. Although a film like *Naked Acts* tries to distance itself from some of the medium's most troubling conventions, it nonetheless uses a baaaddd black mother to create opportunities for the daughter to recognize her own subjectivity and to create a similar type of recognition for viewing audiences, even if it manages to elicit empathy for both mother and daughter in the concluding act.

77. Thomas Schatz, "The Family Melodrama," in *Imitations of Life: A Reader on Film & Television Melodrama*, ed. Marcia Landy (Detroit: Wayne State University Press, 1991), 148.

78. Ibid., 149, emphasis in original.

79. Andreá N. Williams, "Black Women's Labor and the Melodrama of Class Mobility in Sutton Griggs's *Overshadowed*," *African American Review* 45, nos. 1–2 (2012): 50.

80. Williams, *Playing the Race Card*, 42.

81. Perhaps because family dramas create dramatic tension around and within the family unit, I am hard-pressed to think of any black family dramas that are not melodramatic and, by extension, psychoanalytic. Such works may vary in the degree to which they cast obviously baaaddd mothers, and they may vary in the degree to which they are invested in dramatizing successful or failed recognition within the home. Irrespective of these differences in degree, the emotional landscape of black family dramas from *Imitation of Life* to *Precious*, from *Soul Food* to even an innocuous-seeming holiday film like *This Christmas* (2007), is generally consistent.

82. Peter Brooks, *The Melodramatic Imagination: Balzac, Henry James, Melodrama, and the Mode of Excess* (New Haven, CT: Yale University Press, 1976), 14–15.

83. Ibid., 12–13.

84. Ibid., 204.

85. Ibid.

86. Benjamin, *Bonds of Love*, 78.

87. Donald Pease discusses American exceptionalism as built on a chronic "state of exception" and national fantasy. See Donald E. Pease, *The New American Exceptionalism*
(Minneapolis: University of Minnesota Press, 2009).
88. See Allison Berg, *Mothering the Race: Women's Narratives of Reproduction, 1890–1930*
(Urbana: University of Illinois Press, 2002).
89. Laura Doyle, *Bordering on the Body: The Racial Matrix of Modern Fiction and Culture*
(New York: Oxford University Press, 1994), 4.
90. Spillers, "Mama's Baby, Papa's Maybe," 80.

# Chapter 4

1. "Behind the Hustle," bonus documentary on the *Hustle & Flow* DVD, Warner Home
Video, 2006.
2. The character DJay is also a muse or a racial transference of sorts for the film's writer/
director, Craig Brewer, who is white. Brewer gave his black pimp character a backstory
that reflected his own father-son relationship, and in this scene with Shug, DJay
voices details about the death of Brewer's father. In this way, the character functions intersubjectively in additional ways, as a figure of ideation and transference
for Brewer and similarly on-screen for the people around him—the middle-class
"straight-laced" couple Key and Yvonne; the white geeky hip hop enthusiast, Shelby;
and the disenfranchised women around him.
3. "It's Hard Out Here for a Pimp"; "Hustle and Flow (It Ain't Over)."
4. "Behind the Hustle."
5. Ibid.
6. Ibid.
7. Ibid.
8. Jerry H. Bryant provides a capable genealogy of the role that pimps, tricksters, and
other underclass men have played in black literary traditions. See Bryant, *Born in a
Mighty Bad Land the Violent Man in African American Folklore and Fiction* (Bloomington:
Indiana University Press, 2003).
9. Here, I am thinking of the two main ways that Goines and Beck have been influential
in the post–civil rights era: rap and contemporary fiction. Hip hop artists and fans,
including comedians like Dave Chappelle, have memorialized these two popular writers as particularly inspirational figures who have modeled as black men ways to "keep
it real" while they described their relatable, heuristic, lessons learned on the streets.
For example, Ice Cube and Ice-T intentionally chose stage names that are derivatives of Robert Beck's penname, Iceberg Slim. Other rappers like Tupac Shakur have
rhymed, "Machiavelli was my tutor, Donald Goines my father figure." Meanwhile,
Nas waxes that he can be found "sipping Dom out of the bottle" and contemplating
how his life compares to "a Donald Goines novel," as Ludacris explains in his song
"Eyebrows Down," "So I picked up a couple books from Donald Goines / about the
business of this shit and how to flip a few coins." As for the fiction, Justin Gifford
persuasively argues in *Pimping Fictions* that Beck's *Pimp* started the contemporary
trend of pimp literature that continues to thrive in the literary marketplace today. Gifford contributes a valuable analysis of the industrial factors that led to Goines's and
Beck's successes. Although this account pays some attention to the treatment of black

women in these works, the representation of women and mothers is not a central part of the study. The same is true of Gifford's consideration of the psychoanalytic themes that I argue heavily inform pimp culture. Both of these matters are an acknowledged but marginal part of the existing conversation on pimps. See Justin Gifford, *Pimping Fictions: African American Crime Literature and the Untold Story of Black Pulp Publishing* (Philadelphia: Temple University Press, 2013).

10. Although there is very little written on black pulp and popular writers from this time period, in recent years, there has been a boom in scholarship on the various other pulp and popular fiction traditions. As Michael Bronski has noted in *Pulp Friction: Uncovering the Golden Age of Gay Male Pulps*, "This advance in the publishing world, particularly in the late 1940s and early 1950s, also included huge numbers of original novels focusing on illegal or taboo sex—adultery, prostitution, rape, interracial relationships, lesbianism, male homosexuality," Michael Bronski, introduction to *Pulp Friction: Uncovering the Golden Age of Gay Male Pulps*, ed. Michael Bronski (New York: St. Martin's Griffin, 2003), 2. Bronski's volume on the gay male pulps is one recent example of this critical attentiveness, but also see William Darby, *Necessary American Fictions: Popular Literature of the 1950s* (Bowling Green, OH: Bowling Green State University Popular Press, 1987); Greg Forter's *Murdering Masculinities: Fantasies of Gender and Violence in the American Crime Novel* (New York: NYU Press, 2000); Janice Radway's influential feminist scholarship on romance literature, *Reading the Romance: Women, Patriarchy, and Popular Literature* (Chapel Hill: University of North Carolina Press, 1984); Clive Bloom, *Cult Fiction: Popular Readings and Pulp Theory* (New York: St. Martin's, 1996).

11. For an excellent interview about Holloway's evolution as a press and the role writers like Goines and Beck played in its success, see Justin D. Gifford's "'Harvard in Hell': Holloway House Publishing Company, *Players Magazine*, and the Invention of Black Mass-Market Erotica: Interviews with Wanda Coleman and Emory 'Butch' Holmes II," *MELUS: Multi-Ethnic Literature of the U.S.* 35, no. 4 (2010): 111–37.

12. Ibid., 112.

13. In 1973, Richard Milner and Christina Milner published one of the earliest anthropological accounts of black pimp culture. Their research blurs the boundaries between scholarship, biography, and entertainment, but it is perhaps most notable for setting the tone for realist engagements with pimp culture. See Milner and Milner, *Black Players: The Secret World of Black Pimps* (Boston: Little, Brown, 1973).

14. Mark Anthony Neal, "Critical Noir: A Hustler's Legacy," Blackvoices.com, January 5, 2005, www.blackvoices.com/entmain/music/critno10604/20050105 (accessed July 17, 2007; no longer available).

15. Todd A. Boyd, *Am I Black Enough for You? Popular Culture from the 'Hood and Beyond* (Bloomington: Indiana University Press, 1997), 9.

16. Robin D. G. Kelley, *Yo' Mama's Dysfunktional! Fighting the Culture Wars in Urban America* (Boston: Beacon, 1997), 16.

17. L. H. Stallings, "'I'm Goin Pimp Whores!': The Goines Factor and the Theory of a Hip-Hop Neo-Slave Narrative," *CR: The New Centennial Review* 3, no. 3 (2003): 200.

18. Eithne Quinn, "'Who's the Mack?': The Performativity and Politics of the Pimp Figure in Gangsta Rap," *Journal of American Studies* 34, no. 1 (2000): 115–36.

19. Ronald L. Jackson, *Scripting the Black Masculine Body: Identity, Discourse, and Racial Politics in Popular Media* (Albany: State University of New York Press, 2006).

20. Tricia Rose has contributed a good deal in this vein, but I am thinking specifically about her "Never Trust a Big Butt and a Smile," *Camera Obscura* 23 (1991): 109–31; and *The Hip Hop Wars: What We Talk about When We Talk about Hip Hop—and Why It Matters* (New York: Basic Civitas Books, 2008). For Sharpley-Whiting, see *Pimps Up, Ho's Down: Hip Hop's Hold on Young Black Women* (New York: NYU Press, 2007); for hooks, see her essays in *Outlaw Culture: Resisting Representations* (New York: Routledge, 1994); Mireille Miller-Young, "Hip-Hop Honeys and Da Hustlaz: Black Sexualities in the New Hip-Hop Pornography," *Meridians: Feminism, Race, Transnationalism* 8, no. 1 (2007): 261–92. Additionally, for a range of feminist perspectives on hip hop, see Gwendolyn D. Pough, Elaine Richarson, Aisha Durham, and Rachel Raimist, eds., *Home Girls Make Some Noise: Hip-Hop Feminism Anthology* (Mira Loma, CA: Parker, 2007).

21. Donald Goines, *Whoreson: The Story of a Ghetto Pimp* (Los Angeles: Holloway House, 1972), 213.

22. Ibid., 212–13.

23. Ibid., 215.

24. Jacques Lacan, "The Mirror-Stage as Formative of the I as Revealed in Psychoanalytic Experience," in *Écrits: A Selection*, trans. Alan Sheridan (New York: Norton, 1977); Julia Kristeva, *Powers of Horror: An Essay on Abjection*, trans. Leon S. Roudiez (New York: Columbia University Press, 1982).

25. Robert Beck, *The Naked Soul of Iceberg Slim* (Los Angeles: Holloway House, 1971), 19.

26. Ibid., 20.

27. Ibid., 21.

28. Kristeva, *Powers of Horror*, 4.

29. Anne Cheng, *The Melancholy of Race: Psychoanalysis, Assimilation, and Hidden Grief* (New York: Oxford University Press, 2001), 121.

30. See the entry for "phantasy (or fantasy)" in Jean Laplanche and J.-B. Pontalis, *The Language of Psycho-Analysis* (London: Karnac, 1988), 314–19. Laplanche and Pontalis's interpretation of fantasy is also well discussed in Anne Cheng's *Melancholy of Race*, 119–21.

31. Cheng, *Melancholy of Race*, 121.

32. Melanie Klein, "Notes on Some Schizoid Mechanisms," in *The Selected Melanie Klein*, ed. Juliet Mitchell (New York: Free Press, 1986), 186.

33. Ibid.

34. Ibid.

35. Relatedly, Terri Hume Oliver traces the theme of persecution in her reading of Robert Beck and Malcolm X as tragic mulatto figures who fear the predatory nature of white women. Oliver reads the misogynistic portrayals of white women as exposing a reversal of vulnerabilities in the men. See Oliver, "Prison, Perversion, and Pimps: The White Temptress in *The Autobiography of Malcolm X* and Iceberg Slim's *Pimp*," in *White Women in Racialized Spaces: Imaginative Transformation and Ethical Action in Literature*, ed. Samina Najmi and Rajini Srikanth (Albany: State University of New York Press, 2002), 147–65.

36. Beck, *Pimp*, 268.

37. Ibid., 19–20.
38. Ibid., 277.
39. Goines, *Whoreson*, 58.
40. Ibid.
41. Eve Kosofsky Sedgwick, *Between Men: English Literature and Male Homosocial Desire* (New York: Columbia University Press, 1985), 21. Sedgwick's work builds on and challenges the gender biases inherent in Freud's Oedipal configuration and René Girard's triangles on desire. See also René Girard, *Deceit, Desire, and the Novel: Self and Other in Literary Structure*, trans. Yvonne Freccero (Baltimore: Johns Hopkins University Press, 1972).
42. Goines, *Whoreson*, 26.
43. Ibid.
44. Ibid.
45. Ibid., 25.
46. L. H. Stallings reads the significance of Whoreson's name differently—as Jessie's participation in a resistant cultural practice of "un-naming." Stallings argues that "Jessie, a poor single Black mother whom society oppresses, comments on her neo-slave status through the naming of her son. Similarly, the author employs the female character and the name, Whoreson, to express rage, powerlessness, and to produce a fantasy of subversion that suggests what might seem like an embracing of the culture of pimps and whore. However, Goines's use of naming serves as a subversive attack on the society that strangles inner-city dwellers." Stallings, "I'm Goin Pimp Whores!," 194. While I have tried in this chapter to clarify how the pimps' relationship to women and their mothers works in ways that might be subversive but ultimately only oppressed and condemned, Stallings's reading of Whoreson's name as critique does not negate the rich possibilities for erotic association that are also quite apparent in Whoreson's complicated relationship to his baaaddd mama.
47. Beck, *Pimp*, 78.
48. Ibid.
49. Ibid. That this connection between Christ, son, and mother here surfaces as Beck's own dream but also uncannily resembles Shorty's trauma is odd to me. In fact, I am convinced that "Shorty," like Otis Tilson, the gay central character in *Mama Black Widow* is really a fictionalized displacement of Beck's own fears and frustrations. As he says, the lucid dreams about whipping and destroying his mother, at God's direction, haunted him in his waking life as daydreams and there were moments when he was unable to discern the difference between the two when he was in solitary confinement.
50. See Sigmund Freud, "A Child Is Being Beaten" (1919), in *On Psychopathology*, ed. Angela Richards, Penguin Freud Library 10 (London: Penguin, 1993), 159–94.
51. Goines, *Whoreson*, 26.
52. Beck, *Pimp*, 63.
53. Ibid., 255.
54. Ibid.
55. Ibid., 256.
56. Sedgwick, *Between Men*, 1.
57. Gayle Rubin, "The Traffic in Women: Notes toward a Political Economy of Sex," in *Toward an Anthropology of Women*, ed. Rayna Reiter (New York: Monthly Review Press, 1975), 176–77.

58. Beck, *Pimp*, 236.
59. My thoughts here about a black supercock as a dominant but misleading association to pimp culture and masculinist texts is inspired by Peter Lehman's reading of the "sad penis" in Walter Mosely's and Donald Goines's fiction. Lehman's reading offers insight into the "pervasive, shared cultural obsession for both blacks and whites with penis size in general" that casts the big black dick as grandiose opposite to the "tiny" white penis. See Lehman, "A 'Strange Quirk in His Lineage': Walter Mosely, Donald Goines, and the Racial Representation of the Penis," *Men and Masculinities* 9, no. 2 (2006): 228.
60. Beck, *Pimp*, 214.
61. Shengold's work explains why anality expresses both attempts to contain and to destroy or annihilate. See Leonard Shengold, "Defensive Anality and Anal Narcissism," *International Journal of Psycho-Analysis* 66 (1985): 47–73.
62. Beck, *Pimp*, 280.
63. Although not concerned with anality as a metaphor for exchanges between men, in "Bottom Values: Anal Economics and the History of Black Neighborhoods," Kathryn Bond Stockton impressively reads *Sula* through the lens of anality, slowing working through the significance of the verb *tuck* as an anal reference in Morrison's neighborhood, The Bottoms. See Stockton, *Beautiful Bottom, Beautiful Shame: Where "Black" Meets "Queer,"* Series Q (Durham, NC: Duke University Press, 2006), 67–100.
64. Beck, *Pimp*, 303.
65. Ibid., 304.
66. Ibid., 173.
67. Ibid., 153.
68. Ibid., 273.
69. Beck, *Naked Soul*, 34.
70. Ibid.
71. Ibid., 34–35.
72. Klein, "Notes on Some Schizoid Mechanisms," 186.
73. See Robert Reid-Pharr, *Black Gay Man: Essays* (New York: NYU Press, 2001); E. Patrick Johnson, *Appropriating Blackness: Performance and the Politics of Authenticity* (Durham, NC: Duke University Press, 2003); Marlon Bryan Ross, *Manning the Race: Reforming Black Men in the Jim Crow Era* (New York: NYU Press, 2004).
74. Beck, *Pimp*, 160.
75. Ibid., 126.
76. Ibid.
77. Ibid., 130.
78. Ibid., 132.
79. Ibid., 151.
80. Sedgwick, *Between Men*, 89.
81. Ibid.
82. Beck, *Pimp*, 219.
83. Ibid., 212.
84. Ibid.
85. Ibid. 232.
86. Ibid., 77.

254 NOTES TO CHAPTER 5

87. Ibid., 218.

88. Ibid., 315.

89. Ibid., 15.

90. bell hooks, "Postmodern Blackness," *Postmodern Culture* 1, no. 1 (1990), doi:10.1353/pmc.1990.0004.

91. Quinn, "Who's the Mack?," 134.

92. Ibid., 129.

93. Robert Reid-Pharr, "Tearing the Goat's Flesh: Homosexuality, Abjection, and the Production of a Late Twentieth-Century Black Masculinity" (1996), in *African American Literary Theory: A Reader*, ed. Winston Napier (New York: NYU Press, 2000), 603.

94. Ibid., 602–22.

95. Some examples: The women in the film are classically constructed, notably the prostitute whom DJay evicts from his family, Lexus, who is a recognizable construct of black maternity. As for male bonding and homosociality, at times the film resembles a buddy narrative, both in the scenes in which DJay tries to bond with Skinny Black and in the scenes between the men producing DJay's album. On anality, DJ is represented as being "stuffed" full of discourse. He remarks, "Fuck, man, I got this flow I need to spit," and "I ain't putting no shit on top of shit." In response to DJay's linguistic block, Key tells him, "What we doing is a whole bunch of flow. And the shit don't ever stop." Thus, in the early moments of the script, without an intersubjective orientation, DJay only has diarrhea of the mouth.

96. About these types of endings, I am thinking specifically about other black pulp fiction originally published during the civil rights era, including Herbert Simmons's *Corner Boy* (1957; repr., New York: Norton, 1996) and *Man Walking on Eggshells* (1962; repr., New York: Norton, 1997), Clarence Cooper Jr.'s *The Scene* (1960, repr., New York: Norton, 1996) and *Weed* (Evanston, IL: Regency Books, 1961), and Charles Perry's *Portrait of a Young Man Drowning* (1962; repr., New York: Norton, 1996).

97. Goines, *Whoreson*, 291.

98. Ibid., 296.

99. Ibid., 295.

100. Ibid., 296.

101. Beck, *Pimp*, 272.

102. Ibid., 310.

103. Ibid.

104. Ibid.,

105. Ibid.

106. Ibid., 311, 312.

107. Ibid., 312.

108. Ibid.

109. hooks, *Outlaw Culture*, 116.

# Chapter 5

1. At the time of this writing, Cosby has been arrested and arraigned on sexual assault charges. There is much speculation on whether his case will actually go to trial, but one thing is certain: he has fallen decisively from public favor, and most of the conversation

about his stardom has been around how to reconcile the realities of his probable crimes with his televisual legacy. Although Cosby has publicly denied sexually assaulting any of the forty-five women (by some accounts) who have accused him of abuse, previously sealed 2005 court documents have revealed that Cosby admitted to purchasing prescription drugs that he intended to use to drug women. See Graham Bowley and Ravi Somaiya, "Bill Cosby Admission about Quaaludes Offers Accusers Vindication," *New York Times*, July 7, 2015, www.nytimes.com/2015/07/08/business/bill-cosby-said-in-2005-he-obtained-drugs-to-give-to-women.html. There are any number of ways to think about how these charges and potential new court cases impact our interpretations of Cosby's career, but as the popular-cultural scholars Mark Anthony Neal and James Peterson discuss, these issues come as no surprise to anyone who has closely studied Cosby's career. Throughout the many years of conducting research on Cosby, I have always been quite aware of the paper trail and long list of complaints about his various indiscretions, and thus I have always paid close attention to the incongruities and inconsistencies in his star persona. For the Neal and Peterson discussion, see "Cosby's Downfall, Trump's Racism, and Why Rihanna's 'BBHMM' Might Be about Reparations," The Remix with Dr. James Peterson, podcast, July 9, 2015, www.newsworks.org/index.php/local/the-remix/83975-cosbys-downfall-trumps-racism-and-why-rihannas-bbhmm-might-be-about-reparations.

2. While the popular perception about Cosby might not have included some of the skepticism I am inferring here, Michael Eric Dyson's work has long been attentive to some of these issues surrounding Cosby's career. See Dyson, *Is Bill Cosby Right? Or Has the Black Middle Class Lost Its Mind?* (New York: Basic Civitas Books, 2005); Dyson, "Bill Cosby and the Politics of Race," *Z Magazine*, September 1989.

3. See Sut Jhally and Justin Lewis, *Enlightened Racism: The Cosby Show, Audiences, and the Myth of the American Dream* (Boulder, CO: Westview, 1992); Linda Fuller, *The Cosby Show: Audiences, Impact, and Implications* (Westport, CT: Greenwood, 1992); Janet Staiger, *Blockbuster TV: Must-See Sitcoms in the Network Era* (New York: NYU Press, 2000), 141–59; Herman Gray, *Watching Race: Television and the Struggle for "Blackness"* (Minneapolis: University of Minnesota Press, 1995), 79–84; Michael Real, *Super Media: A Cultural Studies Approach* (Newbury Park, CA: Sage, 1989), 106–31.

4. The series changed titles several times throughout its run. The title changes are as follows: *Hey, Hey, Hey, It's Fat Albert* (pilot, 1969); *Fat Albert and the Cosby Kids* (1972–73, twenty-two episodes; 1975–76, fourteen episodes); *The New Fat Albert Show* (1979–81, twenty-four episodes); and *The Adventures of Fat Albert and the Cosby Kids* (1984–85; fifty episodes).

5. Quoted in Gerald Nachman, *Seriously Funny: The Rebel Comedians of the 1950s and 1960s* (New York: Pantheon Books, 2003), 573.

6. Bambi Haggins, *Laughing Mad: The Black Comic Persona in Post-Soul America* (New Brunswick, NJ: Rutgers University Press, 2007), 17.

7. Ibid., 26.

8. Ibid., 27.

9. Mark Twain, preface to *The Adventures of Tom Sawyer*, ed. John C. Gerber (Berkeley: University of California Press, 1982), 33. Also quoted in Gillian Brown, "Child's Play," in *The American Child: A Cultural Studies Reader*, ed. Caroline F. Levander and Carol J. Single (New Brunswick, NJ: Rutgers University Press, 2003), 29.

10. Lynn Spigel, "Seducing the Innocent: Childhood and Television in Postwar America," in *Ruthless Criticism: New Perspectives in U.S. Communication History*, ed. William S.

Solomon and Robert W. McChesney (Minneapolis: University of Minnesota Press, 1993), 259; Jacqueline Rose, *The Case of Peter Pan, or The Impossibility of Children's Fiction* (London: Macmillan, 1984), 2.

11. Caroline F. Levander and Carol J. Singley, introduction to Levander and Singley, *American Child*, 6.
12. Rose, *Case of Peter Pan*, xii.
13. Ibid. Interestingly, Rose also makes a direct connection between claims of innocence and guilt, arguing that "sentimentality about childhood . . . is the other side of guilt" (x). While it is beyond the scope of the project at hand, it does seem worthwhile to explore Cosby's sentimentality and nostalgia around his childhood in the context of his presumed guilt in the current set of scandals.
14. Karen Sánchez-Eppler, "Playing at Class," in Levander and Singley, *American Child*, 41.
15. Levander and Singley, introduction to *American Child*, 6.
16. See Ronald L. Smith, *Cosby: The Life of a Comedy Legend* (Amherst, NY: Prometheus Books, 1997); Bill Adler, *The Cosby Wit: His Life and Humor* (New York: Lorevan, 1987).
17. Smith, *Cosby*, 4.
18. Spigel, "Seducing the Innocent," 264. Also see Lynn Spigel, *Welcome to the Dreamhouse: Popular Media and Postwar Suburbs* (Durham, NC: Duke University Press, 2001), 185–218.
19. Spigel, "Seducing the Innocent," 259.
20. Aya de Leon, "Cliff Huxtable Is the Fantasy. Bill Cosby Is the Reality," *Bitchmedia*, January 13, 2015, http://bitchmedia.org/post/cliff-huxtable-is-the-fantasy-bill-cosby-is-the-reality.
21. Cognitive scientists and linguists have been particularly interested in the use of figurative language, and some have explored the psychological significance of substitutions in rhetorical speech. Although my point is to stress this aspect of Cosby's performance as a fact, close examinations of his use of speech remain to be written; a linguistic analysis of Cosby's stand-up is but one approach that is ripe for future study. For related research, see Raymond W. Gibbs, *The Poetics of Mind: Figurative Thought, Language, and Understanding* (New York: Cambridge University Press, 1994); Sam Glucksberg, *Understanding Figurative Language: From Metaphor to Idioms* (New York: Oxford University Press, 2001); Ludmila Isurin, Donald Winford, and Kees De Bot, *Multidisciplinary Approaches to Code Switching* (Philadelphia: John Benjamins, 2009); Ronald L. Jackson and Elaine B. Richardson, *Understanding African American Rhetoric: Classical Origins to Contemporary Innovations* (New York: Routledge, 2003).
22. Henry Louis Gates Jr., *The Signifying Monkey: A Theory of Afro-American Literary Criticism* (New York: Oxford University Press, 1988). See especially the book's introduction for Gates's metaphor of double-voiced fiction.
23. Ibid., xxvii.
24. "Hey, Hey, Hey . . . It's the Story of Fat Albert," bonus documentary on *Fat Albert and the Cosby Kids: The Complete Series*, vol. 5, Shout! Factory, 2013, DVD.
25. Ibid.
26. Ibid.
27. See Benjamin Spock, *The Common Sense Book of Baby and Child Care* (New York: Duell, Sloan, and Pearce, 1946); Benjamin Spock, John Reinhart, and Wayne Miller, *A Baby's First Year* (New York: Pocket Books, 1958); Benjamin Spock, *Dr. Spock Talks with Mothers* (Boston: Houghton Mifflin, 1961).

28. Karin Obholzer, *The Wolf-Man: Conversations with Freud's Patient—Sixty Years Later*, trans. Michael Shaw (New York: Continuum, 1982), 139.

29. Michelle A. Massé, "Constructing the Psychoanalytic Child: Freud's *From the History of an Infantile Neurosis*," in Levander and Singley, *American Child*, 150, 149.

30. For more on the report, see Gerald S. Lesser, *Children and Television: Lessons from "Sesame Street"* (New York: Random House, 1974); Richard M. Polsky, *Getting to Sesame Street: Origins of the Children's Television Workshop* (New York: Praeger, 1974).

31. Quoted in Robert W. Morrow, *"Sesame Street" and the Reform of Children's Television* (Baltimore: Johns Hopkins University Press, 2008), 5.

32. U.S. Congress, Senate, Committee on Commerce, Subcommittee on Communications, *Extension of Authorizations under the Public Broadcasting Act of 1967*, 91st Congress (1969) (statement of Fred Rogers, Washington, DC), April 30 and May 1, 1969.

33. Ibid.

34. *Brown v. Board of Education of Topeka*, 347 U.S. 483, 494 (1954). Also see *Brown v. Board of Education of Topeka*, 349 U.S. 294 (1955).

35. Kenneth B. Clark, *Toward Humanity and Justice: The Writings of Kenneth B. Clark, Scholar of the 1954 "Brown v. Board of Education" Decision*, ed. Woody Klein (Westport, CT: Praeger, 2004).

36. See Kenneth B. Clark, *Prejudice and Your Child* (Boston: Beacon, 1955); Clark, *Dark Ghetto: Dilemmas of Social Power* (New York: Harper and Row, 1965); Clark, *Pathos of Power* (New York: Harper and Row, 1974).

37. Gunnar Myrdal, *An American Dilemma: The Negro Problem and Modern Democracy* (New York: Harper and Row, 1962); Abram Kardiner and Lionel Ovesey, *The Mark of Oppression: A Psychosocial Study of the American Negro* (New York: Norton, 1951).

38. William Henry Cosby Jr., "An Integration of the Visual Media via *Fat Albert and the Cosby Kids* into the Elementary School Curriculum as a Teaching Aid and Vehicle to Achieve Increased Learning" (Ph.D. diss., University of Massachusetts, 1976), 67.

39. Ibid.

40. "Hey, Hey, Hey."

41. "Cosby's 'Fat Albert' to Star in New Children's Series," *New York Amsterdam News*, June 10, 1972, D7.

42. The cartoon's board was composed of experts with research backgrounds in psychology, social welfare, and children's mental health issues: Seymour Feshbach, Gordon L. Berry, Nathan Cohen, James O. Simmons. Because of their academic backgrounds, there is little doubt that they were aware of the popular discourses on race and psychology during the time, and it is certainly plausible that several were familiar enough with some of the Freudian and Winnicottian analytic concepts I discuss in my readings of the show. I am less concerned, however, with establishing that there was an intentional use of psychoanalysis in the making of *Fat Albert* than I am with exploring how the show is a part of a cultural milieu that tended to appropriate, irrespective of intentionality, discourses of psychology to narrate stories about blackness.

43. "Hey, Hey, Hey."

44. There is ample evidence to indicate that Cosby has been quite intentional in mobilizing the rhetoric of psychology not only in his comedy and television shows from *Fat Albert* to *The Cosby Show* but also in his recent books and public speeches. For example, Cosby has cowritten books like *Come On, People* with the *Cosby Show* psychological adviser (and

Harvard professor of psychiatry) Alvin Poussaint as an attempt to combine psychological research with folk wisdom for black readers, especially parents. Bill Cosby and Alvin F. Poussaint, *Come On, People: On the Path from Victims to Victors* (Nashville, TN: Thomas Nelson, 2007). Similarly, Cosby discusses the sociological and psychological merit of *Fat Albert* at length in his dissertation ("Integration of the Visual Media").

45. Dave Itzkoff, "Hey, Hey, Hey: Bill Cosby on 'Fat Albert,' Yesterday and Today," *ArtsBeat* (blog), *New York Times*, June 12, 2013, http://artsbeat.blogs.nytimes.com/2013/06/12/hey-hey-hey-bill-cosby-on-fat-albert-yesterday-and-today/?_php=true&_type=blogs&_php=true&_type=blogs&_php=true&_type=blogs&_r=2&.

46. D. W. Winnicott, *Playing and Reality* (London: Routledge, 1991), 64.

47. I am simply noting here that the end product and popularized image of Fat Albert is consistent with how a child might have thought of his impressive friend relative to his or her self. Cosby has claimed that all of the Cosby kids are based on real people he knew growing up. At the end of the live-action movie *Fat Albert* (2004), which was based on his sketches and the cartoon, Cosby even appears in a funeral scene at the end of the movie with some of the adult men on whom he based his characters. The fact that Cosby based these characters on people he knew does not, of course, absolve the representations from either intentional exaggeration (as he did often) or unconscious distortion and fantasy. The character Fat Albert is an amalgamation of truth and fiction and fantasy, like the whole of Cosby's sketches and other material.

48. I have written more extensively about the postmodern implications of *Fat Albert* elsewhere. See TreaAndrea M. Russworm, "'Hey, Hey, Hey!': Bill Cosby's *Fat Albert* as Psychodynamic Postmodern Play," in *Watching While Black: Centering the Television of Black Audiences*, ed. Beretta E. Smith-Shomade (New Brunswick, NJ: Rutgers University Press, 2013), 89–104.

49. Michael Swanigan and Darrell McNeil, *Animation by Filmation*, ed. John Reed and Joshua Lou Friedman (Simi Valley, CA: Black Bear, 1993), 46.

50. "Hey, Hey, Hey."

51. Ibid.

52. Winnicott, *Playing and Reality*, 50.

53. See Mikhail Bakhtin, *Problems of Dostoevsky's Poetics*, ed. and trans. Carl Emerson (Minneapolis: University of Minnesota Press, 1984); and Bakhtin, *Rabelais and His World*, trans. Helene Iswolsky (Bloomington: Indiana University Press, 1984).

54. Spigel, *Welcome to the Dreamhouse*, 29.

55. Director Hal Sutherland and producer Lou Scheimer also played influential behind-the-scenes roles in the show's development. As I have suggested here, though, these other creative agents were unlikely to shape the project in ways that Cosby found problematic, and his continued support of the cartoon remained consistent over the years. See "Hey, Hey, Hey." Also see Swanigan and McNeil, *Animation by Filmation*; Lou Scheimer, with Andy Mangels, *Lou Scheimer: Creating the Filmation Generation* (Raleigh, NC: TwoMorrows, 2012).

56. "Dr. Bill Cosby Speaks at the 50th Anniversary Commemoration of the *Brown vs. Topeka Board of Education* Supreme Court Decision," Eight Cities Media & Publications, www.eightcitiesmap.com/transcript_bc.htm (accessed April 16, 2013).

57. Ibid.

58. Booker T. Washington, *The Future of the American Negro* (1899; repr., New York: Negro Universities Press, 1969); Marcus Garvey, *Philosophy and Opinions of Marcus Garvey*,

ed. Amy Jacques Garvey (New York: Arno, 1968); Malcolm X, *The Autobiography of Malcolm X*, ed. Alex Haley (New York: Grove, 1965).

59. John H. Bracey Jr., "Black Nationalism since Garvey," in *Key Issues in the Afro-American Experience*, vol. 2, *Since 1865*, ed. Nathan Irvin Higgins, Martin Klison, and Daniel M. Fox (New York: Harcourt Brace Jovanovich, 1971), 259–79; Also see John H. Bracey Jr., August Meier, and Elliott Rudwick, eds., *Black Nationalism in America* (Indianapolis: Bobbs-Merrill, 1970).

60. "Dr. Bill Cosby Speaks."

61. Ta-Nehisi Coates, "'This Is How We Lost to the White Man': The Audacity of Bill Cosby's Black Conservatism," *Atlantic*, May 2008, www.theatlantic.com/magazine/archive/2008/05/-this-is-how-we-lost-to-the-white-man/306774/.

62. A sampling of the chapter titles from Cosby and Poussaint, *Come On, People*.

63. Ibid., xviii.

64. Coates, "This Is How We Lost to the White Man."

65. Ibid.

66. Ibid.

67. Frazier Moore, "Bill Cosby Talks New Special 'Far from Finished' and Why He Doesn't Tell Jokes," Huffington Post, November 21, 2013, www.huffingtonpost.com/2013/11/21/bill-cosby-far-from-finished_n_4317625.html.

68. Coates, "This Is How We Lost to the White Man."

## Chapter 6

1. David Ehrenstein, "Obama the 'Magic Negro,'" *Los Angeles Times*, March 19, 2007, www.latimes.com/la-oe-ehrenstein19mar19-story.html.

2. "Transcript: Bill Clinton's Democratic Convention Speech," ABC News, September 6, 2012, http://abcnews.go.com/Politics/OTUS/transcript-bill-clintons-democratic-convention-speech/story?id=17164662.

3. Ibid.

4. See, among other sites, "'Cool Obama Burns for America,' Says Bill Clinton after Nominating Him," NDTV.com, September 6, 2012, www.ndtv.com/world-news/cool-obama-burns-for-america-says-bill-clinton-after-nominating-him-498640.

5. Michael D. Shear, "Debate Praise for Romney as Obama Is Faulted as Flat," *New York Times*, October 4, 2012, www.nytimes.com/2012/10/05/us/politics/after-debate-a-torrent-of-criticism-for-obama.html.

6. Katharine Q. Seelye, "BET Founder Slams Obama in South Carolina," *The Caucus* (blog), *New York Times*, January 13, 2008, http://thecaucus.blogs.nytimes.com/2008/01/13/bet-chief-raps-obama-in-sc/.

7. Lauren Berlant, *Cruel Optimism* (Durham, NC: Duke University Press, 2011), 1.

8. Lauren Berlant, "Poor Eliza," *American Literature* 70, no. 3 (1998): 644.

9. Stacey Patton, "After Ferguson, Some Black Academics Wonder: Does Pursuing a Ph.D. Matter?," *Chronicle of Higher Education Vitae*, September 12, 2014, https://chroniclevitae.com/news/703-after-ferguson-some-black-academics-wonder-does-pursuing-a-ph-d-matter.

10. Ibid.

# INDEX